Cheap but Good Marketing Research

Cheap but Good Marketing Research

Alan R. Andreasen

DOW JONES–IRWIN
Homewood, Illinois 60430

This publication is designed to provide accurate and
authoritative information in regard to the subject matter
covered. It is sold with the understanding that neither the
author nor the publisher is engaged in rendering legal, accounting,
or other professional service. If legal advice or other expert
assistance is required, the services of a competent
professional person should be sought.

*From a Declaration of Principles jointly adopted by a Committee
of the American Bar Association and a Committee of Publishers.*

Acquisitions editor: Susan Glinert Stevens, Ph.D.
Project editor: Gladys True
Production manager: Ann Cassady
Jacket Design: Sam Concialdi
Compositor: Carlisle Communications, Ltd.
Typeface: 11/13 Century Schoolbook
Printer: Arcata Graphics/Kingsport

Library of Congress Cataloging-in-Publication Data
Andreasen, Alan R., 1934-
    Cheap but good marketing research / Alan R. Andreasen.
       p.   cm
    Includes index.
    ISBN 0-87094-772-9 : $24.95
    1. Marketing research   I. Title
HF5415.2.A485 1988
658.8'3—dc19   88–2447
Printed in the United States of America

  2 3 4 5 6 7 8 9 0 K 5 4 3 2 1 0 9 8

For Jean and for Maia

PREFACE

This book is designed for managers who want to do marketing research, but feel they cannot afford it. It shows them how to get the information needed to be a better manager and how to do it at low cost.

The basic message of the book is that research need not be expensive, overly complex, or statistical to be extremely helpful to managers in a wide range of organizations. The marketing research community is sometimes guilty of making the research process seem so subtle and complicated that it scares off too many people who could make valuable use of low-cost techniques. One *can* do perfectly decent and useful research without fancy probability samples, complex questionnaires, highly trained interviewers, or the latest in computerized statistical software! This book tells how and gets the motivated reader started.

I believe there is a crying need for this kind of treatment. Conventional textbooks give only passing reference to the potential of many useful low-cost techniques and seem barely interested in the problems of those who are not working in large corporations or major marketing research agencies. And while there are a few books on practical marketing research techniques, they tend to be how-to-do-it manuals primarily for those who want to do field surveys.

This book, then, is a heartfelt response to the cries for help I have heard from practicing and would-be marketing managers of small and medium-sized organizations—a group I call *low-budget researchers*. For them, the pages that follow are designed to achieve four basic objectives.

1. To demythologize marketing research and do away with misconceptions that keep too many managers from doing any kind of marketing research.
2. To offer a basic approach that will assure that any research that is done is needed and useful to the managers for whom it is designed.
3. To describe in a systematic fashion a wide variety of specific research techniques that are low cost, but that, if carried out with care and with appropriate attention to issues of bias, can provide management with crucial market insights to improve marketing decision making.
4. Finally, to motivate the reader to get started, to begin to do the research outlined here and to see how it can lead to better and better decisions.

This book is also written for students. The techniques discussed in the following pages take up only a brief chapter or so of most basic marketing research texts. The treatment is usually cursory and one senses that many textbook writers see these topics as preliminary approaches before getting on to a really serious study, i.e., the major field study or the complex experiment. It is seldom recognized that many of the students who might read such books or attend regular marketing research courses will go on to hold jobs or to advise organizations where they will be able to carry out only low-cost studies. This book is also addressed to these future managers and advisors and to those who would teach them.

OUTLINE OF THE BOOK

Consonant with its twin objectives of motivating and tutoring, the book is divided into four sections. The first and last sections focus on the larger issues of getting started, adopting appropriate philosophies, and setting up the appropriate organization and systems to ensure the gathering of both low-cost and useful marketing research. The middle two sections deal more with the nitty-gritty of specific low-cost research techniques. Three appendices are included. One describes major secondary sources a researcher might wish to use in lieu of his or her own primary research. For researchers with access to a computer and a modem, Appendix B describes a rich array of on-line data bases. The third appendix describes several types of low-cost graphics, database management, decision support, and statistical software for personal computers that can significantly enhance the personal and organizational capabilities of the practicing low-cost researcher.

The first major section of the book is concerned with getting off on the right foot. This may mean sweeping aside some inhibiting misconceptions about research that many readers or their superiors have harbored over the years. Such myths include those that say that good research is inevitably expensive, that research must always involve fancy sampling techniques, complex statistics, and elaborate computer programs, and that too much research is academic and off-target and therefore of little use to busy, budget-minded managers. Chapter 1 indicates why these myths are incorrect. Chapter 2 then turns to problems of deciding how to set up a marketing research program, i.e., how to recognize needs and opportunities for research within individual organizations and how to set in motion both individual studies and a long-term program of information development. The chapter emphasizes the need to be systematic about the task of developing a program of low-cost research and offers a general procedure for doing so.

Chapter 3 continues the discussion of planning by offering an approach to the crucial decision of specifically when it is justified to do research and how much to spend on it. The chapter introduces both formal and rule-of-thumb approaches to the task of estimating the cost and value of research. Chapter 4 then tackles what is perhaps the most important issue in low cost research: how to make sure that every dollar spent on marketing research yields information that is unquestionably useful to managers. The chapter outlines a specific procedure called *backward research design* that can help both the beginning and the more experienced researcher achieve the elusive goal of maximal managerial usefulness.

Section 2 then turns to a detailing of the major alternative approaches to gathering low-cost data for marketing decisions. These chapters cover uses of existing internal and external archives (Chapter 5), systematic observation (Chapter 6), low-cost experimentation (Chapter 7) and low-cost survey design (Chapter 8).

Section 3 takes up issues of quality. For research to be helpful to managers on limited budgets, it needs to be not only low-cost, but GOOD. For the research to be good, the researcher must ensure that the data are valid and that conclusions reached are also valid. In a sense, the researcher must assure that there is not "garbage in/garbage out." Chapter 9 deals with the problems of achieving valid measurements particularly when asking questions in field surveys. Chapter 10 then discusses the often dreaded topic of statistics from the standpoint of its role in making sure that the output of a study (1) properly summarizes the major findings, (2) reports only those differences and relationships that are truly present, and (3) milks the most information out of a given set of input. The reader should rest assured that the treatment here is commonsensical and not highly quantitative.

Researchers with low budgets could obviously use as much low-cost help as they can get. The final chapter, Chapter 11, focuses on the problems of acquiring the financial, physical, intellectual, and manpower resources needed to carry out low-cost research projects. The chapter offers a number of approaches to using libraries, colleges, ad agencies, and commercial research services by researchers with very restricted budgets. The appendices are important supplements to this chapter.

WHAT THE BOOK IS NOT

Before leaving the reader to plunge into the exciting possibilities of the world of cheap but good research, it is important to keep one's expectations within reason. This is *not* a basic marketing research text or a detailed handbook of low-cost techniques. A number of the traditional subjects that one ought to think about to be a really accomplished, sophisticated marketing researcher are not covered here. The reader will not find in these pages detailed suggestions on how to design a questionnaire, or how to word questions, or how to draw a probability sample. The more routine aspects of research administration, data reduction, and data analysis and report writing are also absent.

This is a book about a particular, neglected subset of all marketing research. It chooses not to dwell on what other authors cover well, but on what they no not. It is hoped that the reader finds this to be a volume that provides the raw material and the incentive to begin an innovative program of market research that, even though constrained by limited resources, will prove a significant boon to the organization and to the manager wanting to make more informed and less risky marketing decisions.

ACKNOWLEDGMENTS

Many practicing low-budget managers over the years have provided rich examples of both the problems and possibilities for low-cost research. I owe them my gratitude for stimulating the thinking that has led to this volume. Among those I would particularly like to thank are William D. Novelli of Doremus Porter Novelli, Betty Ravenholt of The Futures Group, Tom Walker of United Way of America, William Wells of Needham Harper Worldwide, and Harold Horowitz of the National Endowment for the Arts. I would also acknowledge the contributions to my understanding of research and its role made by many academic colleagues over the years, most especially Seymour Sudman and Russell Belk. Particular thanks are due Seymour Sudman for his careful reading and insightful suggestions on the present manuscript.

The book, however, would not have been written were it not for the encouragement and support of Jean Manning. Jean provided many of the ideas contained herein and throughout has been both a cheerful goad and a stern critic of what you will read in these pages.

Finally, appreciation must be offered to UCLA's word processing staff which meticulously transcribed my original notes and a great number of revisions over the course of many months. They helped ease the often painful task of putting words in order to offer what should be a very simple, but one hopes highly meaningful, lesson about information use in the era of modern marketing.

Alan R. Andreasen

CONTENTS

SECTION 1

PLANNING A LOW-COST RESEARCH PROGRAM

CHAPTER 1

MYTHS OF MARKETING RESEARCH

Successful marketers are knowledgeable marketers. The world has many intuitively brilliant and sometimes lucky marketers, but the most successful marketers I know are the best informed. They know their customers, know their distributors, and know which marketing tactics work and which ones don't. They know what their competitors are doing almost as soon as they do it. Most important, they are aware of what they don't know and they resolve to find it out. They crave information. They devour it on the job and off the job. They always want to know more and, when they acquire new information, they use it effectively.

Other managers intuitively know this. They know they need more information and ought to be doing marketing research in order to be better marketers. Managers in large enterprises have access to many types of information services and usually a healthy budget for their own research. Managers in small and medium-sized organizations do not have such opportunities. They say, "We know we need marketing information to be good marketers, but how can we undertake it when we have virtually no budgets?"

Other comments include:

- "If I did have the money to do research, how can I do it when I really don't know much about statistics and sampling and computers?"
- "How dare I risk limited resources (not to mention my credibility with my boss) by doing research that I'm told all too often turns out to be a waste of time and effort?"

- "If I decide to go ahead, how can I work effectively with a market research professional when I don't really know what I want, what the researcher can do for me, or how I can tell good research from bad when it gets done?"

This book responds to these cries for help. It is a book about low-cost marketing research designed for both present and future marketing practitioners with limited research budgets and limited experience in carrying out specific research studies or extensive research programs. It offers a rich catalog of techniques for keeping costs down while maintaining acceptable, sometimes high, standards of quality. The book's ultimate goal is to make the user of these techniques a better manager through timely acquisition of relevant, useful marketing information.

The book is not simply a guide for carrying out a specific set of low-cost research approaches. It also is designed to motivate the reader to become an active researcher, to take the first steps toward becoming a frequent, savvy beneficiary of research's rich possibilities. Two barriers keep managers from being active researchers. First, wrong notions about research keep many from even thinking about the topic. Second, many managers simply aren't aware of the wide array of simple, low-cost marketing research techniques that are available today.

This book tackles both issues by confronting the myths and outlining step-by-step procedures for setting up a research program and for carrying out specific, useful studies. It also describes in detail many techniques for doing low-cost, but high quality, research.

We begin by tackling some of the myths that are keeping many managers (consciously or unconsciously) from considering or undertaking marketing research.

RESEARCH PRIESTS AND THE LOW-BUDGET MANAGER

Many managers with limited research experience hold misperceptions about marketing research. These misperceptions can be traced to the marketing research community which has created a forbidding mystique about its own profession and its products. Marketing researchers have developed their own jargon, their own reverence for the most sophisticated approaches, and their own propaganda that implies that only those who are properly trained—i.e., the "research priests"—can conduct valid, reliable marketing research.

In some cases, they are correct! Professionals should be the prime sources of research on such sensitive topics as drugs and sex or of research designed to tap complex or deeply rooted mental processes. Professionals must also be used when results have to be projected with a high degree of accuracy to a general population base or to some distant future period. They must also be used where the research is likely to be subject to close outside scrutiny, for example, by the government or by the courts. And, of course, when a lot is riding on the outcome of a decision or set of decisions that must be based on research, paying for the very best professional work is clearly justified.

But there are many, many marketing decisions that could benefit significantly from marketing research that would *not* involve a high level of sophistication or expenditure levels that mortgage the organization's future! There are a great many research alternatives that can easily be designed and implemented by any minimally knowledgeable manager or his or her staff. This book is designed to encourage and instruct these people to try their hand at marketing research. It is designed to give the neophyte manager-researcher the kind of minimal knowledge necessary to permit frequent and sensible use of a wide range of low-cost marketing research tools.

Many managers, however, are intimidated about carrying out their own marketing research because of myths that have developed over the years. If this book is really to be helpful to its readers, we must first bring these myths into the open and confront them directly.

Myth #1: "I'm Already Doing Enough Research"

Many managers believe they already have enough marketing research information as a by-product of their organization's accounting and control activities. They point to stacks of sales data, expense reports, profitability analyses, and so forth as proof of their contention. While such information may be useful as research, the odds are very good that it is both too much and too little. The problem typically is that no one has ever really sat down and tried to specify just what kind of information the manager should have for day-to-day marketing decisions or for long-range strategic planning. Thus, the manager is offered only what is available and often in overwhelming abundance. Too much of the wrong kind of data can swamp what is really important. The manager is often left to find the proverbial needle in the haystack.

Data overkill, by its sheer bulk, can also intimidate many managers from looking for these needles, while at the same time convincing them that the company is already doing enough marketing research. Certainly the prospect of going into the field and generating even more new and different data will seem highly unpalatable to the overwhelmed manager.

And, of course, the available data may also be too little. As long as the manager keeps making decisions that could have been significantly helped by a few modest additional research projects, we must conclude that the present information is clearly inadequate. It is Gresham's Law applied to marketing research; bad data drives out good data. An overabundance of useless data is bound to quash any modest ambitions to collect more.

The only way to deal with the problem of data overkill is to systematically identify the organization's long-run research needs and ask whether present data meet these needs. In most cases, they will not, and the researcher will have to build a research program to meet those needs and find ways of turning off the supply of useless, inhibiting data. Simply hoping that existing data will be adequate is not enough. If existing data are not carefully designed to help make both short- and long-term decisions, they are probably just accounting or production data and should not be classified as research.

Myth #2: "Research Is Only for Big Decisions"

Many managers in small businesses or in nonprofit organizations suffer from misplaced modesty. They feel that their decisions are small potatoes compared to those of Procter & Gamble or General Motors. They feel they cannot justify the level of expenditures they think any serious marketing research undertaking will require. This kind of thinking has two major flaws. First, there are many circumstances in both small and large companies where relatively trivial decisions can be significantly improved by a little bit of marketing research and where the research is well worth doing because of its modest cost.

Second, despite what many managers think, there are many situations, even in very large organizations, where marketing research is not justified, even though substantial amounts of resources are at risk. The reason a lot of big decisions do not require research expenditures is simply because management already has little uncertainty about what to do. By contrast, as we will see in Chapter 3, it is in cases where managers simply do not know which way to turn (even where the stakes are relatively modest) that research can be most helpful. The dollars at risk will, of course, determine the upper limit of the research budget and therefore, other things equal, bigger decisions will permit more research. But even where relatively modest amounts are involved, if the situation is one of high uncertainty as to what to do, there is usually some level of research expenditure that a manager should accept because it is very likely to tip the balance one way or another.

In many big bucks situations, managers will order research even though it is not justified rationally. Managers often want to feel better about a major decision they are about to make. They may want backup in case the decision is later questioned. In both cases, the manager should recognize that funds allocated to unjustified self-protection are funds that probably should be used to provide information in other contexts which now require management "by the seat of the pants."

Myth #3: "Losing Control"

The lost-control myth in part reflects the deep-rooted perceptions of many managers that marketing research is really some arcane religion to which only a very few priests are admitted. The manager believes that he or she cannot acquire the level of sophistication needed either to do the research alone or to specify what research needs to be bought from outside sources. If managers feel they must go outside for any research, many will refrain from going ahead because they feel that they dare not rely on others to gather and analyze data about their decisions. They feel they will have committed a part of their organization's destiny to an outsider who may or may not understand the situation or the realities of the managers' unique political and market environment. In a sense, the managers feel they have lost control.

This would explain why many managers who recognize possibilities for research do not simply hire smart MBAs to do in-house studies and/or hire outside contractors to fill in critical information gaps. The manager fears losing control. If new information is allowed to become important to decision-making and only certain people (*not* the manager) have access to this specialized information, then they, not the manager, may really have the control. The manager will be beholden to them.

This fear keeps managers from engaging in research, and also keeps them from using the results of research when it is (grudgingly) carried out. This is especially the case if the research results run counter to the manager's own views. Most of us are reluctant to accept new information. But, the problem is significantly exaggerated when managers feel that agreeing with unexpected research results and/or acting on them means giving up real control of their function.

Understandably, this fear of loss of control is a particular problem for middle managers and those in small or nonprofit businesses. Personal survival is very important to them and they often feel they dare not give others the control of their personal organizational fate.

They may also feel that the entire organization is at risk. Organizational fragility is a real and understandable concern of small businesses. If one believes that research is hard to understand and requires a translation to be used effectively, certainly one will be reluctant to delegate one's very livelihood to outside specialists. The outside researcher may not work as hard on the project or on the analysis and interpretation as the manager would like. Worse still, busy outsiders may unwittingly bias the results, understate or neglect key issues, or suppress important reservations.

Finally, many managers worry that outside researchers will be on some theoretical or academic plateau far above the practical realities facing the business. This will be especially so if the manager has glanced recently at specialized journals in the marketing research field with their articles talking of "part-worths," "canonical coefficients," "Mahalanobis D-squared," or "Durbin-Watson statistics."

These fears, of course, are not easily reduced. However, this book is designed to make the manager a more savvy research user, one who knows when to hire outsiders and when to go it alone. It introduces a number of very good, but not-so-fancy, research techniques that the cautious manager can order from outside or can do in-house without fear of being unknowledgeable or unprepared. Should the manager have to go outside, the book also describes (in Chapter 4) an excellent technique that can ensure that what is done is on target and totally useful.

Myth #4: "Market Research Is Survey Research"

Just as many nonmarketing people tend to think that marketing is just advertising, so do many managers tend to think of survey research and marketing research as being virtually the same thing. There is a great range of research techniques that a manager can use that definitely do *not* involve surveys. This includes simple observation, archival analysis, and low-cost experimentation.

Myth #5: "Market Research Is Too Expensive"

This, of course, is the major "straw man" myth that this book is designed to knock down. It exists, in part, because of Myth #4. If one equates marketing research with surveys with their large samples, substantial field costs, complicated computer analyses and so on, it is inevitable to assume that research has to be expensive. Surveys based on careful probability sampling *are* expensive, but, there are many alternatives to survey research that can adequately meet management's information needs at low cost. Further, there are many ways in which the cost of survey research itself can be significantly reduced.

Myth #6: "Most Research Is a Waste"

There are many reasons why research can turn out to be wasteful. However, this book is expressly designed to make sure that managers avoid such a fate.

There can be many culprits behind wasted research. Sometimes research is wasted because the manager has personal motives for not effectively using the research after it is done. Inexperience, time pressure, or relying too much on the research supplier can also lead to miscommunication that will virtually ensure that the research cannot be useful.

Often the researcher is an equally guilty culprit. Some research specialists keep a distance from management simply to protect their own special status. Sometimes the researcher—whether by training or inclination—is simply not adequately concerned about making the research project managerially relevant. This is especially common among academics and freshly graduated Ph.D.s. The researcher may be so into the world of research sophistication that he or she may not really understand, or may have strange ideas about, managerial relevance. It is not uncommon to hear researchers talk about the quality of the design itself or the statistical significance of the results as the true test of whether research was good, rather than how relevant it was to the manager who asked for it.

Finally, the problem may simply not be the fault of anybody or caused by a lack of trying. In many cases where both sides really want to make the research managerially useful, the parties involved simply do not have a procedure that can make a piece of research managerially relevant and useful. Chapter 4 in this volume specifically sets out a procedure that can go a long way toward ensuring a productive manager-researcher collaboration.

MOVING FORWARD

In summary, then, low-budget managers should not be put off from doing research because:

1. They think they already have enough data—almost always they don't. We will suggest a procedure in Chapter 2 for determining what information they really need.

2. They don't face enough big decisions. Research is not only for big decisions, and sometimes big decisions do not need it. In Chapter 3, we will show you how to determine when to do research and when *not* to.

3. They fear loss of control of their destinies because they are not sophisticated enough to be good research users. But, most of the research we will discuss in this book does not require great sophistication—just common sense. Even the discussion of analysis techniques and statistics in Chapter 10 is in very simple terms anyone should be able to follow.

4. They think research is simply conducting surveys and surveys are expensive. But, as we demonstrate in the later chapters, all research is not surveys and even surveys can be done inexpensively.

5. They fear it will be a waste of time and resources. Research *can* be a waste, but it need not be, especially if the approach outlined in Chapter 4 is carefully followed.

An Example: Research for New Product Development

Research is essential for management success. Probably nowhere is this more obvious than in the area of new product development. In this domain, too many managers enamored over an idea that can't miss neglect to do the simplest basic research. For example, Polygon Software Corp. of New York developed a new product, Easy Path, to help professional PC users enhance the "pathing capabilities" of their hard disks. Despite the product's relatively low cost and obvious usefulness, Polygon neglected to find out whether data processors knew they had a need/problem that the software could address. It turned out they were unwilling to pay $99 for something that wasn't apparently needed. For its next product launch, Polygon decided to spend $20,000 on marketing research.[1]

Even those who believe research *may* be valuable in a new product launch may still not embrace it enthusiastically for reasons we've outlined above. John Werner had developed a new coated-peanut snack food and hired a researcher to help with initial marketing decisions. But Werner was "very suspicious of the whole thing. It all seemed like a lot of talk. . . ." Yet, when the researcher got Werner directly involved in the research process (an approach we advocate fervently), he became a believer. Werner was recruited to survey his patrons himself and he found a large number of unexpected comments including one likening the product to dog food. Werner subsequently redesigned the product and used research to decide whether to go into supermarkets (not a good idea as it would require major advertising to build brand recognition), the most effective packaging (stackable bags) and the price ($3.25 for an eight-ounce bag). Despite a considerable outlay, Werner felt that the research ultimately "changed my mind about how to sell the product."

This perception is now much more widely shared. Research on new ventures such as this is deemed to be so crucial that financial sources such as Copley Venture Capital in Boston no longer consider proposals that are not backed by solid market research. As Copley general partner Julius Jensen says, "The professional [entrepreneurs] realize it is part of the process and are willing to do it."[2]

This book is designed to make not only willing, but eager, users out of all entrepreneurs. It is also for managers in large organizations with simpler decisions such as whether to change a direct mail piece, raise or lower a price, or run with a new advertising theme for an existing product. Research is essential in most of these cases. In a surprising number of cases, it is not only essential, it is affordable. The pages to follow will make that point, we hope, crystal clear.

---

[1] Amy Saltzman, "Vision vs. Reality," *Venture*, October 1985, pp. 40–44.
[2] *Ibid*

ORGANIZATION OF THE BOOK

We will assume that the reader is now at least willing to suspend major reservations about the prospect of doing more research and wants to move ahead.

In the pages to follow, we will attempt three things. First, we will show the reader how to decide when to use marketing research even when the budget is small and the stakes are not very high. Second, we will describe an approach that can ensure that, whatever research is undertaken, it is as useful as possible. Finally, we will describe and evaluate a representative range of techniques for carrying out relatively inexpensive research that is still of high quality—or at least of a quality level commensurate with the decisions management faces.

The next two chapters of the book begin by addressing two sides of the issue of when to do research. First, we consider the opportunity for research. Many managers do not see the myriad chances for conducting relatively simple investigations that would significantly improve their decision-making capabilities. They just don't "think research." In part, this is because too many managers are just unaware of the diversity of uses to which research can be put. Further, they may be unaware of the diversity of approaches research can take. Research can consist of something as simple and straightforward as planned, systematic observation of facts and events around us. It can be a simple market experiment or a controlled case study. It can be analysis of secondary data that already exist or a survey study of a convenient nonprobability sample. All are legitimate research approaches that, if they are done right and fit the circumstances, can prove extremely valuable to the openminded manager.

But one must be prepared to gather information, not just hope to recognize chances for research when they appear. Chapter 2 has as its major objective showing managers how to organize to ensure that data are there when they are needed. Research is much better if it is planned. If one is serious about research, it is critical to be systematic about it. A serious manager should prepare an annual plan for research just as one prepares an annual plan for advertising or R&D.

Merely recognizing opportunities to do research does not mean that the manager should plunge forward heedlessly. There are many times when the opportunity to do research ought to be passed by. Sometimes this is because the present state of the research art is just not up to the challenge of providing the needed information at a reasonable cost. This is especially the case when one is talking about research designed to explore customers' psyches—their attitudes, perceptions, motivations, and intentions.

One should also not do research when the economics of the decision situation argue against it. Chapter 3 takes up the general question of when it is economically sensible to go ahead with research and, if so, how much to spend on it. In this chapter, we introduce the concept of decision theory, showing how this formal approach leads to reasonable rules of thumb that will help the manager decide whether to do projects A, B, and/or C or to do nothing at all. It also shows how to determine what the total budget should be.

If research is to meet its promise, the end product must meet the specific needs management sets out to fulfill. In Chapter 4, therefore, we will assume that the manager and the researcher both *want* to make the research as relevant and useful as possible, but do not know how. The chapter offers a relatively simple approach called *Backward Research Design* that makes it much more likely that the research will be as useful as it can be. The reader, however, should be forewarned that a major caution in Chapter 4 is that both manager and researcher must be willing to devote considerable time to thinking through the research problem in advance and both must have *realistic* expectations about what research can do. Research cannot effectively tackle many topics and it can only be partially helpful in a great many others. If this book is to create satisfied users of research, it must ensure that they are not oversold users, especially when the overselling is something they unwittingly do to themselves.

Chapters 5 through 8 get down to the nitty-gritty of the volume by spelling out alternative ways of doing low cost but good research. In each of these chapters, we introduce a particular set of techniques and discuss ways in which they should and should not be carried out. Chapter 9 then considers the problems of collecting valid data, especially when using a questionnaire. Chapter 10 follows with an introduction to statistics designed to make a little less formidable a potentially intimidating topic by showing how statistics can serve rather than confuse the neophyte researcher. Chapter 11 concludes the discussion by outlining ways in which the researcher with a limited budget can acquire outside help and other resources to keep the overall costs of a research program as low as possible.

A CONCLUDING COMMENT

It is important to emphasize two key cautions at this point. First, the low-cost research approaches we are advocating here must be carried out with the highest standards possible (i.e., commensurate with the decisions and with the dollars involved). Second, slovenly low-cost research is, indeed, the most expensive kind since it can lead to worse decisions than those made without the research. The tragedy of much inexpensive research carried out by the untrained and the unsuspecting is that it is really cheap and *dirty* research and worse still—dirty often in ways that are hidden from management. It is always possible that bad research by chance will yield correct insights—sometimes because only a dunce would miss the obvious. But, in the long run, the only way a manager can be sure that the research has a pretty good chance of being right (and, if the procedure outlined in Chapter 4 is followed, on target) is if it is done with as high a level of research standards as the technique and the circumstances permit.

It is this writer's selfish belief that only if managers are satisfied with the research—only if they feel that they got as close to the truth as possible under the circumstances—are they likely to be repeat users of research themselves and to be vocal advocates of the idea of research to business colleagues, co-workers, and employees. Only then will this book achieve its goal of being itself an effective marketing tool.

As a marketer, I believe strongly that a product or an idea (such as the concept of cheap but good marketing research) will sell only if it meets its customers' needs and wants. In this first chapter, we have tried to expose many of the irrational barriers and mystifications that have kept managers with limited budgets from seeing how research can meet their real needs. The following pages provide the tools to achieve this end. But we have only opened the door. It will be up to the reader to make the first daring steps. We can only say that many other managers—some of whom are encountered in these pages—have found the effort extremely rewarding. If it is successful, this book can be only a beginning. On the other hand, if the book does its job and the reader implements many of the proposals made here, it is inevitable that he or she will be our best advocate.

REFERENCES

1. Churchill, Gilbert A. *Marketing Research: Methodological Foundations*. 4th ed. Hinsdale, Ill.: Dryden Press, 1986.
2. Tull, Donald S., and Del I. Hawkins. *Marketing Research: Measurement and Method*. 2nd ed. New York: MacMillan, 1980.
3. Boyd, Harper W.; Ralph Westfall; and Stanley Stasch. *Marketing Research: Text and Cases*. 4th ed. Homewood, Ill.: Richard D. Irwin, 1981.
4. Ferber, Robert, ed. *Handbook of Marketing Research*. New York: McGraw-Hill, 1974.
5. Green, Paul E., and Donald S. Tull. *Research for Marketing Decisions*. Englewood Cliffs, NJ: Prentice-Hall, 1975.

A good general reference from the social sciences:
1. Selltiz, Claire; Lawrence S. Wrightsman; and Stuart W. Cook. *Research Methods in the Social Sciences*. 3rd ed. New York: Holt Rinehart & Winston, 1976.

CHAPTER 2

PLANNING A RESEARCH PROGRAM

Marketing research opportunities are much more numerous than the typical manager thinks! In many cases, a simple, relatively cheap research study can help the manager make a better decision. As with any other important managerial activity it cannot be left to chance, but must be planned. And planning for research requires both an appreciation of the many ways research can help and a systematic approach to specifying and carrying out both continuing and special purpose studies. The low-budget manager must first learn to recognize research opportunities in the day-to-day work environment. For those not trained in research, this may take some time and conscious effort.

Consider the case of Phil Brady (a pseudonym), the Vice President for Development of a public television station in the Midwest. Brady's principal marketing objective was to secure listener and corporate donations to finance the station's day-to-day programming and its long-run capital expenditures. Once or twice a year he designed and conducted an on-the-air pledge drive, a highly successful marketing technique now almost universally employed in public television funding. However, despite the overall success of the technique, Brady felt he could do better in one important respect. Every year, 5 to 15 percent of the viewers who called to volunteer a pledge would, for some reason, neglect to make good on their commitment, requiring the station to undertake some additional follow-up marketing.[1] As a result

---

[1] Bogus or prank pledges were rarely a serious problem.

of these efforts (or perhaps independent of them) about half of the outstanding pledges were fulfilled.

This was a very frustrating situation for Brady. Because the typical pledge week can generate $50,000 to $100,000 in potential donations on each drive, even 5 percent nonfulfillment can mean a substantial loss of revenues. But Brady did not really know why the majority did not fulfill their pledges or exactly how to approach them. Most development managers simply send out reminder notices that treat nonfulfillers as if they fully intended to pledge and had simply let the matter slip their minds. This follow-up note is typically warm and friendly, thanking nonfulfillers for their pledges, welcoming them to the station's "listener family" and then gently reminding them that the pledged amount has not been received. It is assumed that nonfulfillers fall into three groups—those who had forgotten, those who were about to pledge anyway, and those who had changed their minds. It was assumed that those who truly had let the pledge slip their minds would be thankful for the reminder and that those who were about to mail the pledge anyway would not be offended by the letter's tone. Finally, it was hoped that those who had changed their minds about pledging would either respond positively to the warm note or be embarrassed by the fact that the station was counting on them. Brady had no idea what proportion of the no-shows fitted into the third category and whether a stronger letter would be more effective in motivating them to fulfill their pledge.

Brady was also uncertain about whether a mail follow-up strategy was the best way to contact these nonfulfillers. The manager wondered whether there would be any merit in marketing to the recalcitrant pledgers by telephone. This could be easily done by keeping on some of the volunteer telephone operators who worked during pledge week and having them do the follow-up. Brady didn't know whether this modest expense would be worth it.

Here we have an example of the classic problem that this book addresses. The manager was in a situation where not a great deal was at stake but it was enough to worry about. At the same time, he had some important areas of ignorance. He did not know whether to change the follow-up message to offer a stronger motivation and whether to change the form of that communication. Both represent opportunities for research. The manager had two decisions to make but, in the absence of specific research, was inclined to go along with intuition and "what we've always done," i.e., a mailed, friendly follow-up letter.

But Brady did not see this as a research opportunity. Mainly, he did not think it was worth the expense. He saw the potential gain from any kind of study as modest and the mental and financial costs of conducting the research to be significant. Part of the problem, however, was that he also did not really know what research technique might be appropriate and feasible; certainly not one that would also be low cost.

FRAMING THE RESEARCH PROBLEM

In thinking about this modest research opportunity, we must first ask just what might be meant by low cost in the present case? While formal consideration of the question of research budgets will be taken up in the next chapter, a sense of how a manager might proceed may be offered by attempting to make a rough estimate of the maximum the manager might budget in the present case. Assuming, then, that:

1. The typical pledge drive runs twice a year and collects $50,000 each time.
2. Those who need to be contacted for not fulfilling their pledges represent 5 percent of all pledgers.
3. One third of the latter would have fulfilled their pledges without a follow-up message, one third needed to be reminded, and one third had changed their minds.
4. The present mailed message is effective with most of those in the first two groups and only partly effective with the latter.

Given these assumptions, designing a better follow-up strategy could at best increase the station's revenues only by bringing in more of the $833 in pledges in each drive represented by the nonfulfillers who had changed their minds.[2] Assuming the present marketing strategy now motivates payment of $200 worth of these pledges and that the absolute most the station would get with a new tougher message and/or by using a telephone follow-up is $600, then any improvement in marketing strategy could yield at maximum $400 more per pledge drive *if* there was no additional cost to implementing the new strategy suggested by the research. In the case of a new message, the cost of changing to a stronger wording would be close to zero. If any research project recommended contacting nonfulfillers by telephone there would be the added cost of this different approach. On the other hand, the $400 gain would be extended over several pledge drives.

Two studies therefore are possible. One study could focus on learning about motivations and figuring out how to design a better approach to those who had changed their minds. The other study could focus on which medium is better, telephone or mail. Or, the two could be combined. If the two studies had payoffs that were realized over, say, three years (i.e., six pledge drives), the maximum one might invest is $2,400 (i.e., 6 × $400) in one or both studies. However, given that the research will *inevitably* be less than perfect, clearly a manager would want to risk considerably less than this amount, say $500 to $1,000.

The reader of the preceding paragraphs might conclude that a telephone study is probably not worth it because, even if telephone solicitation was found to yield more revenues, it would also incur more costs. On the other hand, the reader might feel that even an imperfect motivational study would be worthwhile because the cost of implementation would be so low. The reader at this point should not be unduly offended to learn that both of these conclusions are wrong! The motivation study represents an opportunity that should probably be passed up. On the other hand, the telephone study is a good, managerially useful research projet that can be carried out for one to two hundred dollars of out-of-pocket cost!

---

[2]One third of 5 percent of $50,000.

The Motivation Study

In the case of pledger motivations, discussions with any station development manager will make it clear that, even if a different set of pledger motives were discovered in a future research project, most managers would be very reluctant to use this information to change the follow-up message. One reason was implicit in the discussion about the target audiences earlier. Although there are three segments within the set of pledgers who do not initially fulfill their commitments, the motivational message would be directed only at those who had changed their minds. The manager will be legitimately worried that the other two groups may react negatively to a stronger, more insistent new message that is perceived as more irritating than the present warm and friendly one. The manager's fear is that for every newly motivated individual converted by a stronger letter, one or more of the others will decide not to pledge because of the more forceful tone. Thus, even if the research did discover the motivations of those who had changed their minds that could be worked on, most managers would probably not be willing to take the risks involved in changing the present approach.[3] For this reason the research should not be done because it will not affect a marketing decision. This is an important point and we will return to it in Chapter 4.

---

[3]A reasonable alternative approach might be to recommend that the manager continue the present mailing, wait several weeks, and then send out the new, tougher motivational appeal to those who have still not fulfilled their pledges. The manager—again legitimately—might express two reservations about this approach. First, a second mailing means additional costs, bookkeeping to keep track of very late nonfulfillers, designing, preparing, and mailing a second letter, and using a new set of stamped return envelopes. While these are not major expenses, they do reduce the amount that could be justified for research. Second, the manager might suggest that a message delivered several weeks after the initial pledge drive may be too late. Attitudes may have hardened by then, the excitement of the pledge week will have worn off, and other economic priorities will have intervened in the pledger's household. The likely payoff, then, from this second mailing will be much smaller than if non-pledgers were reached soon after the pledge drive. Further, one may also question whether a research study presumably designed to discover short-term barriers to pledging will prove valid for barriers remaining after several weeks.

There is, of course, another problem with the proposed motivational study; that is, whether the findings could really be trusted. Without a relatively heavy investment in sophisticated methodology, there is a serious question of whether one could really learn why those in the third group changed their minds. If many are embarrassed by their change of mind, there is good reason to believe that this same embarrassment would also cause many of them to be less than candid in an interview designed to get at the real reasons for their change of mind. This is clearly a research opportunity that should be passed by.

The Telephone Study

The case for a low-cost research study on the telephone versus mail follow-up approach is, however, much more encouraging. Here, one simply has a clear hypothesis to test, namely that the net revenues generated in response to a telephone follow-up with nonfulfilling pledgers will be greater than the net revenues generated by a mail follow-up. In both cases, net revenue is calculated as the return after the cost of the particular method of solicitation is deducted. The research that the hypothesis suggests is a rather simple experiment: take all of those who have not fulfilled their pledges at a particular point (e.g., after 14 days), randomly assign them to a telephone and a mail treatment group, contact them as the treatment indicates, keep track of the full costs of each treatment, and wait for the returns. The allocation of subjects to the two treatments need not be equal. Since telephone solicitation is more costly, one way to keep research expenses in check is to allocate less than 50 percent of the sample to the telephone condition. Whatever the proportion, the allocation must be random for the experiment to be valid.

The proposed experiment is really one that virtually anyone can design and implement with the prospect of a relatively high-quality outcome. The secret is only to make sure that the assignment of pledgers to treatment groups is random and that those doing the telephone solicitation do not behave (perhaps due to the fact that they know they are part of an experiment) in ways that will influence the study such that one cannot realistically project the results to normal future telephone solicitations.

A Low-Cost Study

Just such a study was done for Mr. Brady. The study came about because two students in the School of Business Administration at the local university were looking for a term project. After talking with Mr. Brady, they recognized the research opportunity and went ahead and designed and carried out the required experiment. The only costs to the station were modest additional telephone charges. Although the researchers' services were free, net revenues for the telephone treatment were calculated after estimating what it would have cost to acquire enough telephone lines to handle all the needed calls in the experiment and to pay full-time operators to make the contacts. Even with these costs included, and even though the sample was small, the research clearly demonstrated (in statistically supportable fashion) the superiority of telephone solicitation. The station has since implemented the recommendations as part of a broader telemarketing campaign.

It should be emphasized here that this was a student-initiated project. This reinforces the central thesis of this chapter—namely that most managers do not easily perceive research opportunities that routinely come up in their daily marketing activities. A second point is that there is a surprising array of free or low-cost resources in the outside world that can keep research within manageable budgets. In this case, the students found the station. It could have been the other way around if the station just looked for the opportunity. Students are a good free resource and can be particularly helpful if the project is of the relatively straightforward type described here. Indeed, in Chapter 11 we will outline a wide range of sources of such relatively low-cost or free, sometimes relatively sophisticated, market research help.

LOOKING FOR OPPORTUNITY

The foregoing extended example points out two key features of the problem of looking for and recognizing research opportunities.

The first lesson is that, if managers are to recognize and take advantage of research opportunities, they must learn to suppress the mental barriers to research that they have acquired over the years. As predicted in Chapter 1, the development vice president in the preceding case automatically reacted to the two research possibilities by saying:

- "The decision isn't really important enough to merit research. The dollars involved just aren't great enough."
- "It is impossible to get any reasonably good research done for the few dollars that can be afforded. I can't afford a survey."
- "Even if the research is affordable, it is impossible to imagine *how* to go about getting the research done without spending an arm and a leg for assistance."

As we have seen, all three arguments were really myths, the kind that can get in the way of a systematic program of marketing research.

The second lesson to be learned from the above example is that research opportunities do not usually reach out and tap one on the shoulder as was the case when the students came to Mr. Brady. For cheap but good research to become common practice in any organization, managers have to constantly look for these possibilities themselves. This involves two changes in typical management practice. First, managers must cultivate a sixth sense for the serendipitous research opportunity. From time to time in most organizations, there will appear not only needs for research but also chances for research and managers must train themselves to be alert to both. Second, management must develop an annual research plan as part of its annual planning cycle. The research plan requires that once a year the manager set out a research want-list and then either expressly budget to fill it in or fill it in with serendipitous projects as the occasions arise. We will consider the problem of research planning first.

RESEARCH PLANNING

An appropriate framework for beginning research planning on an annual basis is to start with a cataloging of the major types of marketing decisions that managers in the researcher's organization will face within a typical year's time, including decisions to maintain the status quo. These, then, can be the basis for determining what information is needed to help make each decision better. This, in turn, should yield a list of potential research projects that can be prioritized and implemented. In each succeeding year, the planning task then becomes one of determining whether any new decisions are to be made and/or whether the research programs already in place need to be modified in any obvious ways. This process is outlined in Figure 2–1.

The Decision Framework

While the decisions to be faced by each individual manager will be to some extent idiosyncratic, the kinds of marketing decisions most managers face will require information differing along three

FIGURE 2–1
Research Planning Process

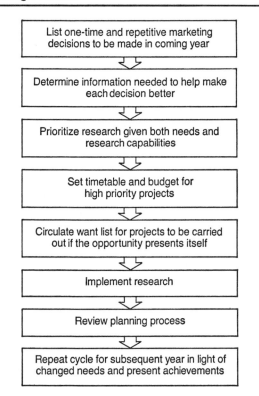

broad dimensions. First, decisions will be either long-run or short-run. Managers often must look down the road for several planning periods in order to decide whether to make investments that would put the organization in the best possible competitive position for that future environment. Contrasted to these decisions are those short-term decisions that relate to this year's, this month's, or even this week's activities.

The second dimension is the distinction between strategy and tactics. In the main, long-run decisions will involve broad issues of strategy—what markets to serve, what products or services to offer, what general approaches to use to match markets and offerings, and what organizational structure, systems, and personnel to employ to carry out these strategies. Short-run decisions, however, while often focusing on strategic questions, usually involve tactical issues such as choosing between advertisements A and B or setting up a new distribution plan to meet sudden shifts in the market and/or to respond to competitors' tactics.

The third dimension for research planning is whether the decisions are about (1) elements of the marketing mix—products, channels, prices, and promotion (advertising, personal selling, sales promotion, public relations), or (2) about the resources and structures needed to ensure that the mix is effectively implemented. The three dimensions, then, yield a basic framework for assessing marketing research needs at the start of the annual planning process. The framework is reproduced in Figure 2–2.

The manager can begin the marketing research planning cycle by listing the kinds of recurring decisions to be made in each of the six major sectors of Figure 2–2 over the course of the year. The next step in the research planning process is to ask what kinds of information are necessary and/or desirable to help make those decisions better. These information needs can then be translated into a funded program of future research and a list of projects to be carried out if the occasion arises.

A suggested list of the kinds of research projects that may evolve is included in Table 2–1. While this table reports the experiences of relatively large and sophisticated organizations in various types of businesses, it does at least suggest the kinds of marketing research that an aggressive low-budget researcher might contemplate.

FIGURE 2–2
Decision Checklist for Market Research Planning

Subject Area	Long-run Strategy	Short-run Strategy	Short-run Tactics
Marketing Mix Products offered Services offered Consumer prices Trade discounts Channels for distribution Advertising levels Advertising channels Advertising messages Salesforce size Salesforce composition Sales promotion Public relations			
Resources and Systems Warehouses and transportation Management staff Line staff Support staff Reporting systems Analysis capabilities Financial requirements			

Information Needs

It turns out that the information management will need in a given year will be descriptive, explanatory, or predictive.

Descriptive Information.   Here management is seeking to learn the state of its present market environment. One approach to specifying these *descriptive* needs is to conduct a *marketing audit.*[4] The market environment will be comprised of the following major dimensions.

Customers: Who is buying what at what price from what outlets with what method of payment? What are their preferences, attitudes, and intentions with respect to the present offerings of the firm and its major competitors?

---

[4]Philip Kotler and Alan R. Andreasen, *Strategic Marketing for Nonprofit Organizations,* 3rd ed. (Englewood Cliffs, N.J.: Prentice-Hall, 1987), pp 637–46.

TABLE 2–1
Percent of Firms Carrying Out Specific Marketing Research

	Consumer Marketers	Publishers & Broadcasters	Advertising Agencies	Industrial Marketers	Financial Services
Advertising research					
Motivation research	61	28	92	29	41
Copy research	78	35	99	55	53
Media research	72	78	93	57	65
Studies of ad effectiveness	86	71	96	67	82
Studies of competitive advertising	73	65	95	54	71
Business economics and corporate research					
Short-range forecasting (up to one year)	97	76	52	98	94
Long-range forecasting (up to one year)	96	76	49	94	91
Studies of business trends	90	76	77	99	92
Pricing studies	91	60	50	90	94
Plant and warehouse location studies	71	46	19	78	84
Acquisition studies	81	53	29	89	79
Export and international studies	69	19	32	82	29
MIS (management information system)	89	56	38	90	89
Operations research	71	46	38	68	78
Internal company employees	73	63	55	80	87
Corporate responsibility research					
Consumers' "right to know" studies	21	12	19	12	25
Ecological impact studies	37	7	4	35	9
Studies of legal constraints on advertising and promotion	58	25	40	46	55
Social values and policies studies	47	32	49	29	37

Product research					
New product acceptance and potential	89	68	76	73	89
Competitive product studies	97	76	83	92	96
Testing of existing products	98	71	81	86	76
Packaging research: design or physical characteristics	91	54	80	61	54
Sales and market research					
Measurement of market potentials	99	89	93	99	97
Market share analysis	99	98	96	98	97
Determination of market characteristics	99	99	93	99	98
Sales analysis	98	89	82	99	90
Establishment of sales quotas, territories	93	80	19	95	81
Distribution channel studies	89	66	26	83	68
Test market store audits	88	31	89	36	49
Consumer panel operations	87	63	90	31	53
Sales compensation studies	83	56	16	73	61
Promotional studies of premiums, coupons, sampling, deals, etc.	82	47	77	36	57
Number of firms	(143)	(69)	(60)	(124)	(100)
Mean Budgets (000)*	$1899	$379	$741	$379	$287
Median Full-time employees*	6	n.a.	7	3	3

*Of firms with formal marketing research departments

Source: Dik Warren Twedt, ed., *1983 Survey of Marketing Research*, (Chicago: American Marketing Association, 1983). Reproduced with permission.

Competitors: What strategy and tactics do competitors currently employ, what marketing mix, what spending levels, and with what organizational structures?

Channels: What channels currently carry the product or service? How do they transport, stock, display, explain, and promote the various offerings? What is the cost of providing these services? What are channel members' preferences, attitudes, and intentions with respect to competitors' offerings?

Marketing system performance: What products, sales-force members, or regional divisions generate what sales and profit levels?

Economic and social conditions: What is the status of general social approval or disapproval of the organization's offerings or marketing tactics? What is the state of employment and economic health in each of the major markets served?

Explanatory Information.   Here management typically seeks cause-and-effect linkages among the bits of descriptive information noted above so that decisions can be made as to whether to continue or to change any elements of the marketing mix. This means eventually getting answers to several questions.

Factors outside management's control: Do competitors' actions, social and economic conditions, consumers' and channel members' goals, attitudes, and preferences significantly influence the organization's marketing effectiveness and how?

Factors within management's control: Does the marketing mix directed at final consumers, channel strategy, personnel, and spending levels significantly influence marketing effectiveness and how?

Changing market factors: What factors make today's explanations consistent or inconsistent with those of the past, i.e., in what ways, if any, are the dynamics of the market changing?

Predictive Information.   Both the descriptive and explanatory information from the previous sections can serve as input into what is most essential to effective management: predictions about the future. Since the actions that the manager will take in the next year will have their consequences in the future, it becomes essential to know what that future will be like, and what will work in that future. Any descriptive and explanatory information gathered may or may not fill this role. It is up to management to determine just which of its present assumptions will hold true for the future.

Additional kinds of predictive information that management may also feel the need for include the following:[5]

- What are competitors' and channel member's likely future strategies and tactics as they might affect the organization's operations?
- Are there important developments in the political and social environment of which the manager should be aware that will pose critical opportunities or threats?
- What will the future technological environment be? Are there developments in techniques of production or delivery that the manager ought to be prepared to adapt to?
- Are significant shifts in consumer attitudes and behavior likely to arise in future that are *not* simply extensions of the past?
- What of the manager's own organization? If kept on the present course, are its financial resources, personnel, and systems going to be up to the tasks they will face?

As may be surmised, predictive information will be mainly useful for strategic decisions with implications for the longer run. Explanatory and descriptive information, on the other hand, is most valuable in shorter-run strategic and tactical decisions.

Getting Started

At this point, the reader may well be reeling from the apparent depth and complexity of the research planning process, espe-

---

[5]The inquisitive manager could do well in this regard to read some of the current popular predictions about the future environment such as Alvin Toffler's *Future Shock* or John Naisbitt's *Megatrends*.

cially when several products or divisions are involved. But three points must be made. First, because something is challenging doesn't mean that it should not be done. Who said planning was easy? If a manager is to be effective, sacrifices are going to have to be made. The hallmark of a modern marketing manager is that he or she does not run the marketing function by the seat of the pants. Careful, necessary soundings must be taken of the environment and then just as carefully merged into thoughtful plans. A manager must be organized and methodical, as well as creative and daring, to be a success. There are, of course, times when a manager must make decisions on the basis of intuition and gut feel because there is no other course. This obviously means going ahead without research or with only partly successful research because either the situation doesn't justify the expenditure or because the state of the art in research technology cannot provide the information needed. Still, a good manager must be systematic in making sure that seat-of-the-pants judgments are made only after—not instead of—the possibility of collecting research information has been carefully and systematically considered. This is the role of the annual research plan.

The second point to be made with respect to the planning process is that many of the possibilities enumerated above may not be relevant. Topics within a category may simply not be important to the manager and others who may be consulted in the research planning process.

Finally, the first time this planning task is carried out, it may prove very formidable, but the manager should take comfort in the fact that in subsequent planning cycles the task will be much more tractable—even easy.

Preparing the First Research Plan

The procedure recommended for the first cycling of this research planning task should have several characteristics that have proven to be important to virtually all kinds of serious planning efforts. To start with, all of the key management personnel who can usefully contribute to the planning process should be brought in on it. This should include not only key marketing staff members, but others who may be expected to use the information generated.

Also, if possible, an advisor from the outside market research community should be included in the initial planning steps. The advisor, on the one hand, can offer creative ideas for research projects based on technology with which management may not be familiar. On the other hand, he or she can introduce some realistic caution to the more ambitious or off-the-wall management suggestions.

It is critical to set aside a specific time for the research planning task early in the organization's planning cycle. Allow enough time to get the job done right! The time blocked off should—at least on the first iteration—be free of other obligations. A good approach is often to undertake the research planning activity away from the office.

Research categories should be covered one at a time starting with longer-range strategic needs in Figure 2–2 and then moving on to short-range strategy and then to short-range tactics. The first time around, the manager must be dogged in insisting that each category be covered and covered thoroughly.

Those participating should be instructed that the major objective of the planning activity is to construct what is in effect a research *want list*. This should make the exercise more enjoyable than many other annual planning tasks. Staff should be urged to be uninhibited, stating what they would ideally like to know to make better marketing decisions. At this step, they should be discouraged from arbitrarily censoring certain research wants as being foolish or undoable. The realities of the organization's budget and its research capabilities can be introduced at a later stage.

Prioritizing

The next stage—preferably after a good pause and perhaps a night's sleep—is to take each of the projects on the want list and group them into categories (see Figure 2–3).

Category A: Projects that are doable, presently essential, and meriting specific funding during the planning year.

FIGURE 2–3
Ranking of Annual Research Projects

Managerial Relevance	Research Capability	
	Doable	Not Doable
Highly important	A. Fund this year.	D. Seek outside suggestions on feasible methodology.
Somewhat important	B. Do not fund. Look for opportunities to fund small studies.	E. Remain vigilant for new methodology that can make study feasible.
Not important	C. Acquire only if free or very low cost.	F. Ignore.

Category B: Projects that are doable, but not so essential as to merit immediate commitment of funds. Category B projects are still high on the want list. Management must constantly seek opportunities and/or funds over the year to carry them out.

Category C: Projects that are doable but represent information it would be "nice" to have. Here, management should be alert to serendipitous opportunities to acquire the information free or at very low cost (for example, using some of the secondary sources or cooperative data collection strategies mentioned in Chapters 5 and 11).

Category D: Projects that would have fit into Category A, but are believed to be not presently feasible because of gaps in research knowledge or because the organization does not have access to the necessary skills. Since they are potentially Category A projects, i.e., they are projects to which management would clearly commit funds if they could bring the study off, some amount of managerial effort should be expended to ascertain whether the assumption about the infeasibility of these project is, indeed, valid. To achieve this end, a simple Request for Proposal (RFP) for a low-cost study on the topic could be sent out to several of the more creative local research suppliers or individual consultants to see if they can come up with ways of researching the problem.

Category E: There are presently nonfeasible projects that might fit Category B. Here, almost all that management should do is maintain the vigilance suggested in the last paragraph. As in the case of Category B projects, learning that a project is now doable still does not mean that the research should be done, only that it be put on hold until the opportunity presents itself.

Category F: These are projects that are both unimportant and not feasible given present methodology. They should be ignored by researchers in *any* organization.

The final stage in the research planning process is a time-table and specific budget for undertaking Category A projects and putting into motion activities needed to carry them out. At the same time, the manager should begin any steps that can be undertaken to explore the feasibility of deferred Category D projects. A list of Category B projects can be circulated to other managers with suggestions as to the kinds of occasions on which serendipitous data gathering might be undertaken.

Future Planning Cycles

Something like this procedure can then be repeated each sub-sequent planning year with important modifications. Taking the previous year's research plan, the manager need simply ask:

1. Which of last year's research projects have been completed that now do not need to be done again, at least for a while?
2. Which of those projects can be deleted as now irrelevant or otherwise unjustifiable?
3. What new projects need to be added either because over the year management has become conscious of the need for them or because circumstances have changed?
4. Which of the projects to be repeated will take the same form and which projects need to be updated to take account of new knowledge or new circumstances?

An additional step should be added after the first year. This is a review of the *process* itself. Management—or perhaps an outsider—should look at the research decisions that were taken on the basis of the first year plan and ask whether the planning process needs to be improved. This would involve investigating at least the following questions:

1. Was the categorizing system appropriate? Were projects in various categories A to E re-categorized over the year? Was there anything that could have been done in the planning process that could have anticipated these reassignments and that could be built into the next cycle?

2. What new wants were added to the list over the year and could these have been anticipated?

3. What Category D and E projects were shifted to Categories A and B and why? Does this suggest any systematic ignorance in the organization about the world of research that would recommend some sort of future management training or the greater use of outside experts?

4. Which Category B projects were actually carried out, if any? What precipitated them and can these "precipitants" be introduced in future to ensure that more low-cost research is actually carried out serendipitously?

All of this involves an evaluation of the research planning process. In the next chapter, we will address more directly the question of evaluating each individual research project in terms of its own specific criteria.

Summary

In closing this part of the chapter, we must restate the two major theses about cheap but good research developed in the first two chapters to this point. We have pointed out that many managers do not do more of this kind of research because they do not see the opportunity for it. Not recognizing opportunities is the result of three, often understandable, gaps in the knowledge of the low-budget manager. First, opportunities may not be perceived because the manager does not know what research can do. Second, they are not perceived because the manager does not want them to be perceived. The manager may fear a loss of control or a revelation of ignorance that is to be avoided at all costs.

Finally, in this last section we have argued that many managers do not see research opportunities because they do not systematically look for them. To overcome this, we have proposed an elaborate, perhaps daunting, procedure for systematically identifying research needs and making room for serendipitous research possibilities. While the task of setting up a research program may be forbidding the first time, we can in good conscience argue that over the long run recognizing and acting on opportunities for cheap but good research will put the organization in a significantly superior strategic position vis-á-vis its competitors. If nothing else, the research planning process can leave the new researcher-manager with a very satisfied feeling that comes from knowing that the organization is making sound, if risky, marketing decisions that have been backed by the best research information that the stakes at issue can justify. These would seem to be adequate rewards for the few grueling days of thinking, evaluating, and planning involved in the research planning process that we have outlined here.

SERENDIPITOUS RESEARCH— RECOGNIZING RESEARCH OPPORTUNITIES AS YOU GO

Of course, not all research projects can be planned ahead. Some come about because occasions for filling in items on this year's "want list" make their appearance.

A recent executive seminar provided the writer with just such an opportunity. I had been asked by the Public Broadcasting System (PBS) to spend an afternoon with their specialists in audience development to discuss several of the topics raised in this book. In preparation for the session, I read a good deal of the literature on the current turmoil in the telecommunications industry and quickly realized that I had limited appreciation of which topics in the broad area of marketing and marketing research might be of interest to this particular audience.

At the same time, I was also actively searching for ways to make my presentation and discussion more realistic and more dramatic. I decided that it would be quite useful to poll the audience development specialists at each of the 170 PBS affiliates around the United States and ask them which current marketing problems they would like to see addressed in my presentation. The poll would also ask about their years on the job, their formal education in marketing (if any), and their marketing experience. Since this request for help was to be a mail solicitation much like those that these audience development specialists send out all the time to potential donors and subscribers, I decided to try to demonstrate how this occasion could provide a serendipitous opportunity for research.

Many of the decisions that face those who use the mails for soliciting financial aid involve the positioning of the letter that incorporates the request for help. Two of the relatively minor decisions are (1) who signs the letter, and (2) how much should the mailing be personalized. In the present study, it was decided to determine whether it would be more effective to have the mail request signed by someone from PBS or by me. Would recipients of the solicitation respond better if the request came from a source with which they were familiar and to whom they might feel a certain responsibility (PBS)? Or, would the response be greater if the source was not personally known to the respondents, but was an independent individual in a high status position (i.e., a university professor) with whom they could be more candid and forthright?

The second issue was whether personalization of the correspondence would be worth the cost. While many direct mailers routinely use computers to make cover letters speak more directly to each recipient, many respondents claim that they know when a letter has been written by a computer.[6] A way to truly personalize the letter would be to include a handwritten note. This would be time consuming and costly but it might yield a higher payoff.

On the basis of the above considerations, it was decided to randomly split the sample of 170 specialists into four groups. One half of the sample was to be sent cover letters with a handwritten note at the bottom stating, "I would very much appre-

---

[6]Betty Furness once reported a bizarre case where a heraldry mail scheme obtained her listing as secretary at Consumer's Union and addressed all future correspondence to "Ms. Secretary" offering to provide her (at a small cost) "the Secretary family's coat of arms."

ciate your help in this request" (the personalized treatment). The other half had no note. One half of each of these groups received notes signed by me and one half received notes signed by the PBS director. One virtue of using this experimental design (formally called a *fully factorial* design) was that it would permit us to see whether the combination of a personalized solicitation from a particular source would be even more effective than the effects of the personalization and the nature of the letter writer taken separately. The criterion in testing the effects of these four experimental treatments was to be the overall rate of response to the request for the questionnaire information.

Before revealing the findings, it should be pointed out that this project was (1) carried out with high research standards, and (2) virtually costless since we were going to send the questionnaires out anyway and we did not feel we needed to place a stamp on the return envelopes.[7] The 170 organizations were assigned to the four treatment groups on a fully random basis. The four basic cover letters were identical in wording. The same handwriting was used for both personalized treatments. The letters were sent out the same day to everyone. All were on PBS letterhead and all were returned to me at UCLA. UCLA's computer was used to analyze the results and care was taken to apply only the appropriate analysis of variance statistics.

The findings were surprising. Essentially, there were no effects! This was significant and important to know. Both the program director and I (and much of the audience when I reported the results) expected that there would be a significant effect at least from the personalized note. Given these expectations, the results were very useful. It appears that the added cost of personalizing this kind of mail solicitation—at least in the way we did it—is not at all worth it! The research would save managers who send out frequent, large mailings considerable amounts of money they might have spent on unnecessary personalization. (Indeed, this is the current conclusion of experienced research practitioners.)

---

[7]The reader may be surprised to learn that the overall response rate for this cheap but good study was 61 percent, a rate achieved without any follow-up letters.

One other step in the analysis was taken. When it seemed likely that the overall response rate was not going to show any significant differences between treatments, it was then decided to go back and see whether there was any effect of the treatments on the speed of response as indicated by the postmark on the return envelope. In this case, there did turn out to be a modest, although still not statistically significant, effect here for one treatment combination. Personalized letters over my signature got marginally quicker responses. However, further computer analysis showed that a better predictor than the nature of the letter of how fast someone would return the questionnaire was how much formal training in marketing he or she had. The more the background in marketing, the faster the response. This would suggest that those who will respond quickest to any solicitation will be those who can most closely empathize with the solicitor's needs. This, too, is a conclusion one can generalize to other contexts.

This last set of analyses illustrates two other features of a well-designed program of cheap but good research. First, it will be noted that I went back to the database when a new research-able question—a research need—occurred to me. Although in this case, it was only a matter of a few days before I decided to take a second helping from the data by looking at the postmarks to gauge the speed of response, this could have occurred months, even years, later (assuming the data base was still available). Digging into an existing archive can be a very productive, virtually free research opportunity (ignoring for the moment the cost of the researcher's own time and effort). We will point out in Chapter 5 that such reworking of an existing data archive, whether already in analyzable form or requiring further modification, can often prove a very rich source of cheap but good research. And—to anticipate a point that will also be made later—a nontrivial advantage of using the PBS data base was that, since it was my own, I knew its flaws and, in fact, could take pleasure in its relatively high quality. This is often not the case when using someone else's data archive.

A second feature of my follow-up analysis is that the measure of speed of response used was not part of the original design. The postmark data were available for me to use as an archive, but I had to recognize this possibility. Then, all I had to do was to go back to each envelope and record its time trace.[8] There are a great many traces such as this available in the marketplace that are free for our use if we only have the imagination to see them and know how to fold them into our research program.

The last lesson that can be drawn from the PBS example relates to the computer analysis. Although our original interest was simply in the effects of the four experimental treatments on the quantity and speed of response, an attempt was made to see whether any of the other information that was collected about respondents along the way (i.e., their marketing backgrounds) was a predictor of the speed of response—as indeed was the case. Wringing as much information out of existing data sets as possible is a major technique for keeping the cost of research low.

THE DECISION OPPORTUNITY

There are a number of situations in which research can be done to contribute significantly to anticipated decisions that face a manager in the day-to-day competitive world of marketing. Daily, managers have many chances to act and, therefore, where there is time, many chances to do research. However, becoming a more effective decision maker through the use of cheap but good research requires the proper mind set. Learning to recognize research opportunities is not just a matter of being more alert for research windows, it is also having research techniques ready to apply. Section II offers just such an arsenal of techniques available at low cost that can be matched with relative ease to specific decision problems when they arise.

But research should not always be done even when a perfectly good low-cost technique is available. What is needed is the judicious use of research. There are many occasions where, even when there is a lot at stake, research should not be undertaken. But we will say more about this in the next chapter.

----

[8]In two cases, it turned out that the cancellation machine missed the entire envelope so that I could not discover the real date; one of the many tribulations of real-world research!

REFERENCES

1. Smith, Stewart. "Research and Pseudo-Research in Marketing." *Harvard Business Review,* March-April 1974, pp. 73–76.
2. Zaltman, Gerald, and Rohit Deshpande. "The Use of Marketing Research: An Exploratory Study of Manager and Researcher Perspectives." Cambridge, Mass.: Marketing Science Institute, 1980.
3. Huber, George. "Organizational Information Systems: Determinants of Their Performance and Behavior." *Management Science,* February 1982, pp. 138–155.
4. Rothman, J. *Using Research in Organizations.* Beverly Hills, Calif.: Sage Publications, 1980.

CHAPTER 3

EVALUATING INDIVIDUAL
RESEARCH PROJECTS

We will assume you are ready to embark on a modest program of preplanned annual research and are much more open to serendipitous research opportunities that might crop up in the future. You and your staff have already set aside a weekend in the woods to hammer out your very first research plan.

But now you are beginning to have second thoughts. "Where does it all end?" you say. "How will I know where to draw the line? How can I determine which projects to move ahead on and how much to invest in each? How do I set an annual budget for the entire research program? Basically, how do I figure out just how cheap the research *has* to be to be worthwhile?"

This chapter will try to answer these questions. To do so, we will introduce some concepts borrowed from what management schools call *formal decision theory*. But before outlining this approach, let us review some alternative rules of thumb for setting research budgets one encounters in less sophisticated organizations.

SETTING BUDGETS

The "Percentage-of-Sales" Pseudo-Equity Approach

This approach is based on some managerially divine notion of proportionality. It says, in effect, that there exists some magical percentage rate that ought to be applied to whatever is at stake in a given managerial decision to establish a reasonable budget for research. For the annual budget, it might be a fixed percent of projected sales. For a specific project, it might also be a percent of the projected sales or of the capital investment involved.

The approach has a nice simplicity. It is easy to compute and easy to justify. It deflects criticism and internal conflict within the organization. For example, suppose your CEO sees that you plan to spend $51,386 on research this year compared to only $36,912 last year and wonders why the great increase. You can easily justify the increase by pointing out that last year's expenditure was just one half of 1 percent of the investment made in new product development and—lo and behold—the current budget is *also* one half of 1 percent of new product investment!

Or, suppose a division complains that the research budget set aside for its problems has been cut 25 percent while another division's budget has been increased 12 percent. The seeming inequities can be resolved again by showing that resulting final figures were one half of 1 percent of sales in both cases!

This approach is like the advertising manager's reliance on percent of sales as the determinant of the advertising budget. The fallacy in research budgeting is the same as in advertising— the percentage chosen may not be adequate or may be excessive for the tasks at hand. In advertising, the reliance on sales as the basis for the budget calculation leads to the peculiar outcome that, when sales are down, when competition is toughest and advertising should be working its hardest, the percentage calculation leads the firm to cut back on its advertising budget. Conversely, when the sales and profit picture is rosiest, when customers are falling all over themselves to buy any and every product the firm and its competition can produce, the Iron Law of the Percentage dictates that the firm should spend more on advertising.

In a sense, the same antilogic applies to research expenditures. Managers seem to think that research *need* is related to the stakes involved in a particular decision. If the stakes are great, you should spend a great deal and when the stakes are smaller you should spend less. Now, of course, what you can spend on research is not independent of what is at stake and, other things equal, the more dollars at stake the more one ought to spend on research. But still, a moment's reflection points to an obvious fallacy in all this. There are many cases where management is going to go ahead with a particular course of action in some major sales category unless the research would indicate that management's assumptions were 180 degrees off base. Although the stakes involved in these projects would allow a significant amount of research, management would not change their minds because of the results. The same logic would apply to a boom market. If sales are expected to be very strong, management may not be worried about making the right decisions about, say, advertising copy. They may believe that almost anything will work. Again, research is less often justified even though sales are high. Conversely, when sales are down, management may be very worried about making just the right decision. On these occasions, despite the smaller stakes, the value of research is much greater.

The illogic of the percentage method for research budgeting can also be seen dramatically when one considers the perfectly performing product line currently experiencing no major competitive problems, no managerial issues. The Iron Law would suggest that one should still spend the Magic Percentage on this category. Does management hope that the research in these circumstances will come up with strategic insights or undetected weaknesses that will justify the research in the first place? This is the kind of fishing expedition we warned against in the previous chapter.

The Affordable or Residual Approach

One rationale for the percent-of-the-sales approach is that it makes sure that the organization can afford the research. If sales are up, it can afford more research. If sales are down, it can afford less.

Although they are similar, the affordable philosophy is a little different from that found in the percent-of-sales approach, in that it is based on a calculus that subtracts from sales or the stakes at issue all other direct justifiable expenditures plus a normal profit and then asks, "What is left for discretionary items such as research?"

Unfortunately, this is a frame of mind that sees marketing research as a highly discretionary expenditure. In part, this attitude reflects years in which too much research has indeed proved to be less than fully useful, if not totally irrelevant, to management's needs. Given this history, in times of financial stringency, managers can easily convince themselves that budgets for research that is likely to be of limited usefulness can be decimated to the immediate benefit of the bottom line with what is assumed are no major long-run negative impacts on the organization.

The affordability approach has the exasperating effect of making the research budget gyrate even more grotesquely than the company's sale curve. When sales are off a little, discretionary research budgets fall quickly to zero and planned research projects are curtailed dramatically if not totally. And when sales are up, discretionary budgets may soar even more rapidly (although one suspects never as high as the research director would like). This volatility under both the percentage and affordable approaches tends to make a career in marketing research even more fragile than one in advertising.

The fallacy here is the very same as that for the percentage of sales approach: there is no logical reason why the affordability calculation will bear anything but the remotest relationship to the *need* for this research. It is this latter criterion that should be management's guide, not some arbitrary, inflexible rule of thumb.

The Free Market or Delegated Approach

This approach usually stems from management's naiveté about what is needed to solve decision problems. In effect, it throws the budget problem into the hands of the research supplier by means of a request for research proposals. In its extreme form, it says in effect, "I have a rough idea about how much is too much—but I don't really understand what kind of research I need, nor do I know how much it will have to cost. You educate me and perhaps I'll buy it."

Ironically, the manager adopting this approach very often feels that he or she will not be really at the mercy of the suppliers in determining the research budget if the project is put out for bids. The manager apparently assumes that there is some sort of competitive market out there. If several organizations respond to a Request for Proposal (RFP) for the project, the manager expects to become pretty well educated as to the cost and design implications of doing the research by reading their submissions. Then, by taking one of the lower-priced alternatives, the manager may erroneously believe that everything possible has been done to keep the cost appropriate to the problem.

The key fallacy in this commonly used approach is that the manager expects the bidding cost somehow magically to be in line with the decision. Yet, the cost-determining processes the manager has set in motion are really driven by the technology the researchers choose to bring to bear and to some extent by market forces and the suppliers' bidding strategies. It is as if, in the days before the motor car, a manager put out requests for bids for a method for moving raw materials over land without relying on fixed rail beds or waterways. Sending this problem out for bids may get a lot of very expensive and very strange proposals (reflecting the state of the art). But unless the manager really has thought through what this thing called a truck will do for the company, the budget may end up 5, 10, or 15 times what it ought to be. So it is with the research RFP. One can, indeed, spend a great deal more than one ought. Different bidders will quote on different designs using different overhead allocations based on different (often arbitrary) accounting standards and profit rates with the final total based in part on the supplier's estimate of the requesting organization's naiveté and/or generosity. Certainly, under this scenario there is no reason to believe that the amount will be at all appropriate to the management's decision.

Other Factors

There are a number of other factors that will come into play to either expand or contract a budget even where the basic criterion is relatively rational. Budgets may be affected by the following considerations.

Customer Relations. Sometimes questionnaires or depth interviews are intended in part to gather information and in part to allow customers to voice opinions. A much larger sample than is necessary (e.g., the entire population) may be surveyed in part to develop goodwill. Sackmary cites a university study of the opinions of all incoming freshmen as excessive from a sampling theory perspective, but desirable from the standpoint of student relations.[1]

External Political Necessity.   Sometimes studies are too extensive because of some perceived external requirement to leave no stone unturned. This is typically the case where data are to be used as part of a legal case or in a regulatory setting.

Internal Political Necessity.   When there is fear that a decision is about to be attacked or where a department is in some organizational jeopardy, research budgets can become bloated as researchers rush to protect their backsides. This is not unlike the effect of growing malpractice threats on the research budgets of physicians and hospitals.

Rhetorical Necessity.   For a researcher or a manager to win specific internal corporate battles, it may be necessary to have a larger study than is statistically essential. There may be some accepted sample size below which those who must be convinced of the results will lack confidence. Sackmary gives the example of a statewide telephone survey for a public health agency where a sample size of 500 was chosen because "prevailing wisdom, past experiences, and previous reports appeared to have conspired to create the myth about the magic of 500." In a corporate setting, it is not uncommon to hear naive managers say, "How could you possibly conclude that when the sample size is so small?"

DECISION-BASED RESEARCH BUDGETING

If the preceding examples outline approaches one should not use to budget research, then how should one do it? It will come as

---

[1]Benjamin Sackmary, "Deciding Sample Size Is a Difficult Task," *Marketing News,* September 13, 1985, pp. 30, 33.

no surprise to the reader that the answer advocated here is *to begin with the decisions or decisions at issue*. This, of course assumes that, by the point at which the question of how much to budget is raised, the potential researcher will have framed the basic research issue in terms of one or more decisions to be made by the organization. If this is not the case, then it is essential that they and/or the managers involved go back and make this determination.

Structuring the Decision

What, then, is it about the decision that will affect what one should spend on the specific research project, indeed, whether to spend anything at all?

To answer this question it will be useful to make a brief detour into the academic world of decision theory. Decision theory may seem intimidating because of the jargon it uses, but it is simply a structured way of thinking about management problems. It says that all decision situations have five major characteristics:

1. The decision alternatives.
2. A decision environment.
3. The expected outcomes.
4. The probabilities of various futures coming to pass.
5. A decision rule.

Decision Alternatives
The first step management must take is to set out all the decision alternatives that they are realistically considering. These alternatives can be very simple—such as whether to leave a price as it is or raise or lower it 5 percent. Or they can be relatively complicated—such as whether to (1) introduce product A containing raw materials one, two and three, at a price of P, an advertising budget of $M and an advertising theme of Q, or (2) introduce product B with raw materials one, four and six, at a price of 2P, an advertising budget of $1/2M and the same advertising theme Q. The only requirement is that each alternative should be mutually exclusive from every other alternative. The

alternatives needn't be exhaustive, but they should cover the major alternatives management is considering.

Relevant Environmental Influences on Decision Outcomes

The next step is to specify the major dimensions of the future environment that will affect whether the choice of alternative one, two or three is a good or bad idea. These could be factors outside management's control such as future interest rates or the proportion of a market already owning a particular electronic appliance or accounting software. Alternatively, they could be factors over which management could have some influence through the alternatives it chooses, such as competitors' prices and advertising budgets. These environmental influences—formally called *states of nature* in the decision theory literature—also can be very complex. For example, one future facing a marketer of VCRs could be that interest rates will be at 11 percent, that 35 percent of the market will own VCRs, that competitors' average price will be $312 and that their average advertising budget will be $3.5 million. Another future could be an interest rate of 12 percent, 20 percent VCR penetration, $350 average price, and advertising at the $4.5 million level. These alternative futures need not be exhaustive, but do need to cover the major possibilities.

Outcomes

For each combination of decision alternative and future environment, management must estimate an outcome. Typically, this outcome will be a dollars-and-cents estimate of the consequences of taking some action in the face of some particular environment, e.g., net profits before taxes. For nonprofit organizations, the outcomes may be stated in other terms such as votes for a candidate or for a referendum, or the number of individuals taking up a good health habit or visiting a museum.

Probabilities about the Future

Managers are usually not neutral about the future. They have hunches or intuitions that some futures are more likely than others. They are often based on years of experience and sometimes on a recent similar situation. Formal decision theory simply requires that management write down these estimates as probabilities. These probabilities are called *prior probabilities*.[2] They must add up to one since they (theoretically) cover all possible "futures."

A Decision Rule

This complex mix of alternatives, future environmental states, outcomes and subjective probabilities must now be combined in order to come up with a final decision. This requires that management decide on a rule that it is going to use to choose among the alternatives. There are several rules that *could* be used by management. Two decision rules that are not usually recommended are outlined in Exhibit 3–1.

A weighted average rule (called the *Expected Value Rule* in formal decision theory) is somewhere between the two extremes outlined in Exhibit 3–1. It requires that the manager explicitly use the probabilities of the various future environments to weigh the outcomes under each decision alternative. The recommended course of action then becomes the one that yields the best weighted sum of all possible future outcomes with each outcome weighted by the probability of its occurrence. This doesn't guarantee one will be correct in any specific case. But, in the long run, the weighted average rule will yield the best average payoffs. This is likely because, in each decision instance, use is made of *all* that management knows about the decision situation.

The framework also gives us the direction we need in deciding when to do research and how much to spend on it.

---

[2]To provide the reader with even more intimidating jargon for cocktail parties, it may be noted that the process whereby prior probabilities are revised in the light of research information uses a mathematical formula called *Bayes Theorem*. As a consequence, the general approach of having managers explicitly introduce their subjective probabilities into their decision making has come to be known in more advanced management circles as Bayesian Decision Making!

EXHIBIT 3–1

Alternative Decision Rules

1. **Going for Broke.** This rule—formally called the maximax criterion in decision theory—advocates that the manager choose that course of action which, across all combinations of actions and future environments, yields the single best outcome. This, of course, is a rule expressly made for the high rollers or for those organizations that, for some reason or other, believe they will stand or fall on the basis of getting one big payoff. The major deficiency of this rule is that it expressly ignores all other (potentially negative) futures that are also possible.

2. **Playing It Safe.** The other extreme is to look at the worst outcome under each alternative course of action and choose the action that involves the best worst outcome. This is known formally as the minimax criterion and is advocated for the very conservative organization. This might be one that is so financially strapped that it cannot survive a very bad loss. For most organizations, however, this approach is also faulty in that it does not consider other possible outcomes under the chosen alternative that may greatly affect its overall desirability.

A Simplified Example

To make this framework more concrete, let us consider a hypothetical, but typical, example of a simple research problem a low-budget manager might face.

Assume that the manager of a university conference center in a woodsy resort area wishes to increase room occupancy on weekends. Weekends are a time with few conferences, yet continuing high fixed costs of operation. Traditionally, the manager has promoted weekend vacations at the center through a general-purpose brochure directed at three markets: university faculty, university staff, and alumni. The brochure describes all of the center's programs and features, trying to offer an incentive for every different taste and interest. He is now considering a carefully targeted brochure aimed at families with young children promoting family weekends at the conference center. He believes such a brochure can be narrowly distributed to those likely to have families by developing a mailing list aimed at (1) assistant and associate professors, (2) staff who have been with the university 5 to 15 years, and (3) alumni who graduated 5 to 15 years ago. Each of these groups can be precisely identified.

The proposed brochure would feature child-centered activities and would cost approximately $800 to produce. The manager's principal concern at this point is that he is not sure that his target audience would be interested in family-centered weekends. He fears that they may rather prefer childless weekend getaways. If that were the case, his new brochure might actually decrease bookings by scaring away those who wish to escape. The key question he now faces is whether to conduct research to assess the target audience's preferences or to proceed with his present best judgment.

Assume that discussions with the manager produce the payoff table outlined in Figure 3–1. If he continues to use the present general brochure, his revenues will be unchanged (except for any trends, etc.) from what they are now. He estimates that if he uses the new brochure and is right about the audience being child-centered, he will reap $3,600 added revenues from which he would have to deduct the cost of the brochure. If he is wrong, he will only lose $400 in revenues, plus the $800 for the brochure. At the moment, he thinks there is a 60 percent chance he is right.

FIGURE 3–1
Formalized Decision Problem (Payoff Table in Terms of Gains or Losses from Normal Campaign)

Alternatives	Market Preferences		Weighted Average Expected Payoff
	Child-Free	Child-Centered	
New brochure	− 1,200	+ 2,800	+ 1,200
Normal campaign	0	0	0
Probability	.4	.6	
Weighted average expected payoff = .4 (− 1,200) + .6 (+ 2,800) = + 1,200			

Figure 3–1 indicates that, using the weighted average criterion, the rational course without research is to go ahead with the new brochure. The expected payoff is $1,200 greater than the payoff with the traditional campaign. What is it worth to him to check out his intuitions through research?

One way to approach the problem is to estimate the *cost of uncertainty,* i.e., formally calculate how much he is worse off by not knowing the truth about his market. Let us assume the manager could acquire perfect information from the all-knowing Madame Olga. If Madame Olga found that the market wanted child-free weekends, it would be better to send out the regular brochure and keep the revenue as it is now (i.e., zero payoff). If Madame Olga said the market wanted child-centered weekends, the manager would use the new brochure and reap a payoff of $2,800. At the moment, as we have already seen, his best guess is that there is a 60 percent chance that Madame Olga will say the market is child-centered and a 40 percent chance that she will say it is child-free. Thus, the weighted expected outcome from perfect research (using Madame Olga) is $1,680 (i.e., [.6 × $2,800] + [.4 × 0]). The difference between this expected payoff with perfect information and the present expected payoff without research is obviously the most he would pay for this perfect study. This amount, $480, is a dollar measurement of the cost of uncertainty. He is $480 worse off by not knowing with certainty what the truth is. It represents the most the manager should pay for any research study since it is the most that should be paid for a perfect study.

Determinants of the Cost of Uncertainty

There are two factors that directly affect the cost of uncertainty. The most obvious one is the stakes involved in the decision. If we were dealing with dollar amounts 10 times greater than those entered in Figure 3–1, the cost of uncertainty would also be 10 times as great.

The other determinant is the manager's uncertainty. But this uncertainty is not what you might think. It is not how uncertain the manager is about the state of the current market or what it will be in the future. Rather, it is the manager's uncertainty about the best course of action to take. There are times when the manager will not need research even though there are great gaps in knowledge about the market if the organization is already quite committed to a specific program or course of action. Alternatively, research may be very important if the manager has strong feelings about the nature of the market, but is still quite unsure about what to do. The latter case often comes about when the manager has strong forebodings about the market, but still sees a particular venture as worth a try. For these reasons, we will refer to this second determinant of the research budget as *decision uncertainty*.

Imperfect Research

Of course, the manager cannot acquire a perfect study. We are, thus, still left with the question of what the manager should do about buying a research study that will not be perfect. The first step in the present example is to ask whether there is any way one could get a reasonable estimate of the truth for a cost less than $480. Since this is the upper boundary on research expenditure, it serves as a quick checkpoint for determining whether the study is feasible under any circumstances.

Suppose the manager, after having read through the remaining chapters of this volume, feels that there are at least some techniques that might be useful for this problem at a reasonable cost—such as convenience sampling or telephone research using present center staff. The question now is how much should be budgeted for such research given that it will be imperfect? There is a formal answer to this question using decision theory and a spreadsheet computer program with which experienced decision makers are familiar. However, most managers at this point simply use judgment and experience in light of the stakes and degree of decision uncertainty involved to decide just how much less than the maximum (perfect study) amount should be committed.

Other Factors

It is important to note that, although dollars and cents of profit have been used as the measure of the stakes involved in the example above, it is possible that the stakes may have some nonmonetary elements. These could include risks to personal careers or to a company's Wall Street image, or could risk the possibility that a government agency will come snooping around. These consequences are difficult to quantify and a consideration of techniques to attempt to do so is beyond the scope of this book. However, it is perfectly valid—and indeed sound management practice—to augment or decrease a particular dollars-and-cents outcome to take account of what are felt to be the nonquantifiable, but important, outcomes in the decision environment. For example, in the present example, the manager might wish to add a value of $1,000 to the payoffs under the new brochure option to reflect an imputed value for the positive effects on staff motivation of simply trying any new approach.

WHEN TO RESIST RESEARCH

This book is premised on the notion that research should be a more frequently used management tool once a wider audience becomes aware that research can be understandable, low cost, and useful.

There are two kinds of danger here. First, if managers become more aware of research approaches that are relatively inexpensive and relatively simple, they may do too much research, arguing that "—since the cost of the research can be kept so low, why don't we go ahead and do the research anyhow?" Such why-not research can lead all too often to wasted research funds. The manager who too often says, "Why not?" may well be one who will eventually shift from a positive attitude toward research to a negative attitude. Since many of the why-not studies will be of little value to the managers, they may well come to conclude that, indeed, research usually is wasted!

There are two major rules one should use in order to resist the urge to do unnecessary research:

> *The manager should resist the "research urge" if (1) the research is not directly related to some decision to be made, and (2) there is some reasonable degree of uncertainty as to the correct action to take.*

The second danger in too much research is that attempts to do cheap but good research will quickly degenerate into the old faithful cheap and dirty research. In later chapters, we will introduce a number of techniques that are relatively simple and straightforward in concept in addition to being low cost. Each of these chapters will contain admonitions to the researcher to observe standards that will differentiate good from dirty research. We will try to make it difficult for the careful researcher to unknowingly carry out dirty research. Where cost constraints force an easing of quality constraints, however, the researcher must know where the potential biases will creep in and how to make allowance for them in subsequent decision making.

Being able to carry out successfully a quality research program, even a low-cost one, requires considerable training (or at least careful reflection about what is written in these pages) and care and conscientiousness.

> *The manager should resist the research urge if the research is likely to be flawed in ways that cannot be estimated or adjusted for when making a decision.*

There are also a number of other situations when one should also be cautioned to avoid research.

1. *A manager should resist doing research if it is really designed to bolster the manager's personal insecurities.* If the manager has worked through the decision framework outlined above and come to the clear conclusion that research is not a rational choice, one should not still go ahead simply because the research is not too expensive and will just make the manager feel better about the risky action about to be taken.

2. *The manager should resist research if it is designed only to provide ammunition to justify a decision to others in the organization.* If experience says that the boss or rival managers will insist on research to back up your actions, research should be done. This is a rational choice, but costs should be kept within reason. However, the research should not be done on the rare chance it will be politically necessary.

3. *A manager should resist research designed just to check up on how things are going.* Unless such checking is part of a consciously designed program of market monitoring or unless there is reason to believe something is up out there, this checking up is—to be candid—just another managerially cowardly act.

One should keep an ear to the ground informally all the time. However, committing research dollars where an informal ear will suffice is an abuse of fiduciary trust.

4. *A manager should resist research that is, at base, a fishing expedition.* Over time, every manager faces spells of corporate malaise and vague uneasiness when someone may say, "Why don't we take a look at . . . ?" If the look can be justified by some concrete suspicions or supporting rationale, then formal research can be justified. A fishing expedition can be pleasurable—to pursue the metaphor—and, if it is just the manager's own time and money involved, it is not irresponsible. Indeed, (like all fishermen, I suspect) the manager may catch fish just often enough to be convinced that the activity is justified by the payoff. However, in research, if the activity is not rationally justified as helping managers make specific decisions now or in the future, it should be avoided.

5. *A manager should resist research that is designed to appeal to the manager's curiosity.* Many wasteful research projects have grown out of the pregnant expression, "Wouldn't it be interesting to know if . . ." (for example) more women used the product than men; corporate ads reached a lot of political bigwigs; the Eastern region was more profitable because it had more large accounts and so forth. Interesting research results are not useful research results unless they affect actions. Whenever the manager hears (or says), "Wouldn't it be interesting . . . ," a loud bell should ring. One should first analyze the decision carefully on paper, asking whether further research information would change the decision materially. If the answer to the question is no, the conclusion should be to suppress the manager's curiosity and not waste company resources.

6. *A manager should resist research that keeps up with the Joneses.* Rare is the manager who hasn't once in a while come back from a conference, a meeting with the advertising agency, or a telephone call to another company division and been frustrated that someone else is doing more or different research than he or she is. This is particularly a problem with research fads. Many years ago I was asked to do a psychographics study for a major Eastern bank. It seems that the marketing director

had just returned from a conference somewhere where everybody was talking psychographics. The manager felt left out, behind the times. His ego was bruised. And darn it, he was going to have *his* psychographic study. A two-hour discussion, however, quickly revealed two things. First, the manager had not at all thought through how he was going to use the psychographic study to affect advertising decisions, product offerings or, indeed, much of anything else. He apparently expected this to emerge from the results (the old fishing expedition problem). Second, our discussions revealed that there were a lot of other, much more important gaps in the bank's marketing knowledge that cried out to be filled before doing a psychographics study. A simple inexpensive research project would analyze internal records to learn which customers used more than one service (i.e., had a checking account *and* a safety deposit box or had a mortgage *and* a Christmas Club Account and so on). This could yield management much valuable information as to which services to sell to customers of other bank services and which to sell to single-service customers. A short survey of multiple-services customers might also be undertaken to assess reasons for heavy use, and motivations and barriers that seemed to affect multiple use. Such insights could then suggest how solicitations directed at single-service users could be worded. (Needless to say, the bank manager found someone else who would do his psychographics study!)

7. *A manager should resist research for the sport of it.* Research can be seductive. Many times, I have found myself going back to do one more computer run or add one more particularly complex questionnaire or conduct a simple little experiment just because I was excited about the project. It is challenging to see whether one can do it! But I try hard to avoid these urges— especially when I am spending someone else's money. Research can be fun. It can provide its own momentum. It is absolutely crucial to make sure that this momentum is towards *useful* research and not towards research for its own sake. To do otherwise will make the researcher in effect an accomplice to misappropriation of corporate resources!

REFERENCES

1. Blankenship, A. B. "Marketing Research Expenditures, Budgets and Controls." In *Handbook of Marketing Research,* ed. R. Ferber. New York: McGraw-Hill, 1975, pp. 1-73–1-84.
2. Raiffa, Howard. *Decision Analysis: Introductory Lectures on Choices under Uncertainty.* Reading, Mass.: Addison-Wesley, 1968.
3. Bass, Frank M. "Marketing Research Expenditures: A Decision Model." *Journal of Business,* January 1963, pp. 77–90.
4. Assmus, Gert. "Bayesian Analysis for the Evaluation of Marketing Research Expenditures." *Journal of Marketing Research,* November 1977, pp. 562–568.

CHAPTER 4

BACKWARD MARKETING RESEARCH[1]

An executive of an entertainment company decided that she knew too little about the consumer segments she was serving or hoped to serve. She had been practicing an obvious segmentation strategy aiming some programs at younger audiences, some at older ones, some at families, and some at singles. She needed a more sophisticated strategy, so she commissioned a research agency to analyze the company's market.

Despite high hopes, glowing promises, and the production of a glossy report heavy with statistics, the executive was disappointed in the findings. She said, "The research mostly told me things I already know."

Her service operated in an industry whose primary consumers had already been studied more than 200 times. Each study said virtually the same thing as this one: the audience was largely female, economically upscale, well educated, urban, and mainly on either end of the age distribution scale.

"Even where the results were new," she said, "they didn't tell me what I needed to know so I could use them." The consumer profile relied on demographics as the principal segmentation variable. "Sure," the manager added, "I know that men attend less than women, but why? Do they see fewer benefits than women or are there barriers to attendance that apply to men and not to women? And what about the age differences? Does

---

[1]Much of the material in this chapter originally appeared as: " 'Backward' Marketing Research," *Harvard Business Review*, May-June 1985, pp. 176–182.

the middle-aged group drop out because we don't meet their needs or are they just into things that we can't match, like building a family?" She had learned who her customers were, but nothing about how to motivate them.

"When the researcher tried to explain the results, it was obvious he hadn't understood what I wanted. The results were all a bit off the mark." Take for example, the measurement of loyalty. The researcher assumed his client wanted a behavioral measure, so he sought information on the proportion of recent entertainment purchases that were from each competitor and on recent outlet-switching patterns. But she also wanted an attitudinal measure revealing consumer intentions. She wanted to know less about their past loyalty than about their likely future loyalty.

HOW RESEARCH GOES WRONG

We can sympathize with this executive's complaints, although clearly she must share the blame for poor study design. She neglected to make the undertaking a real collaboration with the researcher. This is a common fault. Indeed, studies of research successes and failures point again and again to close collaboration between researcher and client as the single most important factor predicting a good outcome.

The typical approach of the two parties starts with defining the problem. Then, they translate the problem into a research methodology. This leads to the development of research instruments, a sampling plan, coding and interviewing instructions, and other details. The researcher takes to the field, examines the resulting data and writes a report. This traditional approach is outlined in Figure 4–1.

The executive then steps in to translate the researcher's submissions into action. She has of course already devoted some thought to the application of the results. From my observations, however, before the research is undertaken, the intended action is left vague and general. Managers tend to define the research problem as a broad area of ignorance. They say in effect, "Here are some things I don't know. When the results come in, I'll know more. And when I know more, then I can figure out what to do."

FIGURE 4–1
Forward Research Design

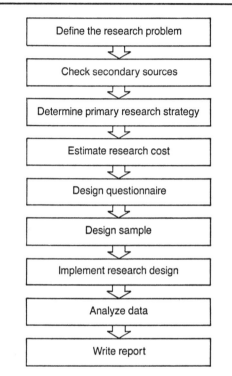

In my experience, this approach makes it highly likely that the findings will be off target.

What I suggest is a procedure that turns the traditional approach to research design on its head. This procedure, a proven one, stresses close collaboration between researcher and corporate decision makers. It markedly raises the odds that the company will come up with findings that are not only interesting, but will lead to actionable conclusions.

There are only two cases in which research is not expected to be immediately actionable. The first is when the research is intended to be basic—that is, to lay the groundwork for later investigation or action rather than have any near-term impact. The second occasion is when the research is methodological—that is, it is designed to improve the organization's ability to ask questions in the future. Except for these two instances, research should be designed to lead to a decision.

TURNING THE PROCESS ON ITS HEAD

The backward approach I advocate rests on the premise that the best way to design usable research is to start where the process usually ends and then work backward. So we develop each stage of the decision on the basis of what comes after it, not before. This approach is outlined in Figure 4–2. The procedure is as follows:

1. Determine how the research results will be implemented (which helps to define the problem).
2. To ensure the implementation of the results, determine what the final report should contain and how it should look.
3. Specify the analyses necessary to fill in the blanks in the research report.
4. Determine the kind of data that must be assembled to carry out these analyses.
5. Scan the available secondary sources and/or syndicated services to see whether the specified data already exist or can be obtained quickly and cheaply from others. (While you are at it, you should observe how others have tried to meet data needs like your own.)
6. If no such easy way out presents itself, design instruments and a sampling plan that will yield the data to fit the analyses you have to undertake.
7. Carry out the field work, continually checking to see whether the data will meet your needs.
8. Do the analysis, write the report, and help management make it have its intended effects.

As one might expect, the first step is the most important.

Step 1. As mentioned before, to most managers the research problem is seen as a lack of important facts about their marketing environment. A manager may say, "The problem is I don't know if formula A is preferred over formula B." Or, "The problem

FIGURE 4–2
Backward Marketing Research

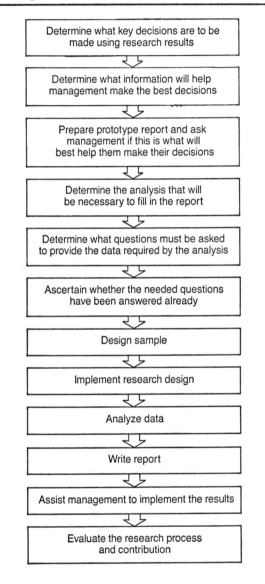

is I don't know if my distributors are more satisfied with my organization than my competitor's distributors are with theirs, and if they aren't, what they're unhappy about."

In this way of defining the problem, the solution is simply a reduction in the level of ignorance. The data elicited may be very interesting and may give managers a great deal of satisfaction in revealing things they didn't know, but satisfaction can quickly turn to frustration and disappointment when the executive tries to use the results.

Take for example a lifestyle study done not long ago on over-the-counter drugs. Some respondents, who claimed they were always getting colds and the flu, were very pessimistic about their health. They frequently went to doctors, but the doctors were never much help. The respondents thought that over-the-counter drugs were often very beneficial, but they weren't sure why. This information, together with other details, caused the researchers to label this group *the hypochondriacs.*

What to do with these results? As is usually the case with segmentation strategies, there are quantity and quality decisions to make. The company has to decide whether to pump more marketing resources into the hypochondriac group than its proportion of the population would justify. The marketing VP might first say yes because the hypochondriacs are heavy over-the-counter drug users.

But the picture is more complicated than that. Perhaps hypochondriacs are sophisticated buyers, set in their purchase patterns, and very loyal to favorite brands. If so, money aimed at them would have little impact on market share. Light users, on the other hand, may have fragile loyalties and throwing money at them could entice them to switch brands. Of course, just the opposite might be true: the hypochondriacs, being heavy users, might prove very impressionable and responsive to compelling ads.

On the qualitative side, lifestyle research could be much more helpful. Since it generates a rich profile describing each group's jobs, families, values, and preferences, this research could tell the company what to say. But the frustrated manager is likely not to know where to say these things. There is no *Hypochondriac's Journal* in which to advertise, and there may be no viewing or reading patterns that don't apply to heavy users in general—hypochondriacs or not.

A self-selection strategy could be tried wherein the company develops an ad speaking to hypochondriacs' fears and worries in the hope that they will see the message and say to themselves, "Ah, they're talking about me!" But nonhypochondriac heavy users who read the ad might say, "Well, if this product is really for those wimpy worrywarts, it certainly is not for sensible, rational me! I'll take my patronage elsewhere." In this case the research will be very interesting (fine fodder for cocktail party banter), but not actionable.

Suppose that the company had first laid out all the action alternatives it might take after the study. If the marketing VP had made it clear that his problems were (1) whether to allocate marketing dollars differently, and (2) whether to develop marketing campaigns aimed at particular, newly discovered segments, he would have set the project in a more appropriate direction.

In the first case, discussions with the researcher would help the VP determine the criteria that would justify a different budget allocation. Naturally, before he can reach a decision the VP needs research on the likely responses of different segments to advertising and promotional money spent on them. In the second case, the manager needs to know whether there are, indeed, channels for best reaching these segments. Only by first thinking through the decisions to be made with the research results will the project be started with high likelihood of actionability.

Step 2. After Step 1, management should ask itself: What should the final report look like so that we'll know exactly what moves to make when the report is in? Now the collaboration between the researcher and the manager should intensify and prove dynamic and exceedingly creative.

"Scenario-writing" is a good technique for developing ideas for the contents of the report. The initiative here lies with the researcher who generates elements of a hypothetical report and then confronts management with tough questions like, "If I came up with this cross-tabulation with these numbers in it, what would you do?"

The first payoff from this exercise arises from improvement of the research itself. These dummy tables can take the project forward by sharpening the decision alternatives and backward by indicating the best design for the questionnaire or pointing out how the analysis of the findings should be carried out. The forward effect is evident in the following case:

> A product manager marketing a high-priced convenience good is considering cancellation of a discount for multiple purchases because she thinks that most people taking advantage of it are loyal customers who are already heavy users, are upscale, and are largely price inelastic. Therefore, she speculates, the discount is just lost revenue. She is seriously considering whether to drop the discount altogether. To determine whether this is a sound decision she needs to predict the responses of both old and new customers to the elimination of the discounts.

Suppose the researcher hypothesizes that long-time customers will be price inelastic and new customers will be price elastic. Results from such an outcome would be like those in Table 4–1. Here, we see that only 8 percent of her sales represents new customers and that elimination of the discount will have little effect on old customers. These results confirm the product manager's decision to drop the discounts. However, reflecting on the results in Table 4–1 showing that new customers *do* respond to the discount, the manager thinks: what if we offered a one-time discount to consumers who have never tried the product? In considering this alternative, the manager realizes that before she can reach this decision she needs to know whether potential new customers can be reached with the special offer in a way that will minimize (or, better, foreclose) purchases at a discount by long-time customers.

TABLE 4–1
Hypothetical Sales Results before and after Discount

	Sales at Discounted Price	Sales at Nondiscounted Price	Number of Respondents
New customers	100	53	40
Old customers	100	92	460

This new formulation of the decision leads to a discussion of the results that indicates that the study *really* needs to ask not only about the permanent discount, but also about a one-time discount. The results of these questions can be captured in another dummy table showing responsiveness to the one-time discount by past patronage behavior as in Table 4–2. This table suggests that it does make sense to go ahead with the one-time discount.

As the manager reflects on this table, she realizes that she still needs a way of minimizing the chance that old customers will take advantage of the one-time discount. One way this could be accomplished is by avoiding announcing the offer in media old customers read or listen to. This indicates to the manager (and the researcher) that the questionnaire should also contain some questions on media habits. And so it goes.

This pattern of presenting possible results and rethinking design needs can be very productive. The process can sometimes have unanticipated consequences. Sometimes the researcher will present contrasting tables or regression results pointing to exactly opposite conclusions, only to discover that management is most likely to take the same course of action despite the results. This is usually a *prima facie* case for doing away with that part of the research design altogether.

Participation by the manager in this process of backward research design has other advantages:

1. It serves to co-opt managers into supporting the research work should it be criticized later by others.

TABLE 4–2

Hypothetical Sales Results under Three Pricing Strategies

	Sales at Discounted Price	Sales at Nondiscounted Price	Sales at One-Time Discount	Number of Respondents
New customers	100	53	76	40
Old customers	100	92	97	460

2. It deepens their understanding of many of the details of the research itself and their appreciation of both its strengths and its weaknesses.
3. Working with hypothetical tables can make the manager eager for the findings when they do appear and ready to implement them.
4. Working with contrasting tables makes it unlikely that the manager will be startled by surprising results, an outcome that sometimes causes a manager to reject an entire study.
5. Participation will also help reveal to management any limitations of the study. In my experience, managers are often tempted to go far beyond research "truth" when implementing the results, especially if the reported truth supports the course of action they prefer to take anyway!

Step 3. The form of the report will clearly dictate the nature of the analysis. If management proves to be leery of multivariate analysis in the earlier interactions, the researcher can design a series of step-by-step cross-tabulations for the report. If management is comfortable with the higher reaches of statistics, the researcher can draw out some of the more advanced analytic procedures. In general, however, the analysis phase should be straightforward. If the exercise of hypothetical table-writing has gone well, the analysis should amount to little more than filling in the blanks.

Step 4. The backward approach is very helpful in the data gathering stage in indicating what kind of data to gather. It can also help in wording questions. One large electonics manufacturer wanted to gauge young consumers' knowledge of, and preferences for, stereo components. Not until the researcher had prepared mock tables, showing preference data by age and sex, did the client's wishes become clear. By "young," the client meant children as young as 10. Moreover, the client believed that preteens, being a very volatile group, undergo radical changes from year to year, especially as they approach puberty.

Original research design plans set a lower age cutoff for the sample at age 13 and grouped respondents by relatively broad age categories—such as 13 to 16 and 17 to 20. This went out the window. If the researcher had been following the usual design approach, the client's expectations may not have surfaced until the study was well under way.

Backward design can also help determine the appropriateness of using strict probability sampling techniques. If, for example, management wants to project certain findings to some universe, the research must employ precise probability methods. On the other hand, if the client is chiefly interested in frequency counts (say, of words used by consumers to describe the company's major brands or of complaints voiced about its salespeople), sampling restrictions need not be so tight. In my experience, researchers often build either too much or too little sampling quality for the uses the company has in mind. Similarly, scenario writing will usually also reveal that management wants more breakdowns of the results than the researcher anticipates, requiring larger sample sizes or more precise stratification procedures than initially planned. Through simulating the application of the findings, the final research design is much more likely to meet management's needs and permit low field costs.

Steps 5–8. The first four steps encompass the major advantages of the backward technique. Steps 5 through 8 revert to a traditional forward approach that applies the research decisions and judgments made earlier. If all parties have collaborated well in the early stages, the last four steps will carry through what has already been largely determined.

One can use the traditional approach and hope that careful thinking about the problem will lead to the needed design improvements. However, the backward approach gives management and the researcher a specific step-by-step technique for ensuring that these improvements will emerge. And, as noted earlier, the approach has the additional advantages of making management (1) able to understand the results once they do appear, (2) unsurprised by some outcomes, and (3) eager and ready to immediately put the findings to use. More widespread adoption of this approach will go a long way toward eliminating the perception of too many managers that research all too often is obvious, off-target, or unimplementable.

Low-budget researchers cannot afford to fund projects that are obviously off-target or unimplementable. The backward approach takes time, but in the long run it is time well spent for both researcher and management. It guarantees the research the best possible chance of being truly useful—and used.

REFERENCES

1. Andreasen, Alan R. " 'Backward' Marketing Research." *Harvard Business Review*, May-June 1985, pp. 176–182.
2. Locander, William B., and Richard W. Scarrell. "A Team Approach to Managing the Marketing Research Process." *MSU Business Topics*, Winter 1977, pp. 15–26.
3. Joselyn, Robert W. *Designing the Marketing Research Project*. New York: Petrocelli/Charter, 1977.
4. Lacander, William B., and A. Benton Cocanougher, eds. *Problem Definition in Marketing*. Chicago: American Marketing Association, 1975.
5. Deshpande, Rohit, and Gerald Zaltman. "Factors Affecting the Use of Market Research Information: A Path Analysis." *Journal of Marketing Research*, February 1982, pp. 14–31.

SECTION 2

ALTERNATIVE LOW-COST RESEARCH TECHNIQUES

CHAPTER 5

USING AVAILABLE DATA

In this chapter, we begin our consideration of various techniques for providing low-cost marketing research information. As we have seen, many managers think that producing market information means going into the field to collect data yourself. Field research *can* be done relatively inexpensively. However, it is always more costly to gather new data than to analyze *existing* data. There is almost always a gold mine of data in every organization which are simply lying about as archives waiting to be milked for their marketing and managerial insights. The primary goal of this and the next chapter is to alert the low-budget researcher to the possibilities for discovering rich motherlodes of information already available that are usually ignored, or at least greatly underutilized, by the inexperienced marketing manager.

One of the solutions is to get more information out of primary data that you have already collected and superficially analyzed. It is my experience that most primary commercial research data are sadly underanalyzed. Researchers sometimes lack the sophistication to take a deep cut into a study's meaning. Sometimes they avoid such sophistication because they believe that the managers for whom they work would not understand the more complex results if they gave them to them! Most often, however, underanalysis is simply a matter of not having enough time. In the commercial world, often one study is just barely done before it is time to move on to the next one.

We will delay a consideration of advanced analytical techniques that could be applied to existing data (if time were available) to Chapter 10. We turn here to considering all of the other existing sources of data that often have never been thought of as a source of marketing research.

ARCHIVES

A Classification Scheme

Existing data ready to be gathered and analyzed at a relatively modest cost represent an extremely diverse array. To put some order on this diversity, it will be helpful to develop a classification scheme. This scheme not only helps organize the material in this and the next chapter, but also offers a checklist to the reader who wishes to make use of the possibilities for just this kind of cheap in-house research.

There are two basic sources of existing information that are readily accessible to the conscientious low-budget researcher. First, there are existing records or documents that enumerate events, actions, and outcomes that have already taken place. These records and documents are usually referred to as *archives*. They include such running records as billing invoices, salespersons' expense accounts, and consumer complaint letters. Archives can be further partitioned into records that are generated by your own organization and records that are generated by somebody else. We will refer to data collected in-house and by others as *internal* and *external* archives respectively.

The second class of readily accessible data are phenomena that are not already recorded, but can be simply observed. Obvious examples in marketing would be observations of traffic flows of consumers in a supermarket, of license plates in a parking lot, or of conversations between salespeople and customers. In the case of observation, some preliminary effort will have to be made by the researcher to systematically record the data before they can be analyzed.

These two types of sources, archives and observations, have an important feature in common. They do not involve questioning respondents or otherwise intruding on the subjects of the research. This helps keep the cost down. It also has another very important benefit in improving research quality. As Webb and his colleagues have pointed out, research that is intrusive can have major distorting effects on the phenomena it is attempting to study.[1] Asking people questions makes them wonder about the researcher's motives, makes them cautious about what they reveal, and/or makes them concerned about how they portray themselves. This can distort the answers they give. Overtly observing people as they shop or watch television or talk to a salesperson can make them behave more cautiously or rationally than they would otherwise. In both cases, *the process of measurement alters that which is measured.* The advantage of the techniques that we will discuss here and in the next chapter is that they can eliminate this potentially major source of bias. Of course, if not systematically carried out, unobtrusive observation or archival studies can have their own biases. But at least they are not compromised by distortions that the techniques themselves create.

In the present chapter, we consider internal and external archives. In Chapter 6, we point out the possibilities of using unobtrusive observations. Appendix A supplements the materials in the present chapter with a list of some of the major external data sources that are available to marketers free or at low cost in various locations, including public libraries.

INTERNAL ARCHIVES

Marketing organizations are rich storehouses of data. These data can be separated into two broad categories. First, there are records that represent measurements of some kind. Sales records are, of course, a good example of these measured records. An excellent cheap but good research project would be one that simply organizes and analyzes such records in imaginative ways.

---

[1]Eugene J. Webb, Donald T. Campbell, Kenneth D. Schwartz, and Lee Sechrist, *Unobtrusive Methods: Nonreactive Research in the Social Sciences* (New York: Rand McNally, 1971)

The other kind of internal record is what might be called *measurable* records. These are data that are transcribed in some non-numerical form and so require as a first step that the researcher attach numerical values to them. Examples of measurable archives that come most readily to mind are consumer complaint letters or salespeople's narrative reports of customer contacts or of competitors' exhibits they have seen at trade shows. A simple enumeration or coding of the data in either measured or measurable records can provide intriguing new insights to a marketing manager. Even in the rare case where the records are biased (as is the case with complaint letters) they can still be managerially useful.

We consider internal measured records first, then internal measurable records and then turn to what others call secondary data (external archives).

Internal Measured Records

Sales Reports

Sales reports are often a rich source of undetected research insights. Consider the following example. In the fall of 1977, Fran Herzog (a pseudonym), the manager of a performing arts facility at a major midwestern university was concerned about the informal way she forecast attendance at various events. Forecasts were used to determine seating configurations for the facility and the number of ushers and concessionaires to be hired, and to estimate the likely revenues and profits (or losses) that would be achieved. She was concerned that most of her forecasts were seat-of-the-pants guesses based on her own experience and that of her staff. She was very anxious to develop a better, more scientific approach, particularly if such a forecast could also serve as the starting point for "what if" speculations about the probable effects of changing prices, increasing (or decreasing) advertising, or spending more for publicity.

Preliminary investigation into the problem by a senior staff member, Ardeth McKenzie, revealed that buried in the drawers of the facility's main office was a wealth of detailed data in the form of sales records on performances over the past 11 years.

Information for most, although not all, of the 264 events over the 11-year period had been recorded on individual sheets of paper on the following performance characteristics:

1. Prices charged in each of three seating categories.
2. Size of the total house.
3. Number of seats assigned to each price category.
4. Number of tickets sold at each price level.
5. Dollars spent on advertising.
6. Costs of the performance (overhead, operating expenses, performers' fees, etc.).
7. Date and time of performance.
8. Weather on the day of the performance.

Ms. McKenzie, a student of the university's MBA program, keypunched this rich trove of archival data into the university computer, and proceeded to apply multiple regression statistical analysis to it. The resulting equation showed management the extent to which sales were affected by price, advertising expenditures, time of year, and weather within each of several event categories holding all the other factors constant. While hampered by small numbers of cases in some categories, the data gave Ms. Herzog the more scientific platform she desired from which to make her future predictions. The new model, of course, only provided ballpark figures. Ms. Herzog and her staff still added to the prediction base their own experiences and intuitions about the likely popularity of groups and events they were thinking of booking. Still, the new forecasting results were considered a major enhancement to what had been a seat-of-the-pants decision-making process. The forecasts were particularly useful at the beginning of the planning year in helping management estimate the effects on annual revenue of different mixes of events. Further use of the equations to explore alternative marketing mixes is contemplated for the future.

In a similar study, Cooper and Nakanishi analyzed season ticket preferences of theater subscribers to the Mark Taper Forum in downtown Los Angeles. They analyzed sales data archives for 108 choices made by subscribers each year from 1970 to 1976 also using a complex multiple regression model. The model was very successful in explaining 79.2 percent of the variation in sales. The researchers were able to tell management that with other variables held constant:

1. Saturday was the best day for performances, followed by Thursday.
2. Matinees were a bit more popular than evenings (other things equal—which they are usually not).
3. Seating in section A was less preferred to section B, suggesting a possible price reduction for the latter.
4. Having a discussion after the performance had a positive motivating effect and should be continued.
5. Subscribers preferred early weeks in the run of a particular show. For this reason, they deserve particular attention as they will have crucial word-of-mouth influence on later individual ticket buyers.[2]

Pseudo-Experiments. Sales data can be the basis for tracking the effects of unexpected occurrences in the marketplace. Because sales data comprise a continuing record, one can monitor the effect of some event or events on a market by looking at performance measures before and after that event. The occurrence of unexpected events, like a competitor's price reduction or a sudden advertising blitz, is sometimes referred to as a *pseudo-experiment*. True experiments involve the random assignment of subjects (e.g., cities, stores, or consumers) to various treatment or control conditions so that effects due to factors other than the treatment (e.g., the new advertisement, the price cut, etc.) can be measured and eliminated. In a pseudo-experiment, the marketer has not exerted such quality control. This often means that the researcher will have difficulty separating out the effects of the event under study from other things going on at the same time.

In a pseudo-experiment, the researcher can dig back into the sales archives to look at the effects of the uncontrolled event

---

[2]Lee G. Cooper and Masao Nakanishi, "Extracting Consumer Choice Information from Box Office Records," *Performing Arts Review: The Journal of Management and Law of the Arts* 8, no. 2 (1978), pp. 193–203.

on sales. For example, compared to the previous period, did a competitor's ad campaign reduce our sales a little, a lot or not at all? A problem of interpretation occurs, however, if the researcher has no market in which the event did not occur (i.e., a market with no competitive ad campaign). There is always the possibility that the change in sales would have occurred even without the competitor's action.

Even where there is a comparison market with no competitive action, the researcher may still have problems. The competitor probably has not assigned the treatment randomly to markets. He or she may cut prices or raise advertising only in those markets where they are already having trouble or where they think their competitors are vulnerable. Sales effects, therefore, may not be generalizable to any other market. Consider a case where one city raises its sales taxes and the researcher wishes to observe its effect on sales. It may be that the taxes were increased only because other city revenues such as corporate or property taxes were very low or declining. The sales archives may show a sales decline after the increase in city taxes compared to the period before the sales tax increase. But the real (or major) cause may be a general decline in the local economy.

Pseudo-experiments using sales archives, however, can be very helpful as a research approach, provided very careful attention is paid to thinking through (and discounting) *all other possible causes* of the effects observed.

An example. In a project in which the author was involved, a sales contest was held among three salespeople of a distributor of contraceptive products in a developing country. Analysis of sales archives for the contest period during the last three months of 1982 indicated three things: (1) sales for the three salespeople overall had risen compared to the year-earlier period, (2) the sales increase had been greater for only one of the two product lines, and (3) only one of the three salespeople had exceeded expected sales.

Management wanted to know whether such contests should be used in future. A first problem was to see whether, in fact, the contest *did* impact sales as total sales had risen over the year-earlier period. The real question was: what would have happened to these sales had there not been the sales contest? The year-earlier figures were the best benchmark assuming there were no major year-to-year increases in overall sales. Unfortunately, the latter was not true. There had been a major increase in sales over the previous year.

Thus, when the sales data archives were reanalyzed, it was found that the increase over the year-earlier sales achieved in the three-month contest period almost exactly equalled the increase in sales for both products for the other nine months of the same year. Thus, it was tentatively concluded that the sales contest's overall effects were due to a general upward trend in sales and not to any special sales efforts on the part of the contest participants.

But that did not explain why one salesperson exceeded the others. One possibility was that the winner was, in fact, able personally to increase sales as the contest intended. However, the winner had a territory that contained the largest retail outlets in the country's capital city, a city containing half the country's population. This fact suggested the possibility that the higher level of sales was made possible by the fact that the salesperson's large accounts could more easily load up inventory under pressure from a persuasive salesperson who was trying to win a contest. The smaller retail stores served by the other salespeople presumably would less often have the financial strength to be so accommodating.

A few simple phone calls to the larger outlets in the winner's territory could reveal the truth. However, if the results of the calls showed no loading up, one would not be able to rule out such behavior. First, it is possible that the retailers might not have recalled their behavior for one or two minor products in one specific three-month period (in this country, one could not rely on their store records). Alternatively, the retailers might simply lie, not wanting to admit that they had been coerced into excessive inventory accumulation.

Since this obtrusive procedure seemed likely to be unsatisfying, an obvious use of another archive in the form of invoices of sales to the individual outlets seemed a reasonable and potentially unbiased alternative. Although the data base was small, the overall indications from this analysis were that excessive loading up by the large retailers was not a factor. It was concluded that sales in this one territory had benefited from the contest. However, the fact that two markets showed no effects led management to conclude that contests were probably not a good way to increase sales.

Individual Sales Invoices

If analyzed as in the above case, sales invoices can give important insight into what is going on in a particular market. They can also be analyzed in other ways.

Invoice details can allow calculation of average sales per transaction. When compared to the *cost* of each transaction, figures can indicate whether some customers are simply not worth visiting or some product lines are not worth stocking simply because the cost of carrying them outweighs the benefit.

Also, dates on invoices can be used to calculate how often salespeople visit customers and the average length of time between visits (assuming that most customer contacts result in sales). Comparisons with dollar sales can show whether salespeople allocate their visit frequencies proportional to the expected sales. They can also reveal which salespeople have favorite customers they seem to like to visit irrespective of sales potential.

In addition, analysis of invoices can allow spot checks of pricing or calculation errors. Are salespeople pricing items correctly and calculating the correct taxes or shipping charges? (Before the advent of check-out scanners, supermarkets routinely found that checkout clerks made over-ring and under-ring errors that, on balance, favored the customers.)

Separate analysis of *sales return slips* can provide early warnings of weak products. Also, the analysis of the number of voided invoices or of the thoroughness with which invoices are filled out can help evaluate the quality of individual salespeople.

Sales invoices can be used to double check other data collected in primary studies, for example, to validate a customer's reported purchases. (A recent study of the family planning product distribution system in Bangladesh made detailed use of DCR's [Distributor's Call Records] to help verify purchases data reported by retailers in a retail audit. These archival data gave the researchers confidence in the primary field data that could not be obtained in any other way.)

Zipcode locations of customers can be analyzed. Is a new outlet suggested for a particular area? Should additional salespeople be assigned? When new items are introduced, invoices can lead to the discovery of new product purchasers by showing whether some kinds of customers or some zipcode areas are more likely to try the item than others.

Field Sales Reports

Many organizations have salespeople report expense information and/or prepare verbal reports of customer comments, tradeshow gossip, and competitive behavior. Evaluation of the quality of such reports can be used as one measure of a salesperson's performance. Also, frequencies and types of clients entertained can portray the styles of salespeople and the extent of possible rapport with clientele.

Mileage per day, when controlled for territory size, can suggest the extent to which salespeople are using their time efficiently. And, mileage data uncontrolled for territory size can support a salesperson's claim that territories are too large and cause too much driving time.

Miscellaneous Records

In some service businesses, purchase orders for various supplies (such as soaps or shampoos for hotel rooms or children's game cards in restaurants) can be good indicators of demand for particular services. In addition, the number and length of long distance calls can be monitored to indicate salesforce activity and pattern of contacts.

When the organization markets services to its own staff, accounting records can often identify important sales opportunities. Recently, a major university's transportation department was seeking new opportunities for renting its cars and trucks to faculty and staff. A computer analysis of accounting archives pinpointed departments that were heavy users of outside auto and truck rental agencies. These departments were then targeted for direct personal and telephone selling by the transportation division's staff.

Internal Measurable Data

Many kinds of archives are not in numerical form. Someone has to sit down and quantify the data to make them usable for research purposes. Some archives of this type are complaint records, and inquiries and comments.

Complaint Records
Virtually all organizations receive letters and phone calls from irate customers. Yet, surprisingly few firms routinely measure the data in these archives or analyze them. What is required is some relatively simple master coding scheme that sets categories for: (1) the product or service involved; (2) the nature of the complaint; (3) the seller; (4) date and location of problem; and (5) complainer characteristics (plus whatever other data the organization may wish to track). Someone then must code each complaint letter or phone call according to the preestablished categories so that the results can be added up and analyzed.

While these data are potentially very rich, it must be remembered that they are biased in two important ways. First, many studies suggest that those who voluntarily complain are not fully representative of all of those with complaints. For one thing, for someone with a problem to actually contact the seller, they must know *how* to complain and be somewhat assertive and articulate. These traits are clearly associated with higher education and higher social status. Poorer, less educated, more timid customers are less likely to speak up. Unfortunately, in many categories the latter can represent a major market and their unrelieved frustration may be the source of significant negative word-of-mouth against the marketer and its offerings in certain communities. To tap the concerns of these noncomplainers, it will be important from time to time to learn of their complaints using some other supplementary research technique, such as a limited telephone study.

The other source of bias in complaint data is that the complaints received are not necessarily representative of all types of complaints out there. Not surprisingly, people are more likely to speak up when there are large dollar amounts involved either in the original purchase or in the inconvenience caused by the defect being complained about. Second, people are more likely to speak up about things that are manifestly wrong and that are clearly the marketer's fault. If they are not sure that there really is a defect (e.g., the paint wore through too quickly or the steam iron did not seem to give off much steam) or if they think they might be partly or wholly to blame ("Maybe Johnny *did* play with that toy too roughly"), they are less likely to speak up and register their complaints. But these unvoiced complaints have the potential to be very important problems for a firm— minor problems that can silently destroy a well-developed market position. Perhaps more importantly, these subtle dissatisfactions are just the kind of thing that cause unhappy consumers to decide not to come back to an outlet or not to buy a product or service again without telling anyone about it. Again, direct telephone studies from time to time may be needed to make sure that there are not whole classes of problems lurking undetected in the marketplace.

Even though complaint data are flawed, they can still be very useful in identifying potentially serious product and service problems. This is particularly the case if complaint data are analyzed repeatedly over time. One may choose not to trust the absolute level of complaints of various kinds at a single point in time because of the biases mentioned above. However, changes in the number and types of complaints over time may be a very significant signal of growing problems on the one hand or (when they decline) of improved performance on the other. Even if the data are not to be used over time, statistically large numbers of complaints may not be needed at all. A few cases may simply be enough to alert a manager to a problem that must be fixed before it sabotages a carefully wrought marketing strategy.

A good example of the latter is an observant analysis by the U.S. Consumer Product Safety Commission. The CPSC noted that, among the medical complaints it was receiving routinely from a small sample of hospital emergency rooms was a noticeable number of cases involving young boys who reported injuring their "private parts" while bike riding. This small number of unusual cases led to further investigation and eventually to the Commission recommending major changes in the placement and design of gear levers on boys' bicycles sold in the United States. What the Commission discovered was that on many models these levers were still located on the crossbar and boys in minor accidents were being thrown painfully into the protruding gearshift levers. Only a few entries in these medical archives were needed by the CPSC to discover and correct a very serious product design problem. This was only possible because the CPSC had set up a system to assemble and track the complaints that hospitals had. Without a system, no one, except by chance, would have put together all the unique occurrences to come up with such an important conclusion.

Finally, analysis of complaint data may have an important secondary value in helping to evaluate personnel or suppliers who handle an organization's products, in addition to evaluating the products and services themselves. General Motors conducts a very large continuing study of new car purchasers and their satisfaction with their cars and with the selling and service dealerships. GM strongly believes that these data provide their best means for evaluating the critical sales and post-purchase performance of their retail dealers.

Inquiries and Comments
Consumers often write or call marketers to complain. But they also write and call to raise questions and offer praise. When properly analyzed, the sum total of these communications can also give management a good notion of what is on people's minds and what might be emphasized in future. An imaginative use of such records has been *Time* magazine's yearly analysis of its letters to the editor. For example, in 1983, *Time* reported that in the previous year, 51,027 readers wrote the magazine. When compared to the same data in 1981, the letters revealed significant shifts in reader interest. Letters about domestic news issues dropped 38 percent while letters on foreign issues nearly doubled.

The letters also revealed shifts to and away from supporting particular groups or positions. *Time* detected a decline in support for Israel and increased concern about war issues, even when controlling for the extent to which *Time* actually wrote about each issue.

Other reader interests surfaced in the 6,000 or so letters that simply asked for more information and 676 letters that took the magazine to task about its grammar and writing style. *Time's* analysis concluded by reporting that its Essay section seemed to have

> ... evoked the most personal and reflective mail. One essay in particular seems to have touched a universal chord: the subject was a passenger among the 74 who perished in the crash of an airliner into Washington's Potomac River in January. Known only as the man in the water, the victim repeatedly passed his own lifeline into the hands of other helpless survivors until he vanished beneath the icy waters. The story moved 387 people to write in honor of his heroism: one person risking and ultimately losing his own life to save others.[3]

Miscellaneous Internal Measurable Records

Other sources of unobtrusive internal measurements include notations on desk calendars or appointment books which, when collated with expense records and telephone bills, can help a manager evaluate how effectively he or she is allocating personal time between meetings, customer contacts, sales supervision, etc.

Also, computers can be programmed to collect data on how people use the system, what software routines they use most, and what features they linger longest over (perhaps because they are interested or because they don't understand something).

Information Centers

One approach that relatively large organizations are using to synthesize and process these internal data is to establish an information center (IC). The information center is, in effect, an internal consulting and service unit that creates software and networks linked to the company's mainframe so that PC users around a corporation can have access to the company's own various internal databases. It helps train managers in what data-

---

[3]"Sorting Through 1982's Mail," *Time,* March 7, 1983, p. 8.

bases are available and how to use them. According to the research firm, Computer Intelligence, IC installations have been growing 20 percent annually since 1980 with 6,000 in place nationwide by the end of 1985. The American Management Association claims that 40 percent of all businesses had ICs in 1986.[4]

IC staff members are responsible for setting up the system and choosing the software and hardware. They then spend many hours consulting and handholding early users to get them effectively on-line. Consulting begins in person and graduates to the telephone. Word-of-mouth spreads and users typically tend to be highly satisfied with what is now really decentralized data processing.

However, IC systems are not cheap, beginning at $1 million. The low-budget researcher should only pursue the IC idea when other company departments will share the cost and where there is an overall company commitment to the concept.

EXTERNAL ARCHIVES

It is also possible to divide data produced by others (i.e., secondary data) into data that are either measured or measurable. Obvious examples in the first case are the major marketing research data sources one could purchase or in some cases (e.g., census data or journal articles) acquire free. In the case of measurable secondary data, the most obvious examples that come to mind are public evidences of competitors' strategies—media advertisements, or prices charged at different locations or types of outlets.

External Measured Records

Raw Data in Secondary Sources
The marketing world contains an extremely diverse and ever-growing array of secondary data which a marketer can acquire at anywhere from virtually no cost to rather healthy one-time

---

[4]Shaku Atre, "Information Center Holds," *PC World,* August 1986, pp. 156–164.

or yearly fees. These data can be separated into two broad categories depending on whether they are raw data or data that have already been analyzed by others to some greater or lesser degree. The former would include census data tapes, purchased panel records, or academic researchers' raw data. These data can often be acquired at the cost of a reel of computer tape or a few floppy disks and a few hours of programmer time. They can then be subject to the purchaser's own analysis. However, when using someone else's raw data, it is crucial to know of the potential biases in the raw data and, if necessary, adjust for them. This is always possible with one's own data, but sometimes it is difficult to learn from external sources. On the other hand, available raw data from outside sources have the distinct advantage that they can be manipulated, categorized, summarized, or otherwise analyzed in any way the researcher wishes.

Predigested Secondary Sources
Sometimes the low-budget researcher may not have the time, equipment, or sophistication to analyze someone else's raw data. On such occasions, predigested external data may be an excellent, often superior substitute.

The very best source of predigested information for marketing managers is state, federal, and local government studies and reports. These data are widely available in libraries and from government agencies. They are extremely inexpensive and usually very accurate. The principal sources of this information are described in considerable detail in Appendix A. Marketers generally find particularly valuable the following:

U.S. Bureau of the Census
- Decennial census of the population.
- Census of housing.
- Censuses of various industries (e.g., retailing, wholesaling, services, manufacturing, transportation, agriculture, and minerals).
- Current population reports.
- County business patterns.

- Current business reports.
- Selected characteristics of foreign-owned U.S. firms.
- Quarterly financial reports for manufacturing, mining, and trade corporations.

Other Federal Government Sources

- Federal Reserve Bulletin (monthly).
- Monthly Labor Review.
- Commerce Business Daily.
- Overseas Business Reports (Annual).
- Statistics of Income Bulletin (Quarterly).
- U.S. Industrial Outlook (Annual).
- Business Cycles: Handbook of Indicators (Monthly).
- Survey of Current Business (Monthly).
- Business Conditions Digest (Monthly).
- Agricultural Outlook (Monthly).
- Consumer Expenditure Survey (Decennially).
- Council of Economic Advisors Economic Indicators (Monthly).
- Current Construction Reports (Various series).
- Current Housing Reports (Various series).
- Consumer Price Index Detailed Report (Monthly).
- Highlights of U.S. Export and Import Trade (Monthly and Cumulative).

These data serve several important research purposes. They can describe the present state of various consumer or business markets and trends in those markets over time. These data, in turn, can help determine desirable opportunities, set quotas for future sales, and help evaluate present performance. They are also often used as bases against which to compare the characteristics of present customers or the profile of respondents in a specific research study.

A growing use of government data sources is in prospecting for business in foreign markets. The costs of gathering data in other countries is usually prohibitive for the low-budget researcher, and U.S. government agencies can tell a marketer the population and business characteristics of most foreign markets including the nature of present competition. These data can often be supplemented by information from foreign embassies or trade promotion services. Both local and foreign sources can also provide critical information on how to access desirable foreign markets.

In the United States, there are a number of regional and local sources that can be used as the marketer narrows his or her focus to specific sites. State agencies, banks, Chambers of Commerce, and local media produce considerable information to attract business to their area. These data are usually free and, in some cases, can be customized for the user. However, since some of these sources have a vested interest in influencing others' marketing decisions, the marketer should be cautious about the completeness and interpretations of data from these sources.

While the array of these secondary sources is substantial and highly complex, access to them is eased considerably with the availability of compilations produced by a growing number of public and private groups. Perhaps the most popular general compendium of federal government data is the *Statistical Abstract of the United States* produced annually by the U.S. Government Printing Office. In the private sector, good summaries for marketers are the *Rand McNally Commercial Atlas and Marketing Guide,* Dun and Bradstreet's *Million Dollar Directory* of companies with assets over $500,000, and *A Guide to Consumer Markets* published by the National Industrial Conference Board.

Other useful private sources include *Consumer Market and Magazine Report* from Daniel Starch and Staff, various manuals of company financial data compiled by Moody's, and Predicast summaries of forecasts made by other organizations on 500 key business indicators.

In addition, lists are produced by private sector organizations and associations on a wide range of subjects of interest to marketers. These would include lists of trade shows and conventions (*Successful Meetings* magazine), American manufacturers (Thomas Publishing Company), available published market research reports (Findex) and, interestingly, other secondary sources themselves (e.g., Ballinger Publishing Company's *Directory of Industry Data Sources*).

Syndicated Services

Increasingly useful secondary sources for marketers are various regular series of data provided for a fee by syndicated services. Among the most prominent of these are:

- Dun's Market Identifiers (3 by 5 inch cards on over 4 million establishments).
- Nielsen Retail Indexes (brand sales in selected supermarkets, drug stores, and mass merchandisers).
- Audits and Survey's National Total Market Index (retail sales).
- Selling Areas-Marketing Inc. reports of warehouse shipments to food stores.
- National Purchase Diary Panel (diary records on consumer goods purchases of 13,000 families).
- Nielsen Television Index (television viewing nationally and in selected metro areas).
- Starch Advertisement Readership Survey (advertising recognition in selected consumer, farm, and business publications).
- Simmons Media/Market Service (magazine readership and consumer purchases).
- CACI/Source Products (PC diskettes on demographics and customer purchases).
- Donnelley Marketing Information Services (interactive databases tied to specific geographic designations).
- BehaviorScan (panel data based on optical scanning of purchases in stores; can be tied to advertising tests).
- IMS International (pharmaceutical product sales in over 50 countries).
- Starter (tracking of trial and repeat purchases of new packaged goods products).
- PRIZM (psychographic profiles and purchases by zipcode).
  National Scantrack (purchase panel based on scanner data).

Predigested syndicated sources are well exemplified by the PRIZM system. For PRIZM, the Claritas Corporation collects a huge amount of primary data on the 35,600 zipcode areas in the United States and then clusters these zipcode areas into 40 categories which are given such colorful names as "Money and Brains," "Shotguns and Pickups," and "Norma Rae-Ville" (see Figure 5–1). A marketer can use these data to help locate new markets or learn what sells in existing markets. For a fee, marketers can acquire a list of all the zipcodes in a selected area in the lifestyle categories that are deemed to be the best targets for their organization's goods and services. Alternatively, PRIZM can help *define* markets. The marketer can learn from PRIZM just which markets are the best prospects for the kinds of products or services they will offer. PRIZM can:

> tell you more than you probably ever wanted to know about [an] area's typical residents: what they like to eat; which cars they like to drive; whether they prefer scotch or sangria, tuna extender or yogurt, hunting or tennis . . . which magazines they read, which TV shows they watch, whether they are more likely to buy calculators or laxatives, whether they're single or are potential customers for a diaper service.[5]

Similar services are provided by Donnelley Information Services. These systems offer several advantages. A much broader and richer database can be brought to bear on a research problem than any individual low-budget marketer could possibly afford (e.g., product purchases, demographic and economic data, TV watching, magazine readership, and other relevant behaviors for each of 35,600 zipcodes in the United States). The data are subjected to much more sophisticated analysis by the research supplier than most low-budget researchers can afford. Finally, purchase of some part or all of these kinds of services usually includes some amount of hands-on consulting help from the database supplier that can materially supplement the low-budget researcher's own skills. The disadvantage, of course, in cases

---

[5]Bob Minzescheimer, "You Are What You ZIP," *Los Angeles Magazine*, November 1984, pp. 175–192.

FIGURE 5–1
PRIZM Cluster Categories (and % of population)

1. **Blue Blood Estates.** The richest of the rich; 0.66 percent.

2. **Money and Brains.** Swank townhouses, apartments and condos; 1 percent.

3. **Furs and Station Wagons.** New money in affluent suburbs; 2.47 percent.

4. **Urban Gold Coast.** Dense, white-collar enclaves; 0.28 percent.

5. **Pools and Patios.** Older, comfortable suburbs; 3.18 percent.

6. **Two More Rungs.** Dense suburbs with conservative buying patterns; 0.94 percent.

7. **Young Influentials.** A younger version of Money and Brains; 2.61 percent.

8. **Young Suburbia.** Child-raising families in outlying suburbs; 5.8 percent.

9. **God's Country.** Well-educated frontier types; 2.81 percent.

10. **Blue-Chip Blues.** The richest blue-collar neighborhoods; 5.68 percent.

11. **Bohemian Mix.** America's bohemia; 0.6 percent.

12. **Levittown, U.S.A..** Suburban tract developments; 4.53 percent.

13. **Gray Power.** Middle-class retirement areas; 1.6 percent.

14. **Black Enterprise.** The black middle class; 1.37 percent.

15. **New Beginnings.** Archie Bunker's children; 4.29 percent.

16. **Blue-Collar Nursery.** Outlying towns and suburbs of small cities; 1.86 percent.

17. **New Homesteaders.** Less affluent version of God's Country; 4.93 percent

18. **New Melting Pot.** New-immigrant neighborhoods; 1.16 percent.

19. **Towns and Gowns.** Midscale college towns; 2.29 percent.

20. **Rank and File.** Aging blue-collar suburbs; 1.11 percent.

21. **Middle America.** Midsize middle-class towns and outlying suburbs; 4.94 percent.

22. **Old Yankee Rows.** Blue-collar areas of older industrial cities; 1.82 percent.

23. **Coalburg and Corntown.** Small, peaceful towns like Lima, Ohio; 2.66 percent.

24. **Shotguns and Pickups.** Large families in crossroad villages; 2.69 percent.

25. **Golden Ponds.** Rustic villages near coasts, mountains, or lakes; 2.81 percent.

26. **Agri-Business.** Ranching, farming, and lumbering areas; 4.17 percent.

27. **Emergent Minorities.** Minorities struggling up from poverty; 2.29 percent.

28. **Single City Blues.** Dense, urban, downscale singles areas; 1.95 percent.

29. **Mines and Mills.** Mining and mill towns where industry is king; 1.9 percent.

30. **Back-Country Folks.** Remote rural towns; 4.34 percent.

31. **Norma Rae-Ville.** Industrial suburbs; 3.21 percent.

32. **Old Brick Factories.** Dense, old factory towns; 1.87 percent.

FIGURE 5–1—*Continued*

33. **Grain Belt.** Farm owners and less affluent tenant farmers; 1.52 percent.
34. **Heavy Industry.** Poorer version of Rank and File; 2.0 percent.
35. **Sharecroppers.** Southern-style tenant farms; 3.83 percent.
36. **Downtown Dixie-Style.** Integrated, dense urban areas; 2.39 percent.
37. **Hispanic Mix.** The nation's Hispanic barrios; 1.7 percent.
38. **Tobacco Roads.** Unskilled rural laborers; 1.12 percent.
39. **Hard Scrabble.** The poorest rural areas; 1.11 percent.
40. **Public Assistance.** The Harlems of America; 2.31 percent.

Source: The Claritas Corporation. Reproduced with permission.

like this is that predigested results may not be exactly what the marketer needs since someone else has done the analysis according to their specifications or according to what they think the average client would want. Thus, the summaries may not be the ones the marketer needs, critical details may be left out and so on. It also means that the data will likely be more expensive than the raw data to buy since one must buy the analysis also. On the other hand, the low-budget manager may choose to accept these limitations and the likely higher cost because he or she doesn't have the time or expertise to carry out the needed analysis.

On-Line Databases[6]
A major source of external data is now available on-line to marketers with a personal computer and a modem or a computer terminal. These external databases include such diverse information as:

- Newspaper and magazine stories.
- Market characteristics for specific geographic areas.
- Economic time series.

---

[6]Much of the information in this section is drawn from *Online Access Guide* 2, no. 2, March–April 1987.

- Census data.
- Stock quotes.
- Company profiles.
- Regulation, legislation, legal cases.
- Yellow Page listings in 4,000 places.
- Patents and trademarks.
- Newspaper, radio, and TV audiences.
- Public relations releases.
- Biographies.
- Bibliographies and citations.
- Ad placements by competitors.

Many of these data are available for both the United States and foreign countries and can be accessed as full texts, data files, and/or indexes. In each case, they originally existed in printed form, but were subsequently computerized for easier access by specific suppliers. A partial list of databases available in 1987 is included in Appendix B.

Using different data files on line, a low-budget researcher can define a specific geographic area to be targeted, develop a demographic profile of the market for today and for five years into the future, develop psychographic profiles, product usage, and media behavior patterns for customers in the market, get Yellow Page listings of possible distributors, learn if competitors are headquartered or have branches nearby, access recent articles on competitors to learn if they have any plans for this market, and review general articles on the geographic area indicating whether there are important economic or political trends that may affect the firm's prospects.

All that is necessary to have access to this rich treasure trove of data is a computer terminal (e.g., a PC) connected to a telephone line and a password to each needed database or database vendor. The password will be provided once the researcher has signed up with the system and sometimes paid an initial or monthly subscription fee.

It is possible in most cases to go directly to the original sources of the data listed in Appendix B. However, most experienced on-line database users sign up with one or more intermediary vendors or information brokers. For one fee, a subscriber can have access to a range of databases. Among the best known and widely used vendors are the following:

1. *BRS* (BRS Information Technologies, Latham, N.Y.). Bibliographic citations, abstracts, and (sometimes) full texts from a wide range of sources. Over 100 databases.

2. *CompuServe, Inc.* (CompuServe, Inc., Columbus, Ohio) Division of H & R Block, Inc. Wide range of business data including S&P ratings, electronic clipping services, travel information, computer shopping, and a base of technical report information.

3. *DIALOG* (DIALOG Information Services, Inc., Palo Alto, Calif.). Over 200 databases, 20 devoted to business. Their "Business Connection" service can provide corporate intelligence (approximately $4 per company), financial screening (up to $3.50 a company), sales prospecting (up to $2 a company) and product/market analysis.

4. *Dow Jones News/Retrieval* (Dow Jones News/Retrieval Inc., Princeton, N.J.). Forty databases support two categories of services: Business and Investor Services (business data, news, stock quotes) and General Services (world news, travel, shopping). 200,000+ subscribers.

5. *Mead Data Central: LEXIS, NEXIS and MEDIS* (Mead Data Control, Dayton, Ohio). Full-text databases of legal, news, business, and general information. Includes medical references, financial and accounting information. 300,000+ users.

6. *SDC/ORBIT* (SDC Information Services, Santa Monica, Calif.). 70 databases primarily in science and technology, although it includes patents and accounting.

7. *I.P. Sharp Associates, Inc.: InfoService, InfoMagic* (I.P. Sharp Associates Limited, Toronto, Canada). 120 primarily numeric databases weighted toward aviation, economics, energy, finance, and news. Data often in time series.

8. *The Source* (Source Telecomputing Corporation, McLean, Va.). Owned by Readers' Digest. Offers business and financial information plus electronic networking. 800 different features.

9. *NewsNet* (NewsNet Inc., Bryn Mawr, Pa.). News and information from newsletters, wire services, and specialty publications on 34 industries and professions.

Costs for these services vary by supplier. In some cases, there may be a signup fee. Beyond this, there will be a basic "connect-time" cost, usually varying by time of day or week (e.g., prime time versus nonprime time) and by the speed with which data are transmitted (e.g., 300 baud, 1,200 baud or 2,400 baud).

There may be additional costs for specific kinds of databases or specific information (e.g., a fee for each stock quote). At first, the costs may seem relatively low. However, the naive online database user should realize that considerable time can be eaten up with unproductive searches. Many of these systems are relatively difficult to use. Indeed, in many communities, there exist independent search specialists who can make searching more efficient by thinking the problem through off line. Finally, even when the search is done, additional costs will be incurred in downloading or printing the accessed information. To the extent possible, online researchers prefer to copy information onto a hard disc and then print it off line, since printers are notoriously slow and can eat up a great deal of connect time.

The data can be extremely valuable as suggested by one company's experience. The company had learned that a competitor might be planning an attack on one of the company's personal care products. The firm considered cutting price to meet the challenge, but first they contacted the Helicon Group Ltd., an Allentown, Pa. consulting firm specializing in competitive intelligence to learn what they could from secondary sources. Helicon developed the following from on-line sources:

- The competitor had been purchased several years earlier by a conglomerate.
- Local business newspaper databases did *not* report the competitor hiring an ad agency for a new product.
- The parent company had once tried to sell the unprofitable subsidiary.
- The parent's commerical debentures were being downgraded and a lawsuit was being filed by a debenture holder.
- A business news database indicated that a senior executive had recently retired with no successor named and two other executives had left.

The company realized from Helicon's data gathering that the competitor posed no threat at all and a hasty price cut would have been a very foolish action.[7]

Measurable External Archives

Some external archives are, of course, not already in numeric form. Among the major examples are the following.

Competitors' Advertising Expenditures
It is critical that managers know what competitors' strategies are and how they are changing over time. There are many archives a manager can use that can provide important clues to these strategies. Competitors' advertisements in newspapers, magazines, the trade press, and even television and radio represent a rich archival database available for measurement and analysis. Sometimes budget levels are reported in the trade press. For example, *Advertising Age* often reports crude expenditure levels for advertising or promotion budgets for various companies, especially where advertising or public relations agencies are involved.

Managers may wish more detail or they may find press reports non-existent. In such cases, they may wish to either access an online advertising database like Adline (Appendix B) or collect the data themselves. If the marketer proceeds alone (e.g., if the database does not include key competitors), it will be difficult to assemble *all* of the newspapers or magazines that competitors may be likely to use for advertising over a year, let alone evidence of television or radio commercials. Still, if the typical span of media use is relatively narrow, for example, if print media are the major vehicles in the industry, the manager may select a few representative print media and set an assistant to sampling such media routinely on a monthly or quarterly basis. Assuming the major media are covered, the manager's repeated measures, although biased, can reveal trends in competitors' advertising levels and themes. Alternatively, commercial clip-

---

[7]*Online Access Guide* 2, no. 2, March–April 1987, p. 44.

ping services can be engaged for just such a task. Hershey indicates that in 1980 such a service would cost a marketer a basic fee of $105 a month for the first competitor, plus $10 for each additional competitor plus 55¢ a clipping.[8] This service would presumably include not only advertising, but several of the other archival sources mentioned below.

Since the manager would have access to the same advertising cost data as competitors from standard rate books, it would not be difficult to estimate the level of advertising expenditure for each competitor and the relative allocation each is using across media vehicles. Again, although biased, comparisons of these estimates from period to period might signal important shifts in competitors' promotion strategy.

Competitors' Advertising Content

There are, of course, numerous possibilities for further analysis of the *content* of competitors' advertisements. Such an analysis can identify major themes, differences in strategy across target markets and, perhaps more important, subtle shifts in strategies over time. Managers may believe that just careful reading or viewing of competitors ads is enough. However, one person's perceptions may be faulty or idiosyncratic. Worse, they may change over time so that changes that seem to be taking place in the market are really changes in the manager's interests and orientation. Systematic content analysis is required to provide objective recorded evidence. It is a technique that can be applied to advertising and several other measurable external archives, like competitor's annual reports, publicity releases, direct mail messages, product packages, or inserts. The content analysis should observe some obvious, but important, precautions.

- Selection of the materials to be analyzed must be objective and randomized in some fashion.
- Characteristics of the content to be measured should be defined in advance so that what the analyst sees does not unduly influence the determination of what *should* be seen.

---

[8]Robert Hershey, "Commercial Intelligence on a Shoestring," *Harvard Business Review*, September–October 1980, pp. 22–35.

(This set of characteristics can, of course, be modified subsequently if the analysis scheme is found to be incomplete
in some important respect.)

- Trial analyses of a subset of the materials should be conducted and rules established for ambiguous cases. (Is a
goldfish a pet? Is the headline greater-than-ever value an
indication of an emphasis on price or an emphasis on
quality?)
- If at all possible more than one individual should be used
to analyze the materials and at least some documents
should be assigned to more than one person simultaneously to establish interanalyst consistency and, indi-
rectly, to test the logic and consistency of the coding scheme.

Content measures, per se, will not tell management anything about which of competitors' messages work and which do
not. However, in some rare cases the manager may notice effects
on his or her firm's sales following some measured change in
competitor advertising. This represents another example of a
pseudo-experiment which may yield some insight into what does
and does not seem to work well in the product category.

Publicity

How the world views an organization and its marketing program
is often clearly reflected in various public and semi-public archival records. Two important sources here are: (1) articles about
an organization and its offerings in newspapers, popular magazines (e.g., *Consumers Reports*), and the trade press, and (2)
evaluations by stockbrokers and investment advisors. Clearly,
management will be interested in what is said about the firm
and about its competitors and undoubtedly will notice such publicity when it chances across the desk. If *systematized,* this casual
reading can be turned into true research if the details of these
public comments are routinely and objectively evaluated and
recorded. Online databases can be very valuable here. Several
of the news sources mentioned in Appendix B can be searched.
PR Newswire Associates is a database specifically designed for
this purpose.

Other Competitive Intelligence Gathering

Repetitive archival records of competitors' activities can tell managers a lot about systematic changes in strategies and tactics over time. One-time critical changes are equally important, but they may be harder to detect. Fortunately, there are a number of archives that can be accessed to provide important intelligence about what is going on within your competitor's management suites. As suggested earlier, among the documents that would serve this function from online data bases would be:

Publicity releases (e.g., from the PR Newswire Association database).

Speeches by competitors' personnel (including nonmarketers such as treasurers, lawyers and the like who often do not realize the value to a marketer of what they are saying).

Articles by company personnel in the trade press, academic journals, and popular periodicals.

Any internal company communication that may be acquired ethically.

Patents applied for.

Court records if the company has been sued lately. These provide rich sources of data on past practices and sometimes reveal strategy. (This is a reason many firms avoid public trials.)

Biographies of key executives whose past may give a good indication of future strategies. This can be particularly valuable when the leadership at a competitive firm changes.

In addition to on-line databases, managers can do the following:

Subscribe to all of the periodicals, trade magazines, academic journals, and conference proceedings where competitor comments and stories about competitors might appear.

Subscribe to an independent clipping service to acquire items missed above (some online electronic database vendors such as CompuServe's Executive News Service will do this for you automatically). Hershey[9] urges that the clipping service should include local newspapers where competitors are headquartered or have plants. One can learn about executive changes, plant expansions, or even manufacturing problems this way. Hershey cites a case where a manufacturer learned of a fire in a competitor's plant that would have a major effect on its delivery capability. This represented a major strategic opportunity for the clipping subscriber.

Subscribe to the *Wall Street Transcript* which reports details of corporate presentations to security analysts or brokerage firms.

Require someone to consult the *Reader's Guide to Periodical Literature* index regularly for reference to your competitors (and to yourself).

Require all company personnel to routinely submit any documents acquired on visits to customers, attendance at conferences, and reading on airplanes that contain even the smallest snippet of intelligence about competitors (and your firm).

Subscribe to the *Official Gazette* of the U.S. Patent and Trademark Office for patent abstracts cross-indexed by corporate owners. Your own product development plans can often be changed dramatically by learning of competitors' new product undertakings.

Purchase a few shares of competitors' stock to secure insiders' data on company plans and past peformance.

Send periodic letters of inquiry to industry analysts at the U.S. Department of Commerce, the Department of Agriculture, or the National Reference Center on industry topics. Hershey cites an example of a firm that dropped a new product when it analyzed salary data on two competitors available in labor agreements made available by the Labor Department. The firm concluded that the competitor's low salary patterns made it too formidable a price competitor for a proposed offering.

---

[9]Ibid.

Whatever the source, it is important to make the data flow *routinely* into a low-cost competitive intelligence data bank. For this purpose, a summary report of each secondary document should be recorded and put into a carefully indexed file to be collated and reviewed periodically. As the examples above indicate, even the slightest advance warnings of changes in competitors' behavior and planning can have major benefits for the alert and rapidly responding marketer.

REFERENCES

1. Berelson, Bernard. *Content Analysis and Communication Research.* Glencoe, Ill.: Free Press, 1952.
2. Kassarjian, Harold H. "Content Analysis and Consumer Research." *Journal of Consumer Research,* January 1977, pp. 8–18.
3. Glossbrenner, Alfred. *How to Look It Up Online.* New York: St. Martin's Press, 1987.
4. Hershey, Robert. "Commercial Intelligence on a Shoestring." *Harvard Business Review,* September–October 1980, pp. 22–35.
5. Stewart, David W. *Secondary Research: Information Services and Methods.* Beverly Hills, Calif.: Sage Publications, 1984.

CHAPTER 6

SYSTEMATIC OBSERVATION

We have seen in the previous chapter that archival data are all around us. One just needs to find them and, in some cases, apply measurements to them to change them from inert data into managerially useful information. What sets the truly superior manager apart is not leaving these insights to chance. The superior manager realizes that a systematic application of low-budget research techniques directed in the right places can make rare insights routine.

Knowing where to look and being systematic about looking for it are the two keys of effective and efficient use of archives. These same two principles apply equally well to mining information from other features of the environment around us that are not written records. In this chapter, we will be concerned with the use of observations of the physical and human environment as a means of conducting low-cost marketing research.

The chapter focuses in turn on each of the steps of the observing process. First, researchers must create the opportunity to observe. These opportunities can be classified as episodic or repeated observation and further divided into natural and contrived occasions. By contrived observations we mean episodes where the researcher intervenes in natural events and watches what happens. Contrived observations are usually found in formally designed experiments which will be considered in the next chapter.

Setting up the opportunity to observe is, of course, not enough. The effective researcher needs to know how to observe. Thus, the chapter considers briefly the kinds of observations that can be made and procedures for doing so.

Systematic observation represents the ultimate in cheap but good research. Observations represent free goods. Marketers already use these free goods daily. They watch customers. They look at and touch and smell their competitors' products and their own. They stay at their competitors' hotels or eat in their restaurants. They have a competitor's muffler installed on their car to see how the competitor treats a customer. And, they try new approaches and see how they work. They try calling customers by their first names for awhile and see if they warm up faster or seem to buy more. They reshuffle their displays or change their room arrangements and see if these make a difference in traffic patterns. Good marketers are doing this kind of free research all the time. But most of it is neither systematic nor purposeful.

Too often, marketers treat casual observation as if it were truly a free good. But they shouldn't. Good observational research is not costless at all. It must be systematic and objective. This can be hard work. It requires that systems be put in place, that at least moderate preplanning be undertaken and that observers be trained to be objective and thorough in what they observe. It is only when these investments are made that chance voyeurship turns into serious research.

COLLECTING NATURAL OBSERVATIONS

Observations and archives can be episodic or continuing. An episodic observation is a one-time look at a phenomenon of interest. This can come about as a result of a particular one-time research interest. For example, a potential gas station owner may observe the ages and types of automobiles passing a proposed station location or at nearby shopping centers to gather information to help decide how many pumps to install in the new station, selling what octane levels, and whether to specialize in servicing particular kinds of cars. A clothing shop owner might systematically observe the number and types of jewelry her customers are wearing to decide whether to add a jewelry line and of what type. The manager of a restaurant might observe the number of orders placed for a new food concoction and then how much of each serving is left on plates after it is tasted to decide whether to keep the item on the menu.

Observations in both episodic and continuing situations will typically comprise one of three activities: *counting, measuring, or seeking patterns*. They can be carried out both obtrusively, as when one visits a competitor's midnight sale and takes notes, or unobtrusively, as when Fisher-Price, the toy company, uses two-way mirrors to observe how children play with their toys. They can be done by people or by mechanical or electronic devices.

Counting

This enterprise typically involves quantifying objects (including people) or behaviors of special interest. Counting typically has as its goal either estimating demand for something or assessing response to some marketing tactic.

Counting was the principle research method used by DioLight Technology Inc. to decide which markets to target for its new long-lasting light bulb. As reported in *Venture*, DioLight's marketing director, Kevin Callaghan, visited office buildings and counted the average number of exit signs that would need long-lasting bulbs.[1] He also developed secondary data to learn the number of hospitals in the United States that would need 24-hour-a-day lighting. Based on these observational and archival data, Callaghan concluded that industrial buyers would comprise a better market than consumer households. In 1985, the firm had $1 million in revenue from its new bulbs, 95 percent of which came from industrial sources.

Other examples of counts of natural phenomena made at very low cost that are helpful for marketing purposes include the following:

1. Counting the number of pedestrians and/or automobiles passing a proposed retail site.
2. Counting the number of competitors within various distances of a proposed retail or service location.

---

[1] Amy Saltzman, "Vision vs. Reality," *Venture*, October 1985, pp. 40–44.

3. Counting the incidence of some correlate of potential product usage such as the number of chimneys in the neighborhood of a fireplace shop, or the number of cars with leather seats coming to a car wash planning to add a leather-cleaning service.
4. Estimating the proportion of men, women, or children at particular promotional events.
5. Counting the number of out-of-state license plates from specific states at a highway roadside diner.

Counting is often the only means of assessing the effects of competitors' actions. Empty spaces in the parking lot can suggest the effects of a competitor's promotions. So can counts of people entering their stores. One can observe their prices or count people stopping at their displays.

A major virtue of simple counting is that it can be carried out by unskilled researchers. For example, one or two teenagers could be hired as a retailer's field research staff and sent out to make observations at competitors' outlets or in the retailer's own outlet or parking lot. Careful training is still necessary and procedures must be carefully specified, but costs can be kept very low.

Measuring

Counting, of course, is the simplest form of measurement. Rather than simply counting people or objects or behavior, observation is more useful if it involves some sort of measurement. This can prove particularly fruitful in the measurement of *physical traces*. Often an environmental characteristic of interest leaves behind a residue which we can observe and measure. The researchers who use these physical traces are in a sense modern-day archeologists.

Physical traces may be divided into three broad groupings: accretion, erosion, and traces. They were all the stock-in-trade of perhaps the best low-budget researcher of all time, Sherlock Holmes. In fact, reading the collected works of Arthur Conan Doyle provides innumerable excellent examples of the wondrous powers of a keen observer routinely using accretions, erosions, and physical traces to solve crimes. Holmes was always astonishing the less observant Watson with the leaps of insight he could derive from observing such things as the type of mud on the shoes of a seemingly innocent houseguest (an accretion) or the size of the footprint near the trellis in the garden (a physical trace) or the missing matches on the left side of the matchbook of the left-handed smoker (an erosion).

In marketing, a good example of the use of accretion data is in the observance of litter. City managers can analyze the amount and type of litter on selected downtown streets for clues as to which areas should be the focus of anti-litter campaigns. Garbage counts of liquor bottles can be used to estimate consumption levels in communities where interview data would be unreliable or where package stores do not exist. Indeed, studies of this type are now so common that an entire field called *garbology* has emerged. Much of this work has been carried out at the University of Arizona. Studies there have been used to estimate market shares in certain neighborhoods, use of specific packaging and the effectiveness of product sampling and direct mail (by noting unopened packages or letters). It is particularly valuable in subject areas where consumers may be reluctant to reveal true behavior.

Other physical measures that have been used by marketers are:

- Wear on particular magazines in physician waiting rooms that suggests popularity and thus potential value of different media for advertising.
- Radio settings of car radios in a repair shop that suggest stations to use for the shop's advertising.
- Clothes tried on, but not purchased, in a clothing boutique as a measure of dissatisfaction.

Mechanical or Electronic Observation

An obvious problem with even such a simple technique as counting is human error. Even the best intentioned individual researcher can be distracted or fatigued or can count the wrong thing. Such failings need not be fatal to studies. Debriefing the researcher or comparing results among researchers can usually detect large systematic mistakes. Distraction and fatigue can also be accommodated if they are essentially random. However, they may not be. Noisy teenagers in a shop may easily distract a researcher (especially another teenager) leading to an under-count of those teenagers and/or their behavior. Fatigue often sets in late in the day or just before meals. If researchers are not scheduled to work at different times over the course of the study, data on late afternoon shoppers or the lunchtime crowd may be systematically distorted.

There may be other problems using human observers. Re-searchers may not want to work late at night or early in the morning, leaving a major potential bias. A more serious problem is that the presence of a human observer during the observation process may itself be obtrusive. A researcher hovering around a particular display or doorway with a clipboard or mechanical counter may discourage customers from looking over the goods on the display or visiting a particular store.

In all of these cases, a desirable low-cost alternative is to eliminate the potential for human error or bias by using elec-tronic or mechanical observation techniques. Indeed, several ma-jor commercial research services are based on just such mechanical or electronic observation. Nielsen's television rating service electronically records (observes) the stations to which its sample households are tuned with a "people-meter." Eye-cameras are used by some advertising researchers to study how people look over an ad.

Probably the most significant recent development in mar-keting research in the packaged consumer goods industry (scan-ner research) is based on the electronic scanning of the purchases of a preselected sample of households as they check out in super-markets. In the more sophisticated scanner research systems, advertising input into sample households via cable is experi-mentally manipulated and the effects on supermarket purchases selectively observed.

All of the above techniques, however, require great cost and/ or levels of sophistication beyond the low-budget researchers. Other options available, however, are the following:

Pneumatic Traffic Counters.   These are the rubber hoses stretched across highways or streets to count automobiles. Although subject to certain errors (e.g., three-axle trucks or playful teenagers recrossing a counter), these counters can monitor traffic passing potential retail locations or cars entering a shopping mall before and after specific promotional events.

Electronic Eyes.   These devices count bodies breaking a beam of light and can be used to note unobtrusively the number of people passing a display or entering a room.

Polaroid Cameras.   Instant pictures can provide important observational data. For example, a marketer in a performing arts center could photograph an audience just before a performance and note which seats were unoccupied. If repeated, this technique could help measure the popularity of different performances or performers. It also could be the basis for follow-up interviews of those subscribers whose seats were empty to assess ways in which the programming could be improved.

Video Tape Recorders.   Customers in many outlets are accustomed to video cameras. Once recorded, their images can provide useful observations of the types of clothing customers wear, the relative number of males and females, the number of elderly attending a particular sale. They can also indicate movement patterns, e.g., how customers look at a package or experiment with a floor model of an appliance. Cameras can record how quickly salespeople approach customers, how long customers stay in the store, which direction they move as they circulate throughout the store and so on.

Computers.   These and other electronic ordering devices can be programmed to record surreptitiously items considered or the length of time a consumer spent viewing a choice alternative.

Seeking Patterns in Natural Observations

Using electronic or mechanical devices to count and measure ignores one of the most important human faculties, the ability to find patterns in what we see. In the field of anthropology, observation is the principle research tool. For the anthropologist, the key concern is finding patterns, getting a full, rich sense of what it is that makes a Trobriand Islander different from a Kwakiutl Indian. While anthropologists count and use physical traces, more often, cultural and social anthropologists simply go into the field, watch what people do, and try to synthesize their observations by detecting the patterns that seem to be there.

A good example of the kind of insight that can be gained from seeking patterns through low-cost, relatively unobtrusive observation of naturally occurring consumer behavior was reported by Wells and Lo Sciuto in a 1966 article. Under a grant from the Benton and Bowles advertising agency, Wells and Lo Sciuto explored the potential for direct observation of supermarket shoppers in three product categories—cereal, detergent, and candy. Fifteen hundred observations were made by three students in supermarkets in Northern New Jersey. The students observed any shopper entering the aisle where the products in question were offered who appeared intent on making a purchase.

The kinds of questions this study methodology can answer are:

- Who actually chooses the products and who influences the choice at the point of sale?
- To what extent are the brand choices made before the shopper enters the store versus at the point of purchase?
- How many people check price?
- Do shoppers check the package before purchase?

The first major finding of the study was that the observations themselves were easy to make. The only problems occurred at the training stage when it was discovered that the observers were not getting sufficient detail into their records. In practice trials, the students were inclined to record only the bare bones of each transaction, omitting the detail which is the essence of the method. A second problem was in getting the researchers to record their observations immediately after the episode. Thorough training overcame both problems.

The study sought both to count behavior (e.g., how many cereal shoppers had children with them) and to seek patterns.

The difficulty inherent in trying to see patterns was exemplified when the researchers attempted to estimate the proportion of shoppers who knew what they wanted when they approached the cereal counter. As Wells and Lo Sciuto note, it is difficult to "infer a state of mind." When the shopper marches right up to a specific spot at the display and grabs a box, the evidence suggesting a preformed choice is all but conclusive. But when a shopper hesitates, searches, and physically inspects several packages, it is hard to guess whether the shopper doesn't know what he or she wants, or knows what he or she wants and can't find it. In cases such as these, the students simply learned to make judgments based on the overall patterns they observed.

Although their study was only a pilot venture, Wells and Lo Sciuto believed the patterns found in their study showed the following:

- Women do more of the family shopping than men, but men do enough to warrant a marketer's attention.
- Husbands who accompany wives and try to influence purchase decisions almost always succeed.
- Children, especially urban children, are also influential, although this varies by product class.
- Urban shoppers show more concern with price than suburban shoppers. This also varies by type of product and by sex.
- Many shoppers of all types inspect packages before they buy.
- The tactile dimension therefore deserves more attention than it usually receives in most package research.

Another example of anthropological research in marketing is a recent study by consumer researchers of a swap meet in Arizona. A team of three professionals with diverse skills in consumer research took a mini-van, a set of tape recorders and TV cameras, portable computers, and large notebooks to a small town and over several days talked, filmed, and recorded both buyers and sellers at a permanent local swap meet. They observed people buying and selling and asked them questions about their activities and the meanings the transactions had for them personally. While the data are only now being analyzed, the researchers believe that such naturalistic inquiry can yield much thicker data on important market phenomena. The technique is very labor intensive but the researchers have found their odyssey has been relatively low cost yet richly insightful.[2]

CONTROLLING THE QUALITY OF NATURAL OBSERVATIONS

Problems of Inference

Some observations, such as garbage counts or observations of clothing preferences, require a considerable leap of inference before the implications for marketing strategy are clear. For instance, if there is an increase in the proportion of all the female customers who enter a clothing store wearing slacks, does this indicate a general preference or simply an indication of what they wear when shopping? Is the style they are wearing then reflecting their general taste (e.g., the price level to be catered to) or are they slumming? The research manager must make strong assumptions before allowing the data to affect marketing strategy. In many such situations it will be desirable to back up the observations with other measurement methods. For example, in the case of the clothing preferences, a few discrete interviews might quickly resolve some of the ambiguities in the observations.

Indeed, when using low-budget techniques, it is always an excellent strategy to attempt to assess key phenomena in many different ways. Many of the techniques proposed in this volume must make some compromises in methodology in order to keep costs down. As a consequence, the results of any given low-cost study must always be taken with at least some skepticism. However, if the researcher can develop multiple measures of several aspects or traits of the same phenomena, preferably using different kinds of research methods, the unique biases of each tech-

---

[2]Russell W. Belk, John F. Sherry, Jr., and Melanie Wallendorf, "A Naturalistic Inquiry into Buyer and Seller Behavior at a Swap Meet." *Journal of Consumer Research* 14, No. 4, March 1988, pp. 449–470.

nique may often cancel each other out. If the same conclusion emerges from several different approaches (e.g., focus groups *plus* a few interviews *plus* observations), the researcher can have much more confidence in what is found. We are strong advocates of what researchers have come to a call the multi-measure multi-trait technique.

Problems of Collection

Observation must be systematic and objective to be valid and reliable. The goal is to secure a representative, accurate sample of the phenomena to be observed. Two steps must be taken to achieve this goal (1) a sampling procedure must be carefully developed to ensure that each potential observation that one *could* make has a known (perhaps equal) chance of being recorded; and (2) the field observer has as little freedom as possible in what is observed when the observation is made.

Sampling Phenomena or Events
Making observations is a method of collecting data just like asking questions with a questionnaire. Yet, many researchers who would be very systematic in designing a careful sampling plan before sending interviewers into the field are often extremely casual about sending individuals out to observe phenomena. Of course, it isn't always the case that a sampling plan is needed for an observational study. Just as with a questionnaire survey, the research objectives may require only a limited number of typical contacts (e.g., to help develop hypotheses or to detect serious problems—for example, with a new toy or appliance). However, if one wishes to project the results to a broader population or to conduct statistical tests, the usual rules of sampling (discussed in Chapter 9) need to be followed.

Typically, this requires procedures for three kinds of observational sampling.

Places.   If one is to observe a phenomenon at different locations, then observations must be taken with either equal observations at each site or with observations proportional to expected occurrence. In both cases, the researcher must first estimate how many events, phenomena, or potential observations will occur at each location. This will permit the results at each location to be post-weighted by the expected number of observations. Alternatively, the prior estimates may be used for assigning quotas for the number of observations at each site.

Times.   All possible times for observations should be sampled. Results can be severely biased if observers always go at the same time, for example when it is convenient for them or when there are few people at the site. Again, one must estimate in advance the likely distribution of events over time and assign observations to cover the spectrum. The time allocations can be proportional or they can be equal and then post-weighted.

Individual Events.   Even if places and times are randomly selected, interviewers should be given some guidance in event sampling. The simplest approach is systematic sampling. The observer can be told to observe every *n*th event, e.g., every fifth person passing on the north side of the Ficus Benjamina just inside the Boulevard Mall's southeast entrance. If this is problematic, an alternative rule could be to take the fifth person after the last observation is completed. Whatever the procedure, the objective is to give the observer a firm *rule* so that he or she will not just observe what seems interesting or easy.

Observing Accurately

Field researchers, of course, can be attentive, objective observers or sloppy and casual. The secret to ensuring the former is to follow four guidelines:

1. Recruit a potential set of field observers who are likely to be attentive and objective.
2. Give them an observation test to screen out the poorer prospects.
3. Establish clear written guidelines specifying what and how to observe.
4. Have the observers practice, practice, practice.

REFERENCES

1. Webb, Eugene J.; Donald T. Campbell; Kenneth D. Schwartz; and Lee Sechrest. *Unobtrusive Methods: Nonreactive Research in the Social Sciences.* New York: Rand McNally, 1971.
2. Nighswonger, Nancy J., and Claude R. Martin, Jr. "On Using Voice Analysis in Marketing Research." *Journal of Marketing Research,* August 1981, pp. 350–355.
3. Stewart, David. "Physiological Measurement of Advertising Effects." *Psychology and Marketing,* Spring 1984, pp. 43–48.
4. Cote, Joseph A.; James McCullough; and Michael Reilly. "Effects of Unexpected Situations on Behavior-Intention Differences: A Garbology Analysis." *Journal of Consumer Research,* September 1985, pp. 188–194.
5. Wells, William D., and Leonard A. Lo Sciuto. "Direct Observation of Purchasing Behavior." *Journal of Marketing Research,* August 1966, pp. 227–233.

CHAPTER 7

LOW-COST EXPERIMENTATION

In the last chapter, we took the world as it is, doing our best to observe and record what it had to tell us. An obvious restriction on observed data is that we must accept reality. This is often desirable because it means the data are not contaminated by our intrusions. On the other hand, we cannot observe something that has not taken place, such as a marketing tactic never tried. Marketers are doers, and it is their mission in the corporate or non-profit worlds to make changes rather than to respond to them. Thus, when managers look to research for help, it is almost always to tell them what to do in the future. (As we argued in Chapters 3 and 4, this is the *only* time they should ask for research help!) Managers are typically very suspicious of research which only tells them what worked in the past or (worse still) that requires great feats of inference and analysis to tell them even that. What managers really want to know is what will work tomorrow. Trying things out on a pilot basis is a very good way to gain just this kind of insight.

This is the role of experimentation—trying things out! Experimentation is immediate. It will help managers learn whether implementing tactic A will lead to result X. And, assuming the rest of the world holds still, it can suggest pretty strongly that doing A tomorrow will lead to X the day after. Experimentation is intentionally intrusive. But the cost in potential bias is often well compensated by four major virtues terribly important to managerial applications:

1. It permits the experimenter to control the intervention so that it closely parallels just what management's strategic options are likely to be.

2. By careful design, experimenters can control a large part of the natural world's chaos, factors that tend to foul up other naturally occurring pseudo-experiments.
3. Experimentation often can prove cause and effect; it can say that, since everything else was held constant, the result X must have been caused by A.
4. Since experimenters can dictate the timing of the intervention, experiments are often speedier and more efficient than many other approaches, especially field observation which has to wait for events to naturally occur.

Experimentation is routinely used by most major marketers in the private sector. Test marketing, a form of real-world experimentation, is a standard technique in most new product development processes. Market tests are used to assess such things as price elasticities, optional advertising budgets, and the desirability of changes in packaging or point of sales materials. In a classic market study, Anheuser-Busch systematically varied its advertising budgets in different markets over several months. Historically, Anheuser-Busch had changed advertising in only small increments and so did not have any experience with big changes. In some of its market tests, it doubled its ad budget; in others it halved it. As a result of the study, the firm gained precise knowledge of the responsiveness of sales to significant changes in advertising and concluded that in general it could cut its budgets significantly and reap substantial rewards in improved profitability.

Unfortunately, experimentation is not a research approach that naturally comes to the mind of the limited-budget manager. Yet it can be a very effective and often very cheap research technique. Experimentation can have an extremely favorable cost/benefit ratio. Yet, it is all too rarely used.

Why is this?

The answer I believe lies in what I have come to call the *one-best-strategy* mentality of many managers. The manager feels under a great deal of pressure to produce and to do so without spending much money. To accomplish this goal, the manager typically tries to be as cautious as possible. The limited-budget manager is usually very risk-averse. This means that he or she changes from the status quo only when the case for such change is very convincing. And, typically, to reduce the insecurity when such a change is made, the manager settles on the one best alternative and, once the decision is made, avoids thinking about any option that is assumed to be less than best. This approach tends to inhibit experimentation. The manager thinks: why try anything that is less than my best choice, even on an experimental basis, since, almost by definition, it is very likely to reduce my revenues?

There are fatal flaws in this reasoning. Most importantly, it assumes that the manager is really correct, that the best strategy has indeed been chosen! But, suppose the cost of an experiment can be kept low. It may well be worth it if there is *some* probability of a major gain in knowing what really is best—for example, if the best strategy is substantially off target. To see why this is so, we must recall our approach to analyzing the costs and benefits of research outlined in Chapter 4.

Suppose a manager is planning to send 10,000 letters to potential buyers at a cost of $800. The present best strategy is expected to yield 500 replies generating an estimated $20,000 in sales and, at a 10 percent rate of profit, net returns of $1,200 after deducting the cost of the mailing. Suppose further that, for an extra $100, a second mailer could be prepared using a strategy that is currently thought to be second best, but which could be better in the long run. Suppose that the manager predicts that, if this second-best mailer is sent to 20 percent of the mailing list, instead of 100 replies, only 80 would be received (because it is second best). At an average return of $40 per response and a profit of $4, the experiment would cost $180 including the cost of the second mailer and the lost profits. But suppose the manager is willing to admit that he or she could be wrong and that the second-best mailer could really be better, should this experiment be conducted?

Suppose the manager estimates that, if the second strategy was really an improvement, it could increase returns at maximum by 15 percent. In such a case, the better strategy would yield 575 replies at an average sale of $40 and an average profit of $4 for a total increase in profits of $300 per mailing. If a strategy lasts say five mailings, this is an overall $1,500 gain in future profits. Further, if the second strategy was better, there would be no loss from this mailing and returns would rise from 100 to 115, meaning that the experiment would only cost $40, and that management would be $1,460 ahead.

Now, if the manager concedes there was a 20 percent chance the second strategy will turn out to be better, there are two possible payoffs associated with experimenting when compared to the strategy of just continuing with the present one best strategy: (1) a 20 percent chance of being better off by $1,460, and (2) an 80 percent chance of being worse off by $180. The weighted expected value then is a positive $148. Management, on average, would gain this amount by conducting experiments like this even if there was only a relatively modest chance the one-best-strategy really wasn't best.

Although the example here is hypothetical and the amounts are small, it clearly demonstrates why the very best managers are always experimenting. First of all, more experimental managers tend to be less risk-averse and are not quite so fearful that a risky second strategy would turn out to be a big disaster—i.e., that expected losses from foregone sales would be very high. At the same time they are more likely to entertain the possibility that they are wrong. Further, their marketing aggressiveness leads them constantly to look for ways of doing things better. And so they will often conclude that, even if a careful estimate of the expected value from experimentation is negative, it is still worth the research because *something* will be learned—even if it is only that this second best alternative can be eliminated in future.

Further, the sophisticated manager is more likely to think strategically about the long run. That is, the manager will be willing to accept quite a number of failures in experimentation in the short run recognizing that, if experiments are done in series, over time the manager can accumulate a very good sense of what does and does not work in a particular market environment. Experimentation for these managers is really systematic wisdom building.

EXPERIMENTAL DESIGN

The opportunities for experimentation are almost boundless, limited for the most part only by the imagination of the researcher. The object of experimentation is to try something different and, by following a few simple rules of proper experimental design, learn what the effect of this difference is, if any, on a result of interest to management, such as brand awareness or product preference. The rules are very important, however, because, while experimentation may seem simple, there are many things that can go wrong.

Experimentation can apply to almost any aspect of the marketing mix. New product and service offerings can be tried out. Prices can be manipulated, cents-off deals promoted, and/or discounts or bonuses to wholesalers or retailers introduced. Different advertising copy or point-of-sale promotion options can be exposed to different target audiences alone or in various combinations. Experimentation can address large and small issues. For example, for print advertising, one can learn whether to use pictures or no pictures; whether to show people or show products; whether the copy should be long or short; or whether the company logo should go on the left side or the right side. One can also study the effect of totally withdrawing advertising from a market or doubling it.

Experimentation can help explore alternative sales presentations, media combinations, timing of ads, sales call frequencies, packages and methods of shipping, or approaches to product service. New distribution outlets can be tried, as can new types of salespeople—even new salary incentive schemes.

Experiments can be done in the real world or in the laboratory. The real world has the virtue of being like the eventual market the organization will face. But a lot of other events will be going on (e.g., competitors' actions) that can cloud a result. In the laboratory, all else can be held constant. But what one gains in control of the experimental setting, one obviously loses in realism.

Results of experiments can be measured in terms of cognitions, actual behavior, or both. Cognitions could include measures of awareness, perception of various product or promotion features, preferences, attitudes toward future patronage or towards passing along favorable word-of-mouth. Behavioral measures could include customer sales, salespeoples' allocations of time, or distributors' warehousing policies.

True versus Pseudo-Experiments

We will begin by discussing what formal experimentation is and what it is not.

To be most useful to a manager, an experiment should ideally possess three characteristics. First, there should be random assignments of different experimental treatments (e.g., different advertisements) to different groups of subjects (e.g., stores, markets, or individuals). Second, the experiment should be designed such that (ideally) nothing else could have caused the results observed. Third, the results of the experiment should be projectable to the future real world marketing situation the organization will face with few doubts as to its applicability. The major variations in experimental design discussed below are simply different ways of controlling one or more of the major kinds of threats to these last two characteristics, sometimes called *internal* or *external validity*.

These requirements help us distinguish between a true experiment and research that seems like an experiment but isn't. The following hypothetical cases *look* like experiments but are not:

- One month after major banks lower the prime rate half a percentage point, a marketer observes that dishwasher sales have jumped 20 percentage points.
- A marketer observes that when competitors reduced the price of its comparable product 10 percent in California and nowhere else in the country, sales of the marketer's product in California fell 20 percent while no changes appeared elsewhere.
- The salesforce's commission rate for a product is increased from 5 to 10 percent and the salespeople then sell 20 percent more as compared to last year.

These all look like experiments in the sense that something is changed and there appear to be consequences that the something caused. But these situations are really what we call *pseudo-experiments*. Can an analysis of the impact of these natural events meet the test of internal validity? That is, can one eliminate the possibility that the observed results are due to something entirely different from the factor we think caused it? In each of the cases above, at least one reasonable alternative hypothesis can be offered.

In the dishwasher case, suppose the banks lowered the prime rate at the same time as (1) a new, aggressive set of modular home builders entered the market who would have bought a lot of dishwashers without the discount rate change, (2) homes under construction had previously fallen to the lowest level in 10 years so that builders would have increased construction in any case just to keep their workers employed, (3) prices of concrete, lumber, and roofing tiles fell from 5 to 30 percent spurring construction (and dishwasher sales); and/or (4) there was the usual seasonal increase in construction.

In the California case, the competitors have cut price because they sensed a decline in sales in California was coming. Your sales may have declined anyway, not as a result of their actions.

In the salesforce commission case, suppose sales of the product were ready to take off even without any added effort and, in fact, because the salespeople became too pushy due to the increased commissions, customers bought 10 percent *less* than they would have otherwise.

In all three cases, the problem with the experiment was that there was no control for other possible explanations. The reasons were threefold. First, since we didn't systematically control the cause (although we could have in the case of the commission rate), there was no random assignment of the subjects of the experiment to the conditions. In the bank rate and sales commission cases, *everybody* was exposed to the condition. In the other case, although California was the target of the intervention, California may have been chosen by the competitor for many reasons (e.g., excess inventory) that had nothing to do with the experimental treatment.

Second, in the bank rate and commission cases, we have the additional problem that because the change affected everyone, we had no comparison or control group. So we don't know what would have happened in the absence of the treatment.

Third, in the California case, since we didn't control the timing of the treatments we cannot even say that the price reduction preceded the sales drop rather than appeared at the same time, thus confusing association with causation.

This then leads us to define three requirements of a true experiment:

1. The experimental treatment must precede the effects it is designed to cause.
2. There must be a comparison group that did not receive the treatment or received a different treatment.
3. There must be random assignment of treatments (or the absence of a treatment) to groups.

The latter is especially crucial. Unless one randomly assigns treatments to targets, there is always the danger that those exposed to the treatment (for example, those who volunteer for it) will be different from those not exposed. Unless there is random assignment, we cannot by definition rule out the possibility that any differences that show up are due to the fact that the two groups are different to begin with.

This is not to deny that pseudo-experiments can be informative. Sometimes they are the only way to observe an effect such as the market's responses to some sudden action by a competitor, or to an environmental shock like a change in interest rates, or a plant closing. In such instances, low-cost researchers should attempt to learn as much as possible from the pseudo-experiment, making every effort to consider and adjust for whatever biases may be present. Often there is simply no reason to believe that the occurrence of the natural event was not randomly distributed. If the results from the pseudo-experiment are believable, this may be quite adequate as a basis for a risk-taking manager to take action.

Types of Experiments

True experiments can take many forms and can be very complicated. We will restrict our attention here to relatively simple experiments. The experiments discussed here differ in two respects; (1) whether measures were taken before and after the treatment or only before, and (2) whether there was a control group with which to compare the group(s) receiving the treatment(s). In this framework, pseudo-experiments would be classified as experiments with no control.

We will consider two of the simplest and most commonly used designs first and then introduce some more complex alternatives for those who have more difficult decision problems to investigate.

After Measure with Control

The simplest experiment to design and administer is called the *after measure with control* design. It requires that the researcher randomly assign subjects to two or more groups, leave one group alone as a control, and apply a treatment to each of the remaining groups. The effects of each treatment are then measured and compared with the untouched control group. The difference provides a measure of treatment effect that eliminates any systematic bias between the groups (as when subjects self-select the treatment they will expose themselves to) although there can still be random differences between the groups.

Let us consider an example. Suppose the owner of a chain of retail clothing outlets is curious as to whether a modest direct mail campaign aimed at residents near the chain's outlets would have an effect on sales. A simple after-measure-with-control experiment could be used with two or more stores assigned to each group:

Group	Treatment	After Measure
1	Yes	Yes
2	No	Yes

To ensure that this is a true experiment the manager must randomly assign stores to the two conditions and not, for example, conduct the mailing around stores nearest headquarters (so one can keep an eye on traffic in the stores). Random assignment has the advantage of eliminating systematic bias. And the presence of the control group not only gives a basis for comparison but helps monitor another harsh reality of real-world market experiments. Many marketers have discovered to their dismay that competitors are not always hesitant to try to foul up a field experiment when they learn of it. This happens very often with new product introductions. A virtue of randomization is that competitors are unlikely to know where and how the tests are carried out and any intervention will affect the control sites just as much as the treatment sites so that the differences in results will still indicate treatment effects.

This approach has one other feature to recommend it. Because measurements are taken only after the treatment, one does not risk the possibility of contaminating a treatment group before applying the treatment. Let us, however, consider why we might want to measure a group before a treatment.

Before and After Measures with Control

Suppose the results of the above experiment turned out as in Table 7–1. The question the researcher must now ask is, Are there any other explanations for the effects other than the treatment? One possibility is that the after measures simply reflect differences in the groups (stores) that existed before the study— and that the treatment had no effect. This is possible even though the stores were assigned randomly.

Suppose the retailer in the example had only four stores to assign to the two conditions described. Suppose further that the stores ranged in size from very small to very large. The problem quickly becomes obvious. If the larger stores by chance were

TABLE 7–1
Hypothetical Experimental Research Results: After-Only with Control

Average Store Sales/Week	
Direct mail	$12,630
No direct mail	$ 9,320

TABLE 7–2
Hypothetical Experimental Research Results:
Before-After with Control

	Average Store Sales/Week		
	Before Mailing	*After Mailing*	*Difference*
Direct mail	$10,510	$12,630	$2,120
No direct mail	$ 8,700	$ 9,320	$ 620

assigned to the direct mail treatment condition, sales will be very high and the treatment will appear to be more effective. On the other hand, if the larger stores end up in the control group, then no treatment would look to be effective. The explanation of the after results then would be confounded by the unmeasured before conditions.

If it is feared that random assignment may leave the groups greatly different even without any systematic bias (e.g., where one is using a small sample), an obvious precaution would be to take a reading on the groups before the treatment as well as after. One could then proceed to compute before-and-after differences for each of the groups and compare the difference for the treatment group with the difference for the control group. This would have the effect of eliminating the effects of differences in starting position across the groups.[1] A hypothetical result is reproduced in Table 7–2. Here we can see that the effects of the mailing were much less dramatic than Table 7–1 suggested.

One might ask, then, why not do this all the time? There are two reasons why a researcher might not want to take a before measure. One is cost; the more measurements taken, the greater

---

[1]An alternative way of handling this problem is called *blocking*. It can be used if one already has a measure of some important prior difference or some characteristic that is believed to be highly associated with it. Blocking in this case would put large stores in one block and small stores in the other. Assignment is random within blocks ensuring that each treatment has one randomly chosen small store and one randomly chosen large store.

the cost. The other is the danger of contaminating the groups. If one takes a prior measure, it is not inconceivable that either (1) the before measure itself will cause a change, or (2) the before measure will cause the treatment to have more impact than it would have if the before measure was not taken.

These two possibilities can most easily be seen in the context of advertising research. Suppose O'Grady's, a manufacturer of packaged tortillas, is going to run a dramatic new billboard campaign to introduce a metropolitan area to the company's brand. The manufacturer wishes to track the campaign's effect on awareness of the brand on the part of householders in non-Hispanic areas. To conduct the experiment, billboards will be randomly assigned to some neighborhoods and not others.

Premeasures are taken in both treatment and control neighborhoods asking householders to name any brand of tortilla that comes to their mind. Scores for each brand are computed. The billboards are set up in the treatment neighborhoods and, after six weeks, the same households in both areas are reinterviewed. The before-and-after results are shown in Table 7–3.

The before measures in the two sets of neighborhoods are very similar. (The researcher should be very suspicious if the before results differ dramatically. This would suggest a nonrandom factor in the selection of treatment and control areas, e.g., putting the billboards in areas where the brand is already successful!) Second, it appears from the results for O'Grady's in the treatment group that the billboards were a great success.

But let us look further. The results have three strange characteristics.

TABLE 7–3
Hypothetical Results of Billboard Study
(percent naming brand)

	Treatment		Control	
	Before	After	Before	After
O'Grady's	22	67	21	38
Major competitors	47	69	44	56
All others (average)	16	39	19	28

1. Awareness rose in the control group. Since there were no billboards there, the only plausible explanation is that the first interview spurred some respondents to investigate tortilla brands on a future shopping trip perhaps because they felt embarrassed that they didn't know more brands when first interviewed. This would be an example of a pre-test effect.

2. Differences between before and after measures for the treatment group are substantially greater than the differences for control groups for *all brands*. Since the only known difference between the two areas is the O'Grady billboards, it would seem that the premeasure and the new billboards may have caused the respondents to be even more curious to improve their knowledge of all brands. This would suggest an interaction between the premeasure and the experimental treatment.

3. In the treatment group, the largest before-and-after difference (45 percentage points versus 22 and 23) is exhibited for O'Grady's. Does this mean that the campaign was a success? We can reasonably conclude that the treatment groups *noticed* the billboards. But, did they notice them only (or largely) because they were subjected to the interview before the billboards went up? The interaction effects on the other brands make it impossible to rule out this possibility.

The bottom line is that, because of all of the problems, we must reluctantly conclude that the experiment is inconclusive.

Most studies involving cognitive changes are very susceptible to premeasure contamination. In such cases, after-only measures are to be preferred. But in many studies, the need for a premeasure will be important and the researcher will simply have to make a judgment as to which set of potential problems is more worrisome: (1) not having a premeasure, or (2) having a premeasure that fouls up the results. In general, the larger the number of cases one can assign to each treatment, the less one has to worry about prior differences across groups and can choose the after-only approach. On the other hand, contaminating premeasures could be ignored if one is only looking at differences between various treatments and there is reason to believe that premeasures will inflate postmeasures for all groups alike and will not exaggerate the effect of any one treatment. In such cases, one can assume that the difference scores are all biased to the same degree and proceed to compare the (biased) treatment differences to the (biased) control group differences. (This is another case of learning to live with bias.)

If a premeasure is crucial, for example where one is worried about important differences across groups (e.g., neighborhoods), *and* if a premeasure may inflate only the treatment effect (i.e., the biases will not be constant), there is sometimes another option. It may be possible to measure different samples of people fore and after the treatments. This could have been done in the billboard study. One could have interviewed one group before the billboard went up and a different group after. However, the conclusions of the study would rely on the assumption that the sample group studied after the billboards went up would have shown the same prior status as the premeasure group, i.e., that there are no differences in starting position between the pre and post groups. But this is not always reasonable, especially where the sample is small. It will be remembered that the reason for the premeasure in the first place was to take into account just such sampling differences between groups! A second problem with using two different samples is that the researcher would not be able to learn which households were affected by the treatment. For example, in the billboard study, O'Grady's would not know if the increased awareness came from young or old, large or small households, or men or women.

Other Biases

Even where the researcher can safely assume that there are no premeasure effects or interactions, other possible sources of bias can appear. Subjects of many experiments may realize they are part of a study. In so-called laboratory studies, this is always a problem. Subjects in laboratory settings (e.g., watching slides of advertising or packaging on a screen) *know* they are part of a study and they will behave strangely. For example, they will likely examine an ad much more carefully than normal. If a control group is subject to the same hothouse effect, then the researcher may safely use the "constant bias" assumption. Even in the real world, the hothouse effect is a possibility. For example, suppose one wishes to experiment with a new in-store display or a new sales presentation method. It is possible that personnel in the experimental group will simply try harder because they know they are part of a study. Higher sales, then, cannot be attributed to the new display or sales presentation but may be due to the hothouse effects of the study itself.

This effect may sometimes apply to the control group as well. In a famous $40 million heart-risk study called MRFIT, the researchers had to inform doctors in the control group that they were part of the study in part because the researchers needed careful records on patients of all physicians. Ironically the researchers found that there was a greater control of heart problems in the control group than in the group practicing the approved regimen, exercising more, and reducing salt intake. They attributed this to the fact that doctors in the control group were more diligent with their patients because they knew they were being watched.[2]

More Complex Designs

In the examples above, we only considered one treatment. In many marketing situations, management will wish to know which of several alternatives is better. In such cases, a simple solution is to increase the number of randomly selected treatment groups—and have a control sample that remains touched. Alternatively, if there is no intention to leave the market as it is now and the managerial action is to choose among several new alternatives, then one really does not need a control group. That is, for management's purposes, one does not need to know whether there is any effect, but only which treatment (if any) has the most effect.

Suppose management is considering new tactics that are not simply substitutes for each other (e.g., different prices for a new product), but which might be used in combination (e.g., different prices *and* different levels of package quality)? Here, managers typically want to know (1) main effects—did any of

---

[2]George D. Lundberg, M.D., "MRFIT and the Goals of *The Journal*," *Journal of the American Medical Association* 248, no. 12, September 24, 1982, p. 1501.

the tactics by itself have a differential effect? and (2) interaction effects—did some combination of tactics yield greater effects than predicted by the separate main effects?

To make this point clear, consider the case of a supermarket chain. The chain wishes to know whether it should put its generic facial tissue on the top or bottom shelf instead of on the middle shelf where it is now and whether they should charge 45 cents instead of the present 49 cents. The criterion is to be total dollar revenues generated. The manager might think that the higher the shelf position and the lower the price, the more sales. However, it may be that the combination of a higher price on the highest shelf would be the most profitable. From an experimental standpoint, the manager is asking:

1. Is there a main effect due to shelf position? That is, do sales differ significantly depending on where the facial tissue is positioned?
2. Is there a main effect due to price? That is, are significantly more revenues generated at the low price than the higher price?
3. Is there an *interaction* effect between price and shelf-position?

To answer these questions, we must have a much more complicated design. Here we need to use *six* experimental treatments, one for each combination of shelf position and price. This is because, without all possible combinations, we cannot estimate the interaction effects. In each of the six conditions or cells, we will want at least six to ten stores so that a good measure of random variation within the cells can be secured. Suppose the results over several weeks turned out as in Table 7–4.

While we must apply statistical tests to each of the three possible effects (see Chapter 10), the results suggest that:

1. There is no main effect due to shelf position. That is, if nothing else were changed, management should not care on which shelf it placed its generic facial tissue.
2. There is a main effect due to price. As economists would have told us, the lower the price, the higher the sales.

TABLE 7-4
Average Revenues for Generic Facial Tissues
Experiment (in $100)

	Shelf Position			
Price	Bottom	Middle	Top	Average
45¢	$300	$190	$170	$220
49¢	50	170	200	140
Average	$175	$180	$185	$180

3. Most importantly, there is an interaction effect. Clearly, the best strategy is to place the toilet paper on the bottom shelf and charge 49¢.

Although this experiment is complex, for a supermarket with many outlets, the cost of the study is very low. In the hypothetical study, the results show that average revenues could be $300,000. This compares to the present strategy which, in the experimental stores, yields $170,000. Assuming a supermarket's typical 1 percent profits, the increase in profits of $1,300 (1 percent of $130,000) multiplied across many stores and many weeks (e.g., perhaps until competitors responded to the price cut) can yield gains from this experiment in the hundreds of thousands of dollars. Compared to this return, the cost of setting up a complex experiment is worth it. However, these costs can be significant. Stores must be carefully chosen, managers alerted, and a separate accounting procedure established. One must make sure that each store carries out the tactic as planned. Stocks must be monitored so that out-of-stock conditions don't contaminate the results. Competitors' responses, if any, must also be monitored. And, store sales personnel must be trained not to influence the findings.[3]

---

[3]There are other complex alternatives to the present design. For example, one could try all combinations in each store so that, in a sense, each store's results can be compared to itself. The order of the combinations, of course, would have to be varied across outlets. If one could only assign a few stores per cell, one could use a technique called *blocking* to make sure that large, medium, and small stores were included in each cell.

There are a great many possibilities for this more complex kind of low-cost experimentation. One of the best places to do complex experiments is through direct mail. A great many organizations spend a lot of effort mailing letters, brochures, price lists, and requests. They are all designed to generate responses. Clearly learning how to increase such responses would be very valuable. Experimentation is the obvious approach here. There are a number of reasons why direct mail experiments are popular:

1. It is very easy to randomly assign subjects to treatments.

2. Because large numbers can be assigned to each treatment, the need for a premeasure is virtually nonexistent.

3. It is easy to keep track of which responses are associated with which treatments. Slightly modified layouts of return envelopes can be used to indicate different treatments. Code numbers can be incorporated on the mail response form itself or on the return envelope. Different P.O. Box numbers can be assigned to different treatments (at a slight added cost) or the return envelope can be addressed to different people, or to one person with different middle initials corresponding to different treatments. For telephone responses (e.g., in catalog sales), callers can be asked to identify the mailing material (treatment) number to which they are responding.

4. The treatment conditions can be very carefully controlled both as to the precise character and timing of the stimulus and as to all irrelevant factors that must be held constant.

5. The private nature of the mail system makes it very unlikely competitors will learn of the experiment. (On the other hand, if they, too, have learned to use low-cost competitive intelligence techniques, they or their employees may already be on several of your mailing lists!)

6. External validity is great because usually what is tried out in a mail experiment is what will be used by the marketer in the long run.

7. Because mail pieces are relatively complicated and because most recipients are only on one mailing list, subjects are unlikely to realize that they are part of an experiment. In this sense, mail studies are unobtrusive.

8. Complete combinations of treatments that can assess interactions are possible because of large sample bases.

Direct mail experimentation should be a routine part of any low-budget researcher's arsenal.

Laboratory Experiments

Despite their problems, laboratory experiments can be valuable alternatives to field experiments. Laboratory studies can be carried out in unreal environments such as hotel rooms, trailers in shopping center malls, university classrooms, or in the researcher's or the manufacturer's offices. The advantage of laboratory studies is that a great many factors can be controlled in these cases. Participants can be carefully assigned to treatments, stimuli precisely introduced, and extraneous factors totally eliminated. For such reasons, laboratory experiments are very popular for taste, touch, or sniff tests, advertising copy studies, pricing studies, and new product or service concept tests. In the laboratory, mechanical measuring devices can be used that would be cumbersome in the field. These could include measures of responses to marketing stimuli in the form of changes in heart beat, eye movement, conductivity of sweat, and pupil diameter.

An example of a simple laboratory study was one conducted by a group of my students at UCLA. At the time of the introduction of new Coke, the students were curious about the effects of the new product's advertising on perceptions of its taste. They set up a table on a quadrangle at UCLA and poured subjects drinks in random order from three cola bottles labeled "New Coke," "Old Coke," and "Pepsi." They asked respondents to rate the three drinks on a number of dimensions, including traits emphasized in early new Coke advertising and their preference among the three samples. They also asked each subject for their favorite cola in the past and whether they recalled seeing or hearing any ads for new Coke in recent days. Comparisons across subjects showed:

1. There were no significant differences in perceptions of the three drinks on all dimensions for all subjects.
2. There were significant differences for those who reported recalling the new Coke ads and the differences were in the direction that were emphasized in the advertising copy.

3. Most respondents had little difficulty indicating a clear preference among the three drinks.

As the reader may have suspected at this point, what was most interesting about this laboratory study was that, unlike the real world, the researchers could control what was in the bottles. And the colas were all the same: they were all old Coke! The study could clearly demonstrate that what advertising leads one to expect is what one thinks one gets! Advertising, even in such a simple product category, is much more powerful than many people suspect. No wonder we are inundated with ads calling colas "the real thing" or part of a "new generation."

However, needless to say, laboratory experiments give up a lot for what they gain. As already noted, subjects who know they are guinea pigs have been known to behave very strangely. Many will try to guess what the researchers want them to do (sometimes called the experimental *demand effect*) and try to please them.

Still, lab experiments are usually inexpensive to set up and can be done very quickly. Often there is little need for representativeness in the samples as long as the participants are (1) members of the target market and, where appropriate, (2) randomly assigned. As a consequence, simple lab experiments are usually a good first step in testing new ideas or alternative strategies. One can recruit friends, church members or, sometimes employees, randomly assign them to groups and see which treatment works best, taking care to control the other sources of explanation outlined earlier in this chapter.

SUMMARY

In the course of outlining these approaches to experimental design, the reader should have begun to appreciate both the potential benefits and the potential problems of the basic technique. There are a great many circumstances, perhaps the majority of cases, where elaborate controls and close checking of outside contamination are not really needed. In the previous paragraphs, we may have made experimentation seem too difficult. Now, we would like to point out instances in which it should be relatively easy.

1. Very often in experimental situations, premeasures will already exist. For example, in studies where markets or outlets are the experimental unit, sales are very often the measurement of primary interest. Since sales data usually are already available (although not always in the form one wants), premeasures can be avoided. If samples within cells must be small due to cost considerations, blocking on past sales or purchases can be used to control for potential bias due to size differences across cells that could occur by chance if there was random assignment.

2. Even where no premeasure presently exists, it may be possible and realistic to record premeasures unobtrusively, again eliminating possible negative premeasure effects. Several examples were offered in the chapter on observation. For instance, the effect of specific shelf layouts in a department store might be tracked by visual counts of the number of people handling the merchandise observed unobtrusively before and after an experiment, for example, by a TV camera.

3. Very often it is the case that the time interval involved between a treatment and a measurement is so short that no external competitor or environmental effects are likely to foul up a field study. Thus, one need not worry about trying to monitor these potential contaminants. The same would be true in longer term studies if the competitive environment was normally highly stable and/or if the researcher could easily disguise an experiment (e.g., with mail studies or in subtle advertising or store layout changes).

4. The population may be very homogeneous and, if randomization is carefully done, a premeasure may be unnecessary.

5. Multiple measures of experimental outcomes can be used if one fears that one or two could be biased. Their individual biases may cancel each other out.

6. As the researcher accumulates experience in experimentation, it will often be possible to make a confident estimate of possible biasing effects. Even using experiments without estimates may be better than doing no experimentation at all if it can be assumed the biases are reasonably constant or proportional across groups.

7. Finally, given an appropriate opportunity (as in the case where human beings are the guinea pigs), there is nothing at all wrong with asking the subjects of an experiment after the study whether they were, in fact, biased by some aspect of the study design and, if so, how. This is usually called *debriefing*.[4]

CONCLUDING COMMENTS

Before leaving the subject, let us recall several key points to keep in mind even when doing relatively inexpensive, simple experiments. Several of these points reflect general themes running throughout this book.

Always be sure that the experiment is designed to help management make decisions. The researcher should get management to think through the uses of a set of hypothetical experimental results to make sure that future actions will be taken. Try out a different but plausible set of results and make sure management is clear that (1) it will accept and act on surprising outcomes, and (2) you know what those actions would be.

Plan to make multiple measures of the experiment's outcomes to ensure that detected effects are real and that measurement peculiarities and biases do not either cover up something important or suggest something that really isn't important. Also, it is important to always randomize the sample population across treatment groups.

In field studies, always monitor potential outside influences by competitors or in the socio-economic environment in which the study is done that may contaminate the outcomes.

Allow enough time after the treatment for the effects to really show up. Make sure that, if lasting effects are wanted, the researcher does not settle for a quick, favorable response. For example, humorous ads always get quick, favorable reactions from subjects. But the effects tend to fade away rather quickly.

---

[4]Debriefing is routine in most professional and academic experiments involving human subjects. Codes of ethics require that subjects be informed of their rights not to participate and that they be told after the fact in the debriefing (except under unusual circumstances) what the aim of the study really was and who was its sponsor.

Other, more boring ads often have much more substantial lasting effects.

Consider the possibility of using multiple treatments in the experiment. The incremental costs of added complexity are often relatively low.

Be careful that employees or other accomplices do not bias the findings. For example, make sure that if a new in-store price or display experiment is tried, the salespeople do not act in ways such that the real results are due to their actions—e.g., more suggestive selling of displayed items—not the experimental treatments themselves.

If possible, debrief the subjects after the study to see if any biases were introduced (this would apply to the salespeople, too).

After the experiment is all over, sit down and write a brief methodological note about what was learned about how to do experiments that you will be sure to incorporate (or avoid) next time. Wisdom accumulates not only by providing findings that improve management's marketing strategies, but also by improving the researcher's abilities to be an even more effective low-budget experimenter in future.

REFERENCES

1. Banks, Seymour. *Experimentation in Marketing*, New York: McGraw-Hill, 1965.
2. Campbell, Donald T., and Julian C. Stanley. *Experimental and Quasi-Experimental Designs for Research*, Chicago: Rand McNally, 1966.
3. Achenbaum, Alvin R. "Market Testing: Using the Marketplace as a Laboratory." In *Handbook of Marketing Research*, ed. Robert Ferber. New York: McGraw-Hill, 1975, pp. 4–31 to 4–54.
4. Ahl, D.H. "New Product Forecasting Using Consumer Panels." *Journal of Marketing Research*, May 1970, pp. 160–167.

CHAPTER 8

LOW-COST SURVEY DESIGNS

As pointed out in the first two chapters, many low-budget researchers automatically think of surveys and questionnaires as their only research alternative. It is important that the reader become aware of, and appreciate the potential of, other techniques before moving on to survey design.

Chapter 7 focused on one such possibility—experimentation. Experiments are relatively easy to do and, because they can determine cause and effect, are usually able to give managers direct insight into what works and what doesn't. Thus, experiments are not only cheap, they are usually highly practical. A researcher with a limited budget has little freedom to conduct research that is not practical.

Chapters 5 and 6 discussed two other alternatives to surveys—archives and observation. These techniques are sometimes less immediately practical since they do not easily lend themselves to assessing cause and effect. They still have the prime virtue of being very inexpensive. Despite inadequacies, they can often help give managers the small edge in decision making that can help them consistently outperform their competitors.

A major reason for first considering these alternatives is that surveys are not only costly, they are difficult to do well. It is not easy to design sensible samples and well-worded questionnaires. Unfortunately, this does not keep amateurs from barging ahead to get something into the field without proper attention to making the research valid. This book is devoted to *good* cheap research, not just cheap research.

Surveys are difficult for two major reasons. First, one must typically draw a representative sample and this is not always an easy goal to accomplish. Second, one must ask people questions. There are a number of reasons the latter can be a major source of problems.

Asking questions is always obtrusive. This means your subjects know they are being studied. And because they know they are being studied, they will usually speculate about why you are asking. This can have one of two effects. On the one hand, it makes people suspicious of your motives and they may decide either not to participate at all (thus fouling up a carefully designed sampling plan) or to withhold or distort important information. A friend of mine always tells researchers studying fast food preferences that he is a heavy, heavy consumer—which he isn't—and that he really would like to be offered healthier ingredients in his burgers, chicken nuggets, and tacos. He always answers this way because he wants to encourage fast-food marketers to offer healthier fare to their *real* heavy consumers.

Awareness of being studied can lead some respondents to try to please the researcher. Well-meaning respondents may try to be helpful and claim they are, indeed, heavy users of whatever it is you are asking about. Or they may try to guess which brand or outlet you are interested in and try to slant their preferences that way.

Asking questions always involves respondents and their egos. Whether we are aware of it or not, we all attempt to influence the way in which others perceive us. We do this with our dress, our choice of our furniture, the way we speak, whom we associate with and so on. It is therefore inevitable that, when we tell researchers things about ourselves, we may answer subtly or directly in ways that will enhance our self-image. *Reader's Digest* fans will say instead that they only read the *New York Review of Books* or the *Atlantic Monthly*. The soap opera lover will swear to a preference for public television. The heavy beer drinker will develop a sudden taste for white wine.

Asking questions always involves language. Words are slippery things. A favorite word in studies of retail and service outlets is *convenient* as in the question "Do you find Store A more or less convenient than Store B?" What the researcher means by convenient may be a lot different from what the typical respondent means. For example, the researcher may assume that respondents are being asked how close the outlet is to their home or normal commuting routes whereas some respondents may think the question is asking how easy it is to park and get in and out of the outlet. Others may think it is referring to the outlet's hours of operation. In such cases, differences across respondents may simply reflect differences in how they interpret what you ask. For example, executives may find Store A more convenient than Store B while homebodies may indicate the reverse. Executives interpret your question to mean ease of parking and homebodies may interpret it to mean closeness to home. The difference in the results is merely an artifact of the language.

All of these types of problems are unavoidable in survey research. Questions will always crop up as to the validity of the study. One can try hard to minimize their effects, but the nasty problem is: you usually NEVER completely know that you have eliminated potential biases or, even, whether you understand them. This is particularly the case if you try to save money in the design by not pretesting the questionnaire thoroughly or training interviewers carefully. Management needs valid research results on which to act. In the last-mentioned example, it would be a mistake to promote the nearness of your outlet to executives as well as to homebodies. The two are very different in their goals and interests.

Conducting surveys and asking questions is often essential to a specific management problem. One must use these techniques in hundreds of situations. If, for example, you want data on attitudes, you have no other recourse. But when surveys are not essential, researchers should exhaust other nonintrusive methods before going forward with a full-blown survey study.

SURVEY ALTERNATIVES

If the researcher has determined that asking questions is the best approach to helping management make a decision, three basic strategic design decisions must be made. The researcher must decide (1) how to ask questions, (2) what questions to ask, and (3) who should answer.

Methods of Asking Questions

Modern technology offers researchers a wide array of approaches to asking questions. They vary mainly in the extent to which the respondent and the question-asker interact. To decide on an approach, the researcher should ask a number of basic questions:

- Should the respondent be given a significant amount of time and the opportunity to talk with others before answering?
- Can the answers to the questions be reduced to a few simple choices?
- Do the questions need to be explained to the respondent if necessary?
- Is it likely that the respondent's answers will often have to be probed or clarified?
- Does anything have to be shown to the respondent such as an advertisement or a package or a set of attitude scales to be filled in?
- Is it likely that many potential respondents will be unmotivated or turned off by the questions or the issue without personal encouragement by an interviewer?

The answers to these questions and several others including those relating to the availability of personnel and financial resources to carry out field work will determine the basic approach. In the majority of cases, the alternatives likely to be considered will be mail, telephone and face-to-face interviews. However, there are other possibilities. For example, one can interview respondents in small groups as in focus group studies. Or individuals can be queried in a shopping mall by a computer video screen or over the telephone by a prerecorded cassette tape with pauses for respondent answers. In some circumstances, a combination of methods may be the best approach. One could ask questions in person that require face-to-face contact and then leave behind a mailback questionnaire on which respondents can record further details such as purchase histories, personal preferences, and socio-economic characteristics.

Mail Studies

To my continuing dismay, when researchers with low budgets think of surveys and asking questions, they inevitably think first of doing a mail study. Many think this is the only alternative possible given their meager resources.

One can see why they might think so. It is often not difficult to get a mailing list. There are many such lists for sale and many list suppliers who will provide labels for a mail sample and even do the mailing at a modest cost. Even without such a commercial list, many researchers feel they can always develop a list themselves using the Yellow Pages, the regular white pages telephone directory, or a list of one's own customers. A mimeograph machine is usually close at hand or a print shop can be hired to run off hundreds of questionnaire forms at low cost. Staff at the office can stuff envelopes at little or no out-of-pocket cost. The office postage meter and bulk mail rates can be used to keep the outbound cost of mailed questionnaires low. Business reply envelopes can be used for the returned responses which means paying postage only for those questionnaires that are, in fact, returned.

Given these low costs, the naive researcher says, "why not?" and sits down and designs a questionnaire and a compelling cover letter and sends out 5,000 forms in the mail. If it is an average study sent to a randomly drawn, but moderately interested, audience, the researcher will be lucky to get 15 to 20 percent of the questionnaires back. (If the audience is not interested, 5 percent would be good!) But, this can mean 1,000 responses returned. The researcher thinks, "Certainly this is a substantial basis on which to make statements about a market. Don't most magazine polls reporting the president's popularity ratings base these on 900 to 1,100 respondents?"

The problem with mail questionnaire studies is not the respondents—it is the *nonrespondents*. The magazine pollsters are very careful to develop probability samples and then attempt to interview everyone in their samples. Because they spend a great deal of money and use face-to-face or telephone interviewing techniques, they usually have very high rates of cooperation. When they do not contact a respondent or are refused participation, they make very careful analyses of just who did not respond and either adjust their analyses accordingly or alert users of the results to potential problems through a "limitations" section in their report. With the typical cheap but dirty mail study with a low response rate, the nature of the nonresponse bias is usually unknown.

Nonresponse *per se* is not necessarily bad. If the nonrespondents would have answered the questions in the study in the same way as the respondents, then there would be no bias. Nonresponse can occur in telephone or face-to-face interview studies when a respondent refuses to cooperate or is out of town or busy for the moment or because the telephone number or address was wrong. Assuming that the interviews were scheduled at random times on weekdays and weekends and there are several follow-up attempts, nonresponse is more likely to be a chance occurrence where one should not expect nonresponders to be greatly different from responders.

In mail studies, this is virtually never the case. Those who get something in the mail asking them to fill in a modest (or great) number of answers will inevitably feel imposed on. (Don't you feel this way—even when you get charity letters?) In a face-to-face interview or telephone study, the personality and skills of a highly trained interviewer can usually overcome these negative initial reactions. But at home at one's desk or at the kitchen table, it is very easy for a potential respondent to throw out a mailed questionnaire. Those who do NOT react this way are likely to be different in one of two important ways. One group will have an inherent interest in the topic of the study. The second group will just want to help the researcher out either because they are a helping kind of person or because they are for the moment swayed by the convincing argument in the study's cover letter. Those that are interested in the topic are likely to be further divisible into two additional types: those who are positively excited about the topic (e.g., those who buy the product or use the service) and those negatively disposed toward the topic who see the study as a grand opportunity to get a few gripes off their chest. As an additional biasing factor, it has generally been found that the higher the education level, the higher the response rate.

What, then, does this imply about the 10 to 20 percent who do respond to the typical mail study? It means they are almost always not at all like the nonrespondents. Unfortunately, too many researchers do not attempt to assess these potential differences because (1) they do not recognize the problem, (2) they do not know how to handle it, and/or (3) they feel they do not have the time or budget to do so.

Not too long ago, I was asked by the publisher of a series of magazines aimed at certain types of retail outlets to give a speech discussing the value of their annual statistical profiles of each retail category. But on reviewing the publisher's methodology, I discovered that the statistics were based on responses to a single mailing from each magazine (with no follow up) and that no checking had ever been made of those who didn't respond. Yet each magazine was publishing its study as a profile of their industry, reporting such data as average store sales, widths of product lines, numbers of employees, various expenses, and profits broken down into various outlet categories.

But what, I asked them, did their profiles really describe? Their response rate was usually 50 percent (which is quite good and not uncommon when mailing to a highly interested group). However, they did not know who really did respond. Although I was not concerned with the response rate, *per se,* I was concerned with possible biases at both ends of the distribution of outlet size. Did the largest outlets participate? They may not have, feeling either that they would be exposing too much internal information that could be identified with them or that they were already part of a large organization that had a great deal of its own internal archival data and so didn't need to contribute to a magazine's profile. At the other extreme, smaller or marginal outlets may not have participated because they were new to the industry, lacked appreciation of the value of such cooperation or perhaps were embarrassed by their small size and/or poor performance. If either of these groups were underrepresented, the profiles really have very limited value. The magazines apparently shut their eyes to these problems, never investigating who did and did not cooperate.

As a consequence of this and a great many similar experiences, I am very reluctant to encourage the use of mail questionnaires for "cheap research."

There are, of course, steps one can take to increase response rates. We will note some of these below. There are also ways to investigate nonresponse bias, although usually at considerable cost. For example, we can conduct telephone interviews of a sample of nonrespondents if they can be identified. Alternatively, characteristics of respondents can be compared to census data or, in a business study, to government business censuses. If there is a close match between the sample characteristics and the universe from which it was supposedly drawn, researchers can be encouraged that their sample may be representative. However, such close matching does not prove that the results are valid.

Even when nonresponse rates are satisfactory or understood, mail studies have a great many other, often fatal, flaws. For example, it is possible that someone other than the intended respondent may fill out the questionnaire. A wife may get her husband to respond or vice versa. A manager may delegate the task to a subordinate. A doctor may ask a nurse to give the necessary particulars. Each of these situations may seriously distort the findings.

Also, there are unlimited chances to improve answers before they are returned. For example, suppose a respondent is asked for "top-of-the-mind" brand awareness early in the mail questionnaire and then later recalls additional brands. He or she may go back and add the newly remembered items. On the other hand, by the end of the questionnaire, he or she may have discovered the study's sponsor and go back to change certain answers to conform more to what is presumed to be the sponsor's objectives.

Despite these problems, there are still three situations in which mail questionnaires should be the preferred choice:

1. There are some situations in which the respondent will need time to gather information to be reported in the questionnaire. In some instances, this might involve consulting with someone else. For example, if one wished to know whether anyone in the household had bought a product, used a service, or visited an outlet, then time would have to be allowed for consultation with others. This usually would not be practical (or sometimes even possible, given people's schedules) in a telephone or face-to-face interview situation. Another, more common, example is where records must be looked up, such as when businesses are asked for expense or sales details or when households are asked to report on last year's taxes or asked what brands of certain products they currently have in their household inventories.

2. There are also situations in which it is desirable to give the respondent time to come up with a well-considered answer. Many years ago, I participated in what is called a *Delphi Study*. This is a technique where respondents (usually a small select group) are asked to make judgments about the future or about some present phenomena. The answers of the group are then summarized by the researcher and fed back to the original respondents who are then asked to revise their answers if they wish. The study in which I participated was an attempt to forecast time usage (e.g., how much leisure or work time we would have and how we would use it) in the last quarter of the 20th Century. The study went on over three rounds of feedback and at each stage, respondents such as I needed several hours, if not a day or two, to give the researcher carefully considered opinions. This could only be achieved by a mail study.

3. A mail questionnaire is probably the only form that many busy respondents would answer. If one has a great many questions, executives or physicians may only be willing to respond to a written questionnaire claiming they do not have the time to participate in a telephone or face-to-face interview.

Even when one or more of these conditions exist, a potential mail study should also meet the following requirements:

- The fact that respondents will have a long time in which to fill in the answers is not a problem.
- It is not a serious problem if someone other than the addressee fills in the questionnaire.
- A mailing list (or a procedure for sampling) that is truly representative of the population of interest can be obtained.
- A careful attempt is made to estimate the nature of the nonresponse bias.
- The respondent population is literate and reachable by mail (requirements that may make mail surveys difficult in some developing countries).
- There is a high probability that a large proportion of the respondents will be interested in the topic and will respond. Interest in the study is likely to be high where the target

population in some way has a tie to the research sponsor. This would be the case, for example, for members of a trade association or a club, patients recently in a hospital, employees in the researcher's organization, holders of a store's credit cards, or subscribers to certain magazines (e.g., *Consumer's Reports*). Even in such situations, it is essential that an estimate of the nonreponse bias be made.

There are two conditions when a biased mail survey can be used. One is when the researcher really does not care about nonresponse. This would be the case whenever projectability is not important. There are a great many situations in which this is the case, for example, when one wants to learn whether there are *any* problems with a certain product or service or with the wording of a particular advertising message or product usage instruction.

A second reason for using a biased study is when one is simply being exploratory, seeking a few ideas for an advertisement, testing a questionnaire, or developing a set of hypotheses that will be verified in a later nonbiased study. If one decides to go ahead with a mail study, there are a number of very important, very basic techniques that should be employed.

The cover letter asking for assistance should be made as motivating as possible (especially the first couple of sentences). The letter should: (1) be enthusiastic (if you are not excited about the study, why should the potential respondent?); (2) indicate the purposes of the study, if possible showing how it will benefit the respondent (e.g., by helping provide better products and services); (3) assure anonymity (for all respondents or for those that request it); and (4) ask for help, pointing out that only selected individuals are being contacted and each answer is important.

Also, the cover letter and the questionnaire should be designed to be attractive and professional. Use dramatic graphics and color where possible. And, the letter should be addressed to a specific individual. If possible, a motivating or prestigious letterhead should be used. If the sponsor of the study can be revealed and awareness of it would motivate respondents (e.g., UNICEF or a key trade association), one should do so.

The questionnaire should be kept as brief as possible but, in all cases, easy to follow and understand. It should be accompanied by a self-addressed stamped return envelope. If the budget permits it, one or more follow-up contacts (even by telephone) should be used to increase response rates.

Giving advance notification to the respondent either by telephone (better) or by postcard (worse) that the questionnaire is coming has been useful to increase the total number of responses, the speed of response and/or the quality of the responses.

In some cases, offering gifts, cash, or a chance at a major prize to those who mail back the questionnaire (or including a coin or a dollar bill "for charity"), and using stamped rather than metered return envelopes increases the number, speed, and quality of responses.

Lovelock and his colleagues strongly urge the use of personal drop off and pick up of what otherwise would be a mailed questionnaire. They believe this technique is particularly appropriate for lengthy questionnaires where considerable motivational effort and perhaps some explanation needs to be carried out. The following results of their study indicate that response rates can be as high as 74 percent. While this rate is achieved by incurring the costs of personnel to handle questionnaire delivery and pickup, they can be lightly trained (i.e., students) and low cost. Cost-per-returned-questionnaire was found to be no different from the traditional mail questionnaire. In addition, those delivering the questionnaire can eliminate individuals obviously ineligible for the study (if anyone is), and data about the respondent's sex, age, nature of premises, and neighborhood can be recorded by *observation* to enrich the database. Reasons for refusals can be elicited, and because the field worker can observe and screen the respondents, field workers can provide the researcher with a very good sense of the nature of the nonresponse bias.

This approach, of course, requires that the study be done in a concentrated geographic area rather than nationally. The technique would be particularly useful in industrial or office studies where respondents are easy to locate, but so busy they would not ordinarily agree to a personal interview.[1]

---

[1]Christopher H. Lovelock, Ronald Stiff, David Cullwich, and Ira M. Kaufman, "An Evaluation of the Effectiveness of Drop-Off Questionnaire Delivery," *Journal of Marketing Research* XIII, November 1976, pp. 358–64.

Telephone Interviewing

Telephone interviewing with or without computer assistance is now the method of choice in most developed countries when a researcher needs to interact with respondents and achieve a projectable sample. A major reason, of course, is the lower cost. A large number of interviews all over the country or even internationally can be conducted from a telephone bank at one site in a very short period of time. Telephone interviewing also has some advantages that alternative techniques do not:

1. The person-to-person contact yields all the advantages of motivating responses, explaining questions, and clarifying answers in face-to-face interviews. However, the number of cues that the interviewer as a person presents to the respondent are very few (sex, voice, vocabulary) yielding fewer chances for biasing effects than if the respondent also could react to the interviewer's clothes, facial expressions, body language, and the like.

2. The facelessness of the telephone interviewing situation can loosen the inhibitions of respondents who might withold a personally embarrassing piece of data if a flesh-and-blood person was standing or sitting opposite them taking down information.

3. Appointments and multiple callbacks permit interviews of precisely defined individuals (e.g., assistant controllers in the widget division).

4. Because telephone interviews are conducted from one location, a supervisor can easily monitor the work of interviewees through systematic eavesdropping, thus greatly increasing quality control and uniformity of techniques.

Despite these advantages, telephone interviewing has three major drawbacks. First it is harder to motivate and establish rapport with potential respondents over the telephone; it is easier for them to hang up the phone than to close the door on a face-to-face interview. This problem appears to be worsening in the age of telemarketing as more unscrupulous sales organizations use the pseudo-telephone interview as a technique for generating sales leads.

Second, some things cannot be done in a telephone interview that could be done in person. No visual props can be used (one can still test radio commercials, though) and certain sophisticated measurements (e.g., scales with cue cards) cannot be used.

The third drawback is that not all households have telephones and even fewer are publicly listed, especially in major cities. For these reasons, the telephone directory is not a good sampling frame for interviewing in most major centers. Telephone books, which typically are published yearly, tend to systematically exclude three kinds of households (1) phoneless households, (2) unlisted households, or (3) not-yet-listed households.

Phoneless households are typically poor or in institutions and, for many marketing purposes, are not of very great interest. However, over 20 percent of all owners of residential lines choose not to be listed. In larger cities like Chicago, Los Angeles, and New York, this figure can be as high as 40 percent! These households are more likely to represent younger heads, single females, middle rather than high or low incomes, nonwhites, and blue collar sales and service occupations. Not-yet-listed households do not include those moving into an area or out of a parents' house since the last directory was published. These may be crucial markets for many sellers such as banks, department stores, and supermarkets.

For these reasons, those planning to do telephone sampling are encouraged to use some variation on random digit or plus-one dialing. These approaches involve first randomly selecting listings from the existing directory to ensure that the researcher is using blocks of numbers the phone company has released. At this point, the last one or two digits in the listing number are then replaced with other randomly selected numbers. Alternatively, the researcher could simply add *one* to the last digit in the selected number. These approaches will still omit blocks of numbers released since the last directory was published, but this should be a nominal bias (mostly affecting new movers) when compared with that of using only numbers in the directory itself.

The random digit dialing approach has its drawbacks. Most importantly, the randomizing technique increases costs because often the randomly selected numbers will turn out to be ineligible businesses or institutions. (Indeed, in one unusual case, an interviewer randomly called a radio call-in show and, to the amusement of both the audience and the interviewer's colleagues and supervisor, proceeded to interview the host on the air!) However, this cost is one that most researchers will usually be willing to bear.

Face-to-Face Interviewing

After mail surveys, researchers planning original field work consider face-to-face or telephone interviews. For a great many purposes, face-to-face interviews will be the ideal medium for a study for several reasons.

For example, respondents (once contacted) can be strongly motivated to cooperate. By choosing interviewers carefully, matching them as closely as possible to predicted respondent characteristics, and giving them a motivating sales pitch, the refusal rate can be kept very low. This can be critical, for example, when studying small samples of high status individuals who *must* be included in the study and who will only participate if a high status interviewer personally comes to them and asks questions. Also stimuli can be shown to or handled by respondents in particular (e.g., rotated) sequences. This is very important where one wishes to assess responses to promotion materials such as advertisements or brochures or where a product or package needs to be tasted, sniffed, or otherwise inspected.

As in telephone interviews, there are opportunities for feedback from the respondent that are impossible in self-report, mail, or computer methods. This permits elaboration of misunderstood questions and probing to clarify or extend answers.

The interviewer can add observation measures to traditional questioning. For example, if a set of advertisements are shown, the interviewer can informally estimate the amount of time the respondent spends on each stimulus. Facial expressions can be observed to indicate which parts of messages are confusing to respondents and need to be refined. Respondents' appearance and the characteristics of their home or office can be observed and recorded. Sex, race, estimated age, and social status can be recorded without directly asking respondents (although some measures, like social class, should be verified by alternative means).

Against these considerable advantages are some important, often fatal, disadvantages.

For example, because the interviewer is physically present during the answering process, two sorts of biases are very likely:

1. The interviewer's traits—dress, manner, physical appearance—may influence the respondent. The interviewer may be perceived as upper class or snooty, or

slovenly or unintelligent, which may cause the interviewee to adjust, sometimes unconsciously, his or her
answers.

2. Simply because there is another person present, the respondent may distort answers trying to impress the interviewer or hide something from them in embarrassment.

In addition, the fact that interviews are conducted away
from central offices means that the performance of interviewers
is very difficult to monitor for biases and errors (say, as compared
to central office telephone interviewing). Also, physically ap-
proaching respondents (e.g., at their home or office) can be very
costly when there are refusals or not-at-homes. Callbacks that
are easy by phone can be very costly in face-to-face interviews.

Finally, delays between interviews are great. Telephone lines
or the mail can reach anywhere in the country (and most parts
of the world) very quickly and with relatively little wasted time.
Travel between personal interviews can be very costly.

The last two factors tend to make the field staffing costs for
face-to-face interviews in most developed countries very high.
They are so high that, except where (1) the technique's advantages are critical to the study (e.g., graphic materials must be
shown or handled or high status subjects must be interviewed),
(2) the sample size is very small, or (3) the study is local, one-
on-one personal interviews are probably prohibitively expensive
for the low-budget researcher. Situations in which these criteria
would be met would include studies in local neighborhoods, malls,
offices, or (quite often) trade shows.

If one does wish to go ahead with personal interviewing,
there are a number of low-cost sampling techniques to consider.

Low-Cost Sampling

If one wishes to carry out a study that is projectable to some
universe of interest (e.g., all adults in an area or all food stores),
one must draw a sample in which each potential sample member
has a known probability of being selected. Two approaches are
typically used. In a simple random sampling study, a list (or
sampling frame) is prepared and enough individuals selected on

a probability basis so that, given expected rates of not-at-homes, refusals, and the like, the desired sample size can be achieved. A variation on this approach is called *stratified sampling*. This approach requires that the sample first be divided into groups or strata (e.g., census tracts or store size categories) and then either proportional or disproportional random samples drawn within each group. This approach has advantages over simple random sampling if (1) there is special interest in some strata, (2) the variation within strata is low compared to the variation across strata, or (3) the costs of interviewing vary significantly across strata.

While simple random and stratified sampling are appropriate for projectable studies, they can raise costs dramatically beyond a limited-budget researcher's capabilities. Where this is the case, the researcher should consider several techniques to cut down on personnel time and increase efficiency in studies that still must use face-to-face interviewing. These approaches, some of which will still yield statistically projectable results include:

1. Focus groups
2. Mall intercept
3. Quota sampling
4. Convenience sampling
5. Judgment sampling
6. Snowball and network sampling
7. Sequential sampling

Focus Groups

One extremely popular low-cost technique for conducting face-to-face interviews is to do so in focus groups. These studies bring together 8 to 12 individuals in a room to talk for one to one and one-half hours about a specific research topic. The discussions are typically led by a trained moderator. Focus groups are qualitative and nonprojectable. They are typically used for the following purposes:

1. Generating hypotheses.
2. Generating information helpful in designing consumer questionnaires.

3. Providing background information on a product category.
4. Securing reactions to new product concepts, a proposed product positioning, advertising messages, or other promotional materials.
5. Stimulating new ideas about products.
6. Interpreting previously obtained quantitative results.

While cost efficiencies are important reasons for using focus groups, they have other desirable features specifically attributable to the group interaction. The latter accounts for much of the technique's popularity among researchers. Even if focus groups were not cheaper per respondent, many researchers would still use them because of the following advantages.

Synergism.   Because each group member can respond to, elaborate on, criticize, modify, or otherwise react to the comments of other group members, focus groups can significantly increase the total volume of information gleaned over what would be the sum of 8 to 12 individual interviews.

Minimal Interviewer Effects.   Although the moderator will act to stimulate the group at times or to move the discussion in a particular direction (i.e., to focus it), for the most part, participants will be responding to the remarks of others like themselves. For this reason and because focus group members are usually actively caught up in the discussion, respondents are less likely to try to guess the purpose of the study or try to please or impress the moderator. The process will be less intrusive.

Increased Spontaneity.   In an individual interview situation, the respondent has to pay attention and answer all questions. In a group situation participants usually feel that they needn't speak if they don't want to. The lack of pressure tends to make respondents feel less up tight and more spontaneous and enthusiastic in their participation.

Serendipity.   Because there are 8 to 12 interviewees in the group, many more questions, perspectives, and comments may be introduced than the researcher and/or moderator would ever have thought of on their own.

Higher Quality Interviewing.   Because several people are interviewed at once, the research organization can afford a more expensive moderator/interviewer than they could if hour-long interviews had to be conducted one by one. This is a very important point because the moderator's role is a crucial one in what is really a group depth interview. (A focus group session can sometimes appear not unlike a group psychotherapy session!)

Natural Setting.   A one-on-one interview situation is usually highly artificial. In a focus group, one can create an atmosphere of a "bunch of people sitting around chatting" about a product or a set of advertisements. This will seem to the participants to be much more like the real world. The comments and reactions therefore will have much more projectability to the actual marketplace.

Guidelines for Focus Groups.   High quality focus group interviews are achieved by following a number of basic guidelines.

First it is necessary to keep the group size from 8 to 12. Smaller groups tend not to have enough input to be valuable and run the risk of being dominated by one or two individuals. Larger groups are likely to find many members who are frustrated at not having enough time to talk or are just plain bored.

It is also important to select participants carefully. Usually, focus groups should be kept relatively homogeneous so that members share the same values, experiences, and verbal skills and so that some members do not intimidate others. Those with previous group experience should be avoided and members should not be previously acquainted. In most major cities, there are commercial organizations which, for a fee, will recruit focus group participants designed to meet precise specifications. One focus group I recently observed was composed of twelve women 21 to 35 years old who had two or more children and did not work outside the home. This group was asked to evaluate new cake mix products. A local focus group recruiter provided the group.

Make the atmosphere for the group session as nonthreatening and natural as possible. Ideal focus group locations include a respondent's home or a hotel or motel room. Many research agencies now maintain their own focus group rooms at their offices with comfortable chairs, cookies, soft drinks, coffee, and minimum distractions. Many agencies try to make the focus group interview area resemble a kitchen or living room as much as possible.

Keep the session to two hours or less. Fatigue and repetitiveness set in quickly after two hours. The modal length of focus groups is around one and one-half hours.

Hire the very best moderator the budget can afford. The moderator will be responsible for guiding (focusing) the discussion without seeming to, and for catching hidden or subtle points and bringing them out for elaboration (e.g., by frequently indicating, "I don't completely understand that point"). A good moderator also will draw out shy or inhibited participants, and be able to quiet or distract those who wish to dominate the group. To establish and maintain a conflict-free, permissive environment the effective leader will encourage participants not to criticize the thoughts of others, but instead to elaborate on them or provide another perspective. Also the moderator must stimulate participants to talk to each other (not always look to the moderator for guidance), and be able to close off the discussion at the appropriate moment. Last, a review and summary of the major findings after the session ends is the moderator's responsibility.

If possible, tape record and/or videotape each focus group session. This puts less pressure on the moderator to take notes or remember everything that goes on and allows concentration on group dynamics and the focus of the session. The existence of such a permanent archive also permits (1) going back over tapes for additional insights or clarification of unclear points, and (2) having two or more experts review and summarize the same material. The archives can also be used for comparisons over time, for example, as the cake mix or ad message is improved.

Have two-way mirrors available for others to observe and hear the group without influencing the participants. This is usually only possible in the specially constructed focus group rooms at research or advertising agencies. Many research clients like to observe focus groups, although one must be careful not to let an attending executive's instant analysis influence later, more carefully considered findings. Two-way mirrors also permit other focus group experts to watch the proceedings and share in the eventual interpretation.

Have very clear objectives for each session and, if possible, a hidden agenda of topic sequences. It is typical in focus groups to begin the discussion generally (e.g., discussing food preparation) and then gradually narrow the topic to the researcher's specific interest (i.e., reacting to this specific new cake mix concept). It is this approach that led to the term *focus* group.

If the budget merits, conduct several focus group sessions, if possible using more than one moderator. Some of the additional focus groups should replicate the original group's composition while others should be quite different. This will allow the researcher some insight into the extent to which the original insights tend to generalize or have to be modified for specific populations.

Mall Intercepts[2]

Mall intercepts are now probably the second most popular technique for commercial survey research in the United States after telephone interviewing. As Sudman has noted, they are the modern-day equivalent of the old street-corner interview.[3] They are relatively inexpensive since interviewees in effect come to the interviewer rather than vice versa, significantly reducing travel costs and keeping the interviewer perpetually occupied with questioning.

While the efficiencies are considerable, the major worry with mall intercepts is the quality of the sample. Two concerns are typically raised. First, it is suggested that those coming to a mall do not represent the population about which the study wishes to say something (e.g., all households in the community). It is argued that mall shoppers constitute a biased sampling frame of the universe; for example, they are more likely to have automobiles and are not bedridden. The second problem with mall interviews is that there is a danger that interviewers will choose to interview atypical people such as those who are (1) alone; (2) of the same characteristics as the interviewer in terms of age,

---

[2]Much of the material for this section is drawn from Seymour Sudman, "Improving the Quality of Shopping Center Sampling," *Journal of Marketing Research,* November 1980, pp. 423–31.

[3]*Ibid.*

race, sex, and social status; (3) not in a hurry; or (4) appearing to be the kind of person who would be unlikely to reject the interviewer's advances.

Controlling for Sampling Frame Bias. Fortunately, it has been reported that virtually all households shop in a shopping mall at least once a year and two thirds have been there in the last two weeks. So, unless the population of interest is the very ill, the elderly, or the very poor, the mall sampling frame is, in principle, a reasonable one. Those who never go there may be of little interest to most marketers! The problem then is: if one wants a projectable result, how does one account for the fact that some people go to malls more often than others? In a mall study, two steps are taken to deal with this problem. First, malls in a given study area can be selected on a probability basis with their probability of selection proportional to the number of customers they serve.

Second, a procedure can be developed to sample individuals on a random basis within each selected mall.[4] If done correctly, such a procedure would assume that everyone in the mall over a given time period has a non-zero chance of being in the sample. However, the more a given individual goes to shopping malls, the greater his or her chance of selection. Fortunately, this possibility can be explicitly taken into consideration if, in the course of an interview, the researcher obtains an estimate of the repondent's frequency of mall shopping in a given period, say, the last year. All that is then necessary to get a projectable representative sample is to reweight the final sample proportional to the *inverse* of each respondent's frequency of visits. In this way, those who come rarely will receive greater weight than those who come often.

---

[4]The terms *random* and *probability* sampling are used interchangeably here. Strictly speaking, the former is a special case of the latter where all members of the sampling frame have an equal probability of selection. On the other hand, if we sampled twice as many men as women because we were interested in a new men's fragrance, then the two sexes would have a known (e.g., a .67 and .33) probability of selection, but not an equal probability.

Controlling for Interviewer Selection Bias. Interviewers can sabotage a carefully designed mall sampling procedure if they tend to pick easy subjects. Basically, all that is needed to control for such potential interviewer selection bias is to develop and enforce a tightly specified procedure that allows the interviewer virtually no degree of freedom in the choice of interviewee. People within a mall must be selected on a probability, not judgment, basis either when they arrive or while they are moving around the mall. If the latter is the approach used, several locations must be chosen to account for traffic patterns and the differential popularity of stores in the mall.

One needn't worry about how long the interviewee was in the mall if the researcher decides to sample people when they arrive. With such a procedure, it is necessary to select several entrances at random and then interview every Nth arrival at each chosen entry. (Two persons will be needed, one to count and select arrivals, one to carry out the interviews.) This would effectively weight the entrances for the number coming through, i.e., one would secure more respondents at busy entrances than at less busy ones.[5]

Several entrances must be used because different types of customers may park at different sides of a mall (or arrive on public transportation) and because major retailers at different ends of the mall will attract different clienteles. Finally, the researcher should be careful to conduct mall interviews on different days and at different times of the day.[6]

If the sampling procedures outlined above are followed and proper reweighting is introduced, mall surveys can often yield

---

[5]If, however, one wished to have equal interviews per hour at an inlet, then a preliminary estimate of arrivals at each entrance would be necessary, with entrances then selected with a probability proportional to their volume and the fraction N established as inversely proportional to the entrance volume.

[6]Again, it would be desirable to set the probability of selecting a day or time period proportional to the number of customers expected to be in the mall at that time. All of this may seem very complicated. However, malls that will cooperate often will have already collected some of the preliminary data the researcher needs on number of customers per day and hour and perhaps even the proportion using each entrance.

good population estimates and the advantages of face-to-face interviewing at costs the low-budget researcher can afford.

It should be recognized, however, that not all malls will permit interviewing to be done on their premises. Some malls will restrict interviewing only to commercial agencies or to those firms with a permanent interviewing site in the mall. In the latter case, it still may be economically feasible for the low-budget researcher to contract for these agencies' services.

Finally, it should be noted that malls have one advantage over in-home face-to-face interviews. Large displays of products can be set up at mall sites, movies or TV commercials run, and mechanical measurements taken with sophisticated equipment. It would be rather expensive for car manufacturers to bring two or three new models to everyone's house to preview. But they can be brought to a central mall location (and also kept relatively well-hidden, a nontrivial advantage) where interviewees can study and evaluate them.

Quota Sampling

A popular technique for keeping down field costs in commercial market research is quota sampling. Quota sampling, in fact, is frequently used in combination with convenience or mall interviewing. It is also very common in telephone studies. The approach is extremely simple, highly cost-effective and, its advocates claim, virtually identical to results that would be obtained from a strict probability sample. However, quota sampling is *not* a probability sampling technique and, strictly speaking, the researcher should not apply to quota studies statistical tests that require the assumption of random selection.

The procedure involved in developing a quota sample is to first develop a profile of the population to be studied and then set quotas for interviewers so that the final sample is forced to fit the major dimensions of the population profile. Thus, for example, if one wished a projectable sample of opinions of retailers in a town, one could take a Chamber of Commerce publication and find that, say, 3 percent of all outlets are shoe stores, 13 percent are restaurants, 27 percent are grocery stores, and so on. A sample size of 200 is set and interviewers are sent out to interview owners or managers in 6 shoe stores, 26 restaurants, 54 grocery stores and so on. The quotas may be more complex than this, however. The interviewers could be asked to meet the above distribution while at the same time making sure 30 percent of the respondents were female and 10 percent were black.

The advocates of quota sampling argue that, if the quotas are complex enough and if interviewers are directed not to interview just easy or convenient cases, the results will be as projectable as any probability sample. And, the costs will be dramatically lower than probability sampling. The key to this cost saving is the fact that *any* 6 shoe stores or *any* 60 female respondents will be as good as any others. The field workers need not worry about sample members' refusals. The field worker just keeps trying to interview anyone who will cooperate until the various cells of the quota are filled.

There is a legitimate role for quotas in some telephone studies. Here, quotas can be used to help control for possible nonresponse biases. The initial sample may be drawn probabilistically (e.g., by random digit dialing methods). However, in some designs, to keep costs at a minimum, it will be desirable to conduct few or no callbacks. In other studies, callbacks may not be possible because of the topic under investigation, for example, when one is seeking instant reactions to a significant political or social event or a specific television show. In such cases, quotas are used to minimize the chances that the sample is grossly unusual.

The major risk of error in quota sampling is, of course, due to the fact that the final sample members are still selected by the field workers. If they are biased in their choices, then the research will be biased. The answer to getting cheap but good quota research is, as usual, careful control and systemization of the process.

Convenience Sampling

Mall intercepts are efficient because they include a very high proportion of most populations of interest and because respondents come to the researcher rather than vice versa. There are a number of other situations in which the advantages of convenience may be important. Convenience samples would include people in university classes, in an office, or in a social or religious organization, or those coming daily to a restaurant, to the lobby of the researcher's building, and so on.

There are four kinds of occasions in which convenience samples may be useful. First, there are a few rare occasions when the results of a convenience sample can be generalized to make some projectable statements. Second, convenience sampling can be used for some kinds of experiments where the researcher needs a reasonably representative group to assign randomly to various treatment and control conditions. Third, convenience samples can be useful when the researcher simply wants exploratory data. Finally, convenience samples may be used if one wishes to conduct so-called *depth interviewing*. We will discuss each of these situations briefly in turn.

Projectable Convenience Samples. If one wishes to learn something about the convenience population itself, then there is every reason to study them. Obvious examples would be a study of those patronizing a firm's outlet or one or more of its services, patrons at a single mall or neighborhood center, and those working in a given building or simply passing a particular location (e.g., if a marketer were planning to open an outlet there or to change an existing product/service mix there).

It would be easiest to draw a projectable sample for such convenience samples if one had a list of possible respondents or an approximation to it. Suppose, for example, someone considering opening a delicatessen or offering video movie rentals in a specific office building wishes to sample the building's workers. It may be possible to obtain in advance a list of offices in a building and the number of employees per office. Offices could then be selected with probability proportional to size (PPS) and every Nth worker on a list the office could supply then interviewed or given a questionnaire to fill out. If, in addition, the researcher wanted to study not just the workers in a building, but also everyone entering it, the approach would be identical to that described for mall intercepts above.

Finally, there are some kinds of studies where it can be assumed that any warm body will suffice. This would be the case in many explanatory studies where one can assume one brain processes information from the marketer in about the same way as any other brain, or where the relationships between, say, age, sex, and product experience and some purchase characteristic can be assumed to be the same for the convenience sample as for any other. These arguments explain why many academic studies are not at all apologetic about using student samples when seeking to understand the principles of basic consumer behavior.

Convenience Experimentation. Taste, feel, or sniff experiments or tests of ads or packages, or even new product concepts are naturals for convenience sampling if one can assume that the population conveniently nearby is not odd in some obvious way. One simply needs to develop a procedure for randomly assigning subjects to treatments, ensuring that the presentation of stimuli is carefully controlled, that there is no cross-talk among participants during or after the study, and otherwise adhering to the tenets of quality laboratory experimental design outlined in Chapter 6.

Qualitative Research with Convenience Samples. Convenience samples are ideal for a great many qualitative research purposes. These purposes could involve developing a set of attitude or other scales or a set of questions to be included in a later questionnaire, learning what words people use to describe something, what features they evaluate, or what motives they bring to bear in a particular purchase context.

It is also an effective method for pretesting the questionnaire for a later study, or testing advertisements, brochures, packages (or any other graphic or written materials). In this way the researcher can determine whether there are glaring problems with the materials (e.g., does *anybody* notice the possible sexual connotation in a phrase or the portrayal of teenagers in a food ad), whether a situation portrayed or the models used seem realistic, or whether a message seems to get across what the marketer intends it to. The convenience sample may also be used to develop hypotheses to be tested later.

In qualitative studies, it is merely necessary to use "normal" people, including those not especially knowledgeable about the subject matter.

Depth Interviewing with Convenience Samples.   Many researchers advocate the use of lengthy in-depth interviews of a limited number of convenient individuals as a very valuable approach for drawing out deep-seated *basic* motivations, hidden meanings, and/or fundamental longings and fears that may be kept hidden from other researchers in group situations or in responses to superficial questionnaires. In comparing these so-called depth interviews with focus groups, Sokolow suggests the following advantages.

1. The respondent is not influenced by the need to conform to group norms or to avoid embarrassment for unusual thoughts or behaviors.

2. The respondent is the sole focus of the interviewer's attention and therefore is more likely to open up.

3. Because of the intense involvement of the interviewer, the respondent is highly focussed and therefore yields richer data, more clearly to the point of the study.

4. Most interviews are brief and the time a respondent may have to speak in a focus group is limited. In a depth interview, the respondent has 90 minutes or more to talk about the topic. This inevitably leads to richer data that is both broader and deeper than in the alternative face-to-face formats.

Solokow points out that depth interviewing is especially valuable for sensitive topics, for interviews with individuals, such as teenagers, who are especially likely to be influenced by group pressure, and for interviews with groups that may be especially worried about confidentiality. The latter would include salespeople discussing their employers and business managers talking about their collaborators and competitors.[7]

Judgment Sampling

Sometimes it is desirable to seek out particular informants because their answers are good predictors of what the general population would say. Thus, to develop a forecast of future general market trends, one might interview leaders in an industry

---

[7]Hal Sokolow, "In-Depth Interviews Increasing in Importance," *Marketing News*, September 13, 1985, pp. 26–27.

who are thoughtful, expert observers of the target population. Alternatively, one could simply concentrate interviews in an area of the country (or the world) which is seen as especially representative of the target market or which is often a leading indicator of what will come about in future. To predict high fashion trends, designers say one should study Paris, Milan, and New York. More adventurous designers study the market in Los Angeles. Political analysts look to key precincts to predict elections (quite accurately) and most marketers have their favorite test cities. In all cases, these researchers are judging that they will learn more from intensive study of a few nonrepresentative individuals than a broader, shallower study of a statistically representative group.

Another judgment sample often used by marketers is key informants. In the commercial sector, key customers, journal editors, stock analysts, or knowledgeable suppliers can often be a firm's best source of trend information and what is called *commercial intelligence*. To tap this information, many marketers assign salespeople to routinely conduct lengthy interviews with editors, stock analysts, and suppliers and to ask key customers specific questions about the market, competitors' plans, and activities every three to six months. These interviews (often really structured conversations) can yield early warnings which the marketer can use to considerable advantage. What is critical is that, although not random, they be conducted on a systematic, routine basis.

The major problems are two. First, there is the possibility of selection bias. Researchers may try to choose people who are "average." Second, if experts are used, there is the danger that they may be too familiar with the subject to be objective about it.

Snowball and Network Sampling

Many techniques that involve probability sampling of the general population are very inefficient and costly if one is interested in studying a small, very special population. For example, if one wished to study VCR owners, 60 to 70 percent of the telephone calls one would make in most markets would be wasted. Because the stakes involved in the VCR market are so high, most researchers would use a procedure called screening. Screening involves asking each randomly selected individual a set of qualifying questions which determines whether he or she falls within the population of interest (e.g., "Do you own a VCR?"). In many studies, the researcher will reluctantly absorb high screening costs in order to get projectable results. But what if the research is about a topic such as the use of hearing aids where screening would be prohibitively expensive because of the high proportion of ineligible respondents who would have to be contacted?

One technique that can be used in such cases is network sampling. The technique is based on the notion that individuals are involved in networks of other individuals and is very simple. One begins with a few respondents possessing the characteristic of interest and then asks them for the names of any others with the same characteristic within a precisely defined network (e.g., immediate family, uncles, aunts, grandparents, nieces, and nephews) who can be contacted later. This approach takes advantage of interpersonal networks. Not surprisingly, many people with unusual traits tend to know others with the same trait. The sampling approach is not only more efficient in finding potential sample members, it makes it much more likely that those contacted on second or third waves will agree to cooperate since the researcher can say, "so and so suggested I contact you." Sudman and Kalten have recently developed techniques whereby network sampling can yield projectable population estimates.[8]

A similar procedure can be used to obtain a sample to contrast with a convenience sample. For example, suppose a hospital does an attitude survey of its own past patients (sampled from accounting archives). But the hospital realizes that it is not studying potential new customers. To do so, it could ask its patient-respondents for the names of one or two friends who had not been patients. The advantage of this snowball approach is that the second sample will be closely matched socially and economically to the patient sample (and probably live in the same

---

[8]Seymour Sudman and Graham Kalten, "New Developments in the Sampling of Special Populations," *Annual Review of Sociology, 1986*, Vol. 12, pp. 401–29.

areas). Neither sample, of course, is projectable and the results, accordingly, should be treated as only suggestive.

Sequential Sampling

This technique is a form of probability sampling that can yield projectable results while keeping costs low. Sequential sampling simply involves taking successive dips into the pool of randomly chosen respondents and checking the results after each dip. As soon as the results are acceptable (e.g., in precision or some other dimension), the sampling stops. Often this occurs well below the sample size specified initially, obviously at significant savings in cost.

Sequential sampling is also appropriate in studies with largely qualitative objectives. If a researcher is seeking to learn, say, about any problems with a new product or about the reasons people give for vacationing in Barbados, sequential dips can be taken until the researcher stops getting any new insights.

OTHER ALTERNATIVES FOR ASKING QUESTIONS

Mail surveys, face-to-face interviews, and telephone interviews are, of course, the major alternatives a researcher typically considers as a means of obtaining answers to questions from individuals. There are other low-cost approaches that may be valuable from time to time.

One of the most common is the so-called *self-administered questionnaire* which is really a hybrid of a mail study and a face-to-face or telephone interview technique. Here, the interviewer asks the respondent for cooperation personally (as in a store, office, shopping mall, or other public place) or by telephone. The questionnaire is then handed or mailed out for prepaid return. It is frequently used in hotels and restaurants. This hybrid technique has some obvious advantages:

1. Respondents can be personally asked to cooperate.
2. Any questions about the purpose of the study can be answered in advance.

3. A large number of people can be contacted and recruited for relatively little cost in personnel time.
4. Questionnaires (or stamps) are not wasted on those unlikely to respond.

One area in which the self-administered survey is used very effectively is in hospitals. Patients scheduled to be released are given satisfaction/complaint questionnaires by a nurse or customer relations specialist who returns at a prearranged time to retrieve the completed instrument. Participation rates are extremely high in such studies, yielding extensive, valuable tracking data for hospital marketing managers.

Another approach to the self-administered questionnaire only now being used by some research organizations is the use of the computer. Many people are unfamiliar and perhaps fearful of computers, but where respondents will cooperate, the machines can be used to administer questionnaires to consumers in malls or offices. Portable computers can be taken into the field and left for interviewees to use while the researcher sets up other interviews. Computers have important advantages in conducting interviews. Perhaps the most prominent of these are the following:

1. Complex skip patterns can be handled without confusing respondents. One of the very serious problems with self-administered and mailed questionnaires is that one can only use limited skips. *Skips* are necessary where different respondents must be directed to different parts of the questionnaire depending on their answers to a specific question. For example, in an alcohol consumption study, one might wish to ask different questions of beer, wine, and scotch drinkers and those who don't drink at all. If a respondent is a wine drinker, one may wish to ask different questions of heavy and light consumers and different questions of those preferring foreign over domestic wines, those whose spouses or mates do or do not *also* drink wine, those who are recent wine converts, and those who are veteran oenophiles. This complex set of subcategories requires a great many branching instructions (e.g., "If you answered No to Question 6, go to question 23. If you answered Maybe, go to question 30. If you answered Yes and also answered Yes to question 5, go to question 15!") One could not possibly get a respondent to follow all the implied arrows in such a written instrument. (It would even be difficult to prepare an instrument that didn't look frighteningly complex.) But with a computer, it is easy.

2. The respondent does not know how long the instrument is and will not be intimidated by a long questionnaire which (because of elaborate branching) he or she would only answer in part.

3. Unlike traditional mail and self-administered question-naires, respondents can't go back and correct an answer or can't skip ahead to see what is coming and anticipate it. Thus, in a computerized study, a sponsor could be revealed at the end of the instrument without worrying that this will cause bias in earlier answers.

4. Inconsistent answers can be corrected on the spot. While the advantages mentioned above also apply to telephone and personal interviews (e.g., skip patterning and disguising spon-sors until later), catching inconsistencies may be very hard for interviewers to do. Further, if the inconsistency is the inter-viewer's fault, they would not catch it. But the computer would be infallible in this connection and could ask the respondent to indicate what the correct answer should be.

5. Finally, the computer can instantly create the database for the analysis just as the respondent inputs the answers. This has two payoffs. First, it leaves out one or two steps in the typical research design that can cause errors. Where an interviewer transcribes the answer and someone else enters it into a com-puter, minor or major errors can creep in. In large studies, this will only create "noise." In the small studies that will be typical for low-budget researchers, errors made in the answers for only a few respondents may seriously distort the results.

The second advantage of creating an instant database is that management can get a daily (even hourly) summary of the results to date. This, in turn, has three uses. First, analysis of early returns may suggest problems with the questionnaire. For example, if there are preset categories for, say, consumption of a product, the researcher may discover that 90 percent of the answers fall in one category. This may require changing the category boundaries for the study from that point on. The second possibility is that further questions may be suggested. For example, respondents may report large numbers of complaints about product or service features that management thought were noncontroversial. This could well prompt new questions probing the nature of the problem.

Third, the availability of daily analyses may permit the research manager to terminate the study with fewer respondents than originally planned. This is, in effect, an example of the sequential sampling method mentioned above.

Computers are still rarely used as a means of interviewing respondents, but computers are now being used extensively to guide telephone interviewers. Computer Assisted Telephone Interviewing or CATI is now a central part of most sophisticated research supplier services. It works as it would with final respondents, but it presents on a computer screen questions the telephone interviewer is supposed to ask. Because CATI has the computer's advantages of elaborate branching, self-monitoring, and instant databasing, it is becoming extremely popular. While not something a low-budget researcher could presently afford, CATI is a feature used by those research suppliers that the low-budget researcher might hire. Use of CATI can be a reason for choosing a specific supplier because of the complicated studies CATI will permit, the lower error rates, and sometimes the lower research charges. Someday, software may exist so that low-budget researchers can do CATI studies themselves.

REFERENCES

1. Sudman, Seymour. *Applied Sampling*. New York: Academic Press, 1976.
2. Goodman, Leo A. "Snowball Sampling." *Annals of Mathematical Statistics*, 1961, pp. 148–170.
3. Higgenbotham, James B., and Keith K. Cox, eds. *Focus Group Interviews: A Reader*. Chicago: American Marketing Association, 1978.
4. Sudman, Seymour. "Improving the Quality of Shopping Center Sampling." *Journal of Marketing Research*, November 1980, pp. 423–431.

SECTION 3

MAKING LOW-COST RESEARCH GOOD RESEARCH

CHAPTER 9

ASKING VALID QUESTIONS

For any curious human being, asking questions is easy. But for professional researchers, it can be a daunting challenge fraught with innumerable chances to destroy a study's validity. The basic objective is simple: the researcher wishes to record the truth accurately. The closer the questioning process comes to this ideal, the more one is justified in claiming to have valid measurements of what one is trying to study. There are, however, a great many points where bias—major and minor—can creep into the process of transferring what is in a respondent's brain to numbers and symbols that are typed into a computer.

Consider the problems of measuring consumer preferences. Suppose a California householder has three favorite department stores. She greatly prefers Nordstrom's to Bullocks and slightly prefers Bullocks to The Broadway. All of the following things could go wrong:

- The respondent may not reveal the truth because she (1) doesn't understand the nature of her own preferences; (2) wants to impress the interviewer; (3) is trying to guess what the right answer is (e.g., what the sponsor would prefer her to say); or (4) simply misunderstands the question.

- The question used to measure the preference may be worded vaguely or not capture the true relationship (distance) between the stores.

- The interviewer may record the response incorrectly because he or she (1) mishears the respondent; (2) misconstrues what the respondent meant; or (3) records the wrong number or symbol by accident (or someone else assigns the wrong number or code to what the interviewer wrote down).

- The data entry person may enter the wrong information into the computer.

If any or all of these events transpire (or many others we will point out below), the researcher will have a clear case of "garbage in." No amount of sophisticated statistical manipulation can wring the truth out of biased data—it is always "garbage out."

In keeping with the backward approach introduced in Chapter 4, we will first consider data entry and coding errors and then turn to the more complex problems of eliciting and recording human responses.

NON-QUESTION SOURCES OF ERROR

Data Entry Errors

Data entry errors will almost always occur in large studies. In expensive studies, entry error can be virtually eliminated by verifying every entry (i.e., entering it twice). However, this option is not open to the low-budget researcher. Four alternative solutions exist. First, separate data entry can be eliminated by employing computer-assisted telephone interviewing (CATI) or having respondents sit at a computer terminal and record their own answers (this, of course, would also eliminate a lot of interviewer errors). Second, if more than one data entry person is used, a sample of the questionnaires entered by each operator can be verified to see if any one operator's work needs 100 percent verification. Third, a checking program can be written into the computer to detect entries that are above or below the valid range for a question or that are inconsistent with other answers (e.g., the respondent who is recorded as having a dog, but who records zero dog food purchases). Finally, if it assumed that the entry errors will be random, they may be accepted as simply random noise in the data.

Coding Errors

There are different kinds of values one can assign to any phenomenon we can observe or ask about. They can be nonnumerical values, such as words like "positive" or symbols like plus or minus, or they can be numerical. Numerical values are the raw material for probably 99 percent of all market research analyses and all cases where statistical tests or population projections are to be made.

Assigning numbers (or words or symbols) is the act of *coding*. In a questionnaire study, coding can come about at various stages of the research process and can be carried out by different individuals. There are three major possibilities for coding. The first possibility is that precoded answers can be checked by the respondent (as in mail studies or any self-report instrument). Also, precoded answers can be checked by the interviewer (as in telephone or face-to-face interview studies). Finally, postcoded answers can have codes assigned by a third party to whatever either the respondent or the interviewer wrote down.

Most researchers would, I think, prefer it if answers could be precoded and checked or circled by either the respondent or the interviewer on the spot. Precoding has several advantages, such as reducing recording errors, and speed, so that a telephone interviewer, for example, can ask more questions in a given time period. Precoding makes mail or self-report questionnaires appear simpler for respondents which, in turn increases their participation rate. Also, it permits data to be entered into the computer directly from the questionnaire (thus keeping costs down by eliminating a step in the research process).

Sometimes, precoding helps clarify a question for the respondent. For example, it may indicate the degree of detail the researcher is looking for. Thus, if asked, "Where did you seek advice in choosing a vacation site?" a respondent may wonder whether the correct answer is the name of each travel agent or each co-worker or just the type of source. Presenting precoded categories will help indicate exactly what is intended. It may also encourage someone to answer a question where they otherwise might not. Many respondents will refuse to answer the following question, "What was your total household income last calendar year?" But if they are asked, "Which of the following categories includes your total household income last year . . . ?" many more (but still not all) will reply. In addition, precoding ensures that all respondents answer the *same* question. Suppose respondents are asked how convenient several shopping malls were for them. Some respondents may think of convenience in terms of ease of parking, number of entrances, and so on. Others may think of it in terms of travel time from home. If you ask respondents to check whether the malls are "10 minutes or less away," "11 to 20 minutes away," and so on, this will ensure that every respondent will be using the same connotation for the term *convenience*.

Suppose respondents are asked, "Where have you seen an advertisement for a cancer treatment program in the last three months, if anywhere?" Unaided by precoding, respondents will offer fewer answers than if offered a checklist. For example, one can ask: "Have you seen an advertisement for a cancer treatment program in any of the following places . . . newspapers, magazines, billboards, or in the mail?"

There are, however, two main drawbacks in using precoded questions.

First, it assumes the researcher already knows all the possible answers or at least the major ones. While research can always leave space for an "other" category on a mail questionnaire, most respondents will ignore anything that is not prelisted.

Another drawback to precoding is that it may frustrate a respondent who does not quite agree with the categories or feels unduly restricted. For example, if someone is asked: "Do you think President Reagan is doing a good job; Yes or No?", many respondents would like to answer "Yes, but . . ." or "No, but . . ." If they experience such frustration, many respondents will terminate an interview or not reply to a mail questionnaire.

Post-coding involves coding a set of answers some time after a questionnaire is filled in. It is typically necessary under one of the three major circumstances:

1. The researcher does not know in advance what categories to use. For example, if the researcher is rushed or has a very limited budget, it may not be possible to conduct any preliminary focus groups or pretests to develop the appropriate precodes.
2. The researcher is afraid that presenting precoded alternatives will bias the answers.
3. The researcher wishes to accumulate verbatim answers that can be used to give "flesh and blood" to a final report.

If a third party is brought in to do the post-coding, there is always the possibility that the wrong code will be assigned to a particular written answer (of course, the interviewer could make this mistake also). The main difficulties will crop up when the answers are ambiguous. Suppose a coder is asked to assign a "liking" rating for a series of perfume descriptions. The coder has three categories: (1) likes a great deal, (2) likes somewhat, or (3) doesn't like. The description is "Enchanting Perfume is very strong smelling. Very feminine. My boyfriend would really notice it." A coder would really like to have the respondent nearby so that a number of clarifying questions can be asked such as: "Do you *prefer* strong smelling or feminine perfumes? Is it important to you that your boyfriend notice the perfume or is it better that he *doesn't*?" Interviewers who do the coding on the spot can interrogate the respondent. Third-party post-coders may simply have to make intelligent guesses that can introduce bias into the study.

The example above is truly ambiguous and probably should be coded as a fourth category, "not clear!" In most studies coding problems can be minimized if one follows some well accepted procedures.

After a set of questionnaires is completed, it is helpful to review a sample of verbatim answers and, along with some or all of the prospective coders, develop a clear, exhaustive set of coding categories. If necessary, write these down in a code book, with a number of examples for each category. It is important to make sure coders understand the categories and how to use the codebook.

Coders should practice on sample questionnaires to ensure they assign the correct codes. And, if possible, use multiple coders and have them code a sample of each other's work to detect inconsistencies among coders or to discover questions where the coding scheme is producing a great deal of inconsistency among coders.

ASKING QUESTIONS

Most of the threats to measurement validity discussed to this point are partially or wholly controllable. But even where control is minimal, their potential for bias pales in significance compared to the problems in eliciting the truth from respondents. Problems can arise from three sources: the interviewer, the respondent, and the instrument. We will consider them in turn.

Interviewer-Induced Error

Respondents may report something other than the truth because he or she responds to the way the interviewer looks and how he or she asks the questions. Interviewers can induce respondents to exaggerate, to hide, to try to impress, to be distracted. As a general rule, one would like the interviewer to be as unobtrusive a "tool" as possible. This means that in a face-to-face interview situation the interviewer should possess socio-economic characteristics as much like their respondents as possible; one should avoid having young blacks or Hispanics interview whites, or having attractive young women interview teenage boys. A neat and unobtrusive appearance (while still being enthusiastic and motivating in behavior) is important. Personal interviewers with distracting handicaps (or unusual clothing or make-up) may be effective over the telephone, but not in the field.

The interviewer should keep physically and emotionally nonthreatening to respondents, and avoid body or vocal cues that may give away or distort answers. The more the interviewing involves difficult questions and interaction with the respondent over the course of the interview, the more the interviewer's characteristics, style, and specific actions can influence the results. If the interviewer must explain questions, probe for details, or encourage fuller responses, his or her manner of doing so can have profound consequences for both the quantity of data elicited and its quality. For these reasons, the researcher should be very careful in selecting and training both telephone and personal interviewers. Someone with a limited budget may be tempted to hire low-cost (or free) amateurs and think that minimizing training sessions is a good way to cut costs. This is usually *very* short-sighted behavior.

If one is forced to use amateurs, then careful training, extensive use of precoded questions, and a detailed set of interviewer instructions ought always to be built into the study design.

Even then, the dangers of interviewer-induced error will be great. In a classic study, Guest had 15 college-educated interviewers apply the same instrument to the same respondent who was instructed to give the same responses to all. The number of errors was astonishing. No questionnaire was without error and the number of errors ranged from 12 to 36! Failure to follow up questions for supplementary answers occurred *66* times.[1]

Another problem with amateurs is that there is always the small possibility that they will fabricate total interviews or responses to particular questions (e.g., those they are fearful of asking such as income, drinking, and sex habits). Fortunately, it is almost certain that such amateurs will not know how the results to particular questions should be distributed. Consequently, his or her answers will look markedly different from the rest of the study and can be detected in computer checks. In a study I conducted many years ago on radio station preferences using student interviewers, one interviewer apparently chose to do his field work in his dorm room. And, of course, when it came time to record station preferences, he used his own preferences which, not surprisingly, were not at all like the general population in the area studied. Such cheating can also be controlled by recontacting respondents in a small percentage of each interviewer's work to verify that they were contacted. Postcards or brief telephone calls can serve this purpose. Such validation is routine in most commercial research organizations.

Respondent-Induced Bias

There are four major sources of respondent bias: (1) fogetting, (2) deliberately withholding information, (3) simple mistakes or unintentional distortion of information, and (4) deliberate distortion of information.

The largest source of respondent bias in surveys is forgetting. With time, subtle details of purchases can be lost and even major facts, such as brand names or prices, disappear. Aided

---

[1] L.L. Guest, "A Study of Interviewer Competence," *International Journal of Opinion and Attitude Research*, 1 March 1977, pp. 17–30.

recall can help reduce this problem (although potentially introducing its own biases) as can carefully limiting the time period for recall to that for which the respondent's memory should be reasonably accurate. The low-budget researcher should guard against the tendency to be greedy for information, asking for recall of data farther and farther back in time where such recall may be highly suspect.

Mistakes or neglect of information can be minimized by proper questioning. First, one must make sure that definitions of each desired bit of information are very clear, possibly with the use of precoded answers. A frequent problem is household income. Respondents may not know what to include as household income or may forget critical components. Worse still, different respondents may have different definitions which could make them appear different when they are not. For example, there is the problem of whose income to include, e.g., spouses, teenage children, live-in parents? What if one has a boarder, is this included? What about spending money earned by a daughter away at college? Are dividends included? What about the $1,000 lottery winning? Is social security included if one is old, or dividends from an IRA? While not all contingencies can be handled in a simple questionnaire format, questions can be worded so as to specify most of the information desired. In face-to-face or telephone studies, interviewers can be instructed about the real intention of the question and armed with prompts to make sure that respondents do not inadvertently give biased or incomplete information.

Another broad class of unintentional respondent problems is time distortion. Often a study will ask for a summary of past experiences. That is, a researcher may wish to know how many head colds respondents have had, or vacations they've taken, or salespeople they have seen within some specified period. The typical problem is that people will telescope experiences beyond the specified time frame into the period in question. A questionnaire may ask about six months' worth of head colds and really get eight months' worth! If everyone used the same amount of telescoping (e.g., eight months into six), this would not be a problem. But if they differed, this will produce artificial differences across respondents. The solution is again a matter of design. First, the study should involve as few of these kinds of questions as possble. Second, questions requiring memory should only ask about relatively prominent events (e.g., do not bother asking how many cans or bottles of beer a respondent has consumed in six months). And third, whenever possible, each question should clearly *bound* the starting point of the period. This boundary would depend on the subject, the respondent, or the date of the study. For example, one could anchor the period to the start of the year, Thanksgiving, the beginning of the school year, or the respondent's last birthday.

Telescoping is an unconscious distortion on the part of the respondent. Respondents can distort results in other ways. If given a scale of answers, some respondents will use the full range of the scale, others may use only a small part in the middle. *Naysayers*, as they are called, will tend to use the negative end of the scale and, *yeasayers*, the positive end. These systematic biases can often be controlled by having the computer normalize an individual's responses after the data are collected, in effect rescoring each answer in terms of the respondent's answer tendencies (see Chapter 10).

Harder to detect and control are deliberate efforts by respondents to portray themselves as they are not or to answer as they think the researcher would like them to answer. Deliberate response bias in general is much harder to analyze and adjust for because the researcher doesn't know what the truth would have been. About all that can be done is to make the stimulus (i.e., the question and/or the interviewer) as unlikely as possible to encourage such distortion and to stress to the respondent the importance to the study that they be as candid and objective as possible. Repeating the researcher's initial guarantee of anonymity when introducing particularly worrisome questions can sometimes help.

Questionnaire Design

This book is not intended to make an expert question writer out of the reader. To some extent, writing questions that both motivate and get at the truth is a skill acquired only by considerable practice. The beginning low-budget researcher is admonished not to think that writing a good questionnaire is something any intelligent person can do. It takes considerable experience. One way the low-budget researcher can appropriate experience quickly is to borrow questions from others, preferably questions used by several other researchers. Using questions from secondary sources not only assures that the questions have been pretested, it also guarantees that a database will exist elsewhere to which the researcher can compare the present results.

The U.S. Census is a good source of such questions in part because its categories (e.g., for income or occupations) are the ones used by most researchers and in part because the Census Bureau provides vast quantities of data against which to validate the researcher's own work.

Once the borrowing possibilities have been exhausted, the naive researcher should seek the help of an expert question writer, if one can be afforded. Alternatively, once a questionnaire is prepared, the draft instrument should be reviewed by as many colleagues as possible (especially those who will be critical). Finally, one should test the instrument with real potential respondents even if it is only the office staff and inlaws. I have never yet written a questionnaire that did not have major flaws, ambiguities, and even missing categories despite the fact I was sure that this time I had finally done it right. It takes a thorough pretest to bring these out. My own preference is to continue pretesting each redraft until I am confident the instrument is right. I keep reminding myself that if I do not measure whatever I am studying validly at the start, all the subsequent analysis and report-writing I might do will be wasted!

Following are possible questionnaire biases that could crop up in research instruments.

Question Order Bias

Sometimes questions early in a questionnaire can influence later ones. For example, asking someone to rank a set of criteria for choosing brands or outlets makes it very likely that a later request for a ranking of brands or outlets will be influenced by the very criteria already listed. Without the prior list, the respondent may have performed the evaluation using fewer or even different criteria. The solution here is to try different orderings during a pretest and *see* whether the order makes any difference. If it does, then the researcher should either place the more important question first (i.e., are the criteria or the rankings more important?) or change the order in every other questionnaire (called *rotating* the questions) to balance the effects overall.

A second, more obvious, questionnaire order effect is what might be called *giving away the show*. This problem seldom survives an outside review of the instrument or a pretest. However, I have seen first drafts of a questionnaire where, for example, wording that mimicked an advertising campaign was used as one of the dimensions for evaluating a retail outlet. Later, a question asking for recall of advertising themes got a surprisingly high unaided recall of that particular theme.

A third kind of questionnaire order effect involves threatening questions that, if asked early, can cause a respondent to clam up or terminate the interview altogether. If a researcher must ask questions about sex, drugs, cancer, or income, it is better to leave these as late as possible in the instrument.

A final order effect applies to lengthy questionnaires. It is known that, as respondents tire, they give shorter and less carefully thought out answers. Here again, one should either put the more important questions early or rotate the questions among questionnaires.

Answer Order Bias

There is one major problem when respondents are given a choice of precoded categories to answer to a question. There is a tendency for respondents, other things equal, to give higher ratings to alternatives higher on a list than those lower on a list. In such instances, pretesting and (usually) rotation of answers are recommended. Practically, rotation is achieved during face-to-face or telephone interviews by having the supervisor red-check different precoded answer categories where the interviewer is to begin reading alternatives. (A CATI computer can do this automatically.) On mail questionnaires, the researcher simply must have the word processor reorder the alternatives and print out several versions of the questionnaire to be mailed out randomly.

Scaling Bias

Wording and formatting of individual questions that attempt to scale attitudes, preferences, and the like can be an important source of bias. If the researcher must construct his or her own scales (e.g., to measure perceptions or preferences), the best approach is to use one of a number of pretested general techniques that can be customized for a specific study.

Thurstone Scales. In this approach, a large number of statements about an object of interest (such as a company, a retailer, or a brand) are sorted by expert judges into 9 or 11 groups separated along some prespecified dimension such as favorableness. The 9 or 11 groups or positions are judged by the experts to be equally far from each other. One or two statements are then selected by the researcher from each group to represent each scale position. The final questionnaire then presents respondents with all statements and asks them to pick the *one* that best portrays their feelings about each object. Their choices are then assigned the rating given by the judges to that statement. The ratings are assumed to be interval scaled.

Likert Scales. A problem with Thurstone scales is that they do not indicate how intensely a respondent holds a position. Likert scaling involves giving respondents a set of statements and asking them how much they agree with each statement usually on a five-point continuum: (1) strongly agree, (2) somewhat agree, (3) neither agree nor disagree, (4) somewhat disagree, or (5) strongly disagree. Responses to a selected series of such statements are then analyzed individually or summed to yield a total score. Likert scales are very popular, in part, because they are easy to explain and to lay out on a mail questionnaire. They are also very easy to administer in telephone interviews. One problem with the technique, however, is that the midpoint of a Likert scale is ambiguous. It can be chosen by those who truly don't know and by those who are indifferent. For this reason, some researchers allow respondents a sixth option, "don't know," so that the mid-point will really represent indifference.

Semantic Differential. Here respondents are asked to evaluate an object such as a company, store, or brand on a number of dimensions divided into segments numbered from 1 to 9 or 11. In contrast to Likert scales, each position is not labeled. Rather, the scales are anchored on each end with opposing (semantically different) adjectives or phrases. Examples might be:

Strong |_|_|_|_|_|_|_|_|_| Weak
        1 2 3 4 5 6 7 8 9

Friendly salespeople |_|_|_|_|_|_|_|_|_| Unfriendly salespeople
                      1 2 3 4 5 6 7 8 9

Respondents indicate where on each scale they perceive the object in question to be. Two problems are common with semantic differentials. First, there is again the confusion of whether the midpoint of the scale represents indifference or ignorance. Second, there is the problem that the anchors may not be true opposites; e.g., is the opposite of healthy, "unhealthy" or is it "sick"?

Stapel Scale. Some dimensions on which the researcher may wish to rate something may not have obvious opposites, for example, "fiery," "cozy" or "classic." Stapel scales were designed for this contingency. Here, the interviewer merely asks the respondents to indicate the degree to which a particular adjective applies to an object in question. Usually Stapel scales are easier than semantic differentials to explain over the telephone and require little pretesting.

Graphic Scales. If the respondent can be shown a scale graphically, for example in a mail, self-report, or face-to-face interview study, then a scale where the positions look equal can be used. Researchers sometimes use a ladder to represent social class dimensions along which respondents are asked to place themselves. The latter can also be used on the telephone as can the image of a thermometer to give people unfamiliar with scales an idea of what they look like.

Threatening Questions
Many studies will touch on issues that are threatening to some or all respondents. As suggested earlier, this would include topics

like sex, alcohol consumption, mental illness, or family planning practices—all of which may be of interest to a marketer. These are touchy issues and hard to phrase in questions. Respondents usually do not wish to reveal to others something private and/ or that they feel may be unusual. Some seemingly innocuous questions may be threatening to some respondents. For example, a man may not wish to reveal that the reason he chooses a fast-food outlet is because of the attractiveness of a waitress. Or a housewife may not be anxious to admit she likes to shop at Neiman-Marcus for minor items just so she can get a shopping bag to impress her middle-class neighbors.

There are several approaches to reducing threat levels. One is to assure respondents at the start of the study that they can be as candid and objective as possible since the answers will be held in complete confidence. This point can then be repeated in the introduction to a specific threatening question (e.g., asking about income).

A second approach that tends to ease individuals' fears of being unusual is to preface the question with a reassuring phrase indicating that unique answers are not unusual for a specific question. Thus, one might begin a question about alcohol consumption as follows: "Now we would like to ask you questions about your alcohol consumption in the last week. Many have reported consuming alcohol at parties and at meals. Others have told us about unusual occasions on which they take a drink of whiskey, wine, or beer—like right after they get out of bed in the morning, or just before an important meeting with a co-worker they don't like. Could you tell us about each of the occasions on which you had an alcoholic beverage in the last week, that is since last (day-of-the-week)?"

Another approach is to use an indirect technique of some kind. Respondents may often reveal the truth about themselves when they are caught off guard, e.g., thinking they are not talking about themselves. For example, a questionnaire may ask respondents to talk about "a good friend" or "people in general." In this case, the assumption is that, in the absence of direct information about the behavior or attitudes of others, a respondent will bring to bear their own perceptions and experiences.

Finally, the researcher could use so-called *in-depth interviewing* techniques (mentioned in Chapter 8). Here, the interviewer tries not to ask intrusive questions. Rather the topic (e.g., alcohol consumption) is introduced and the respondent is kept talking by such interjections as, "that's interesting" or "tell me more." In the hands of a skilled, supportive interviewer, respondents should eventually dig deeply into their psyches and reveal truths that might be missed or hidden. However, such approaches: (1) are very time consuming; (2) can only be used with small (and probably unrepresentative) samples; and (3) require expertise that is often unaffordable for the low-budget researcher.

Constricting Questions

Respondents may withhold information or not yield enough detail if the questions do not permit it. They may also terminate out of frustration. The questionnaire should almost always include an "other" option where there is the real possibility that all the possibilities have not been precoded. Multiple choices should be allowed where they are relevant and people should be able to report that some combination of answers is truly the situation.

Generalization Biases

Bias can often creep into answers by respondents who are asked to generalize about something, particularly their own behavior. For example, naive questionnaire writers often ask respondents to indicate their favorite radio station, the weekly newsmagazine they read most often, or the beer brand they usually order when they go out. The problem is that these questions require the respondents to summarize and make judgments about their own behavior. Yet, how they make these generalizations will be unknown to the researcher. For example, when asked for a favorite radio station, one person may report a station they listen to while in the car, another may report a favorite station at home, while a third may report one that pleases them most often rather than the one they listen to most frequently.

When asking questions about behavior, it is almost always better to ask about specific past behaviors than have a respondent generalize. Rather than asking about a favorite radio station, a respondent can be asked, "Think back to the last time you had the radio on at home, work, or in the car; what station were you listening to?" In this case, the respondent perceives the task as reporting a fact rather than coming up with a generalization. In such cases, one is likely to get much more objective, error-free reporting than if consumers are asked to generalize.

REFERENCES

1. Sudman, Seymour, and Norman M. Bradburn. *Asking Questions: A Practical Guide to Questionnaire Design.* San Francisco, Calif.: Jossey-Bass, 1972.
2. Payne, Stanley L. *The Art of Asking Questions.* Princeton, N.J.: Princeton University Press, 1951.
3. Tyebjee, Tyzoon. "Telephone Survey Methods: The State of the Art." *Journal of Marketing*, Summer 1979, pp. 66–78.
4. Heeler, Roger M. and Michael L. Ray. "Measure Validation in Marketing." *Journal of Marketing Research*, November 1972, pp. 361–370.
5. Haley, Russell L., and Peter B. Case. "Testing Thirteen Attitude Scales for Agreement and Brand Discrimination." *Journal of Marketing*, Fall 1979, pp. 20–32.

CHAPTER 10

ALL THE STATISTICS YOU
NEED TO KNOW (INITIALLY)

As we noted in Chapter 2, management's needs are for three types of information: descriptive, explanatory, and predictive. Management will want to know what it is, what caused it, and/ or what it will be in future. Answering these kinds of questions correctly is a two-part process. First, one must have the right raw material. That is, valid measurements are needed. Second, the right meaning must be extracted from those measurements. That is, we need valid descriptive summaries, valid measures of association and causation and valid predictions. We have considered some of the problems of developing valid measures in Chapter 9. Now, we will outline the major analysis techniques. We will describe both simple techniques and a few of the more complex multivariate techniques for those who wish to extract even more from a given data set.

FEAR OF STATISTICS

Most people are frightened of statistics. They seem to think that statistical analysis is some kind of mystical rite not to be comprehended or used by ordinary people. They avoid statistics like the plague and take a curious pride in doing so. The view seems to be that those who avoid statistics are somehow more plain-speaking and down-to-earth, while those who use statistics are either trying to make something simple appear unnecessarily complex and sophisticated or trying to hide something from others. One often hears, "Don't confuse me with all your statistics."

In my view, this fear of statistics is irrational, but understandable. Unfortunately, sometimes simple truths have been obscured by statistics and statisticians. But statistics can be very valuable tools for the budget-minded researcher. They make it significantly more likely that management will make decisions based on a valid interpretation of the information at hand.

Statistics, as we use the term here, can serve researchers and managers in two critical roles. First, there are descriptive statistics. These include simple frequency counts, measures of central tendency like the mean, median, and mode, and measures of variability like the range. These statistics do not frighten most people. However, some fancier descriptive measures like standard deviation and standard error do. Descriptive statistics perform a crucial function for the harried manager. They provide ways of reducing large amounts of data to more concise, comprehensive values. A sales manager would rather not be faced with a report of sales for every product for every salesperson in every outlet in every region. Descriptive statistics such as means, modes, and ranges will be much more manageable and therefore much more useful. By comparing these summary numbers, insights that would be lost in the mass of original data may become clear and causes of remedial or reinforcing action suggested.

The second, and more fearsome, connotation of statistics is more properly called *statistical testing*. It is readily conceded that statistical tests are a bit intimidating if one focuses on the method of applying the tests—the calculations, the theory, the assumptions. We will try to avoid this as much as possible, and instead, will concentrate on the uses of statistical tests. These uses can be boiled down to one expression: statistical tests are designed to keep management honest. Statistical tests make sure that, if management thinks that sales are up in Atlanta, or that Sally is really out-selling Irving, or that only middle-size cities have large sales of the new laundry detergent, these conclusions are truly there and not artifacts of management's imagination. There is a great temptation to all of us to want to find something in a set of data, particularly if that something supports a prior assumption or will lend strong support to a course of action management was planning to take anyway. But if that something has an unacceptably high probability of just being a chance aberration, a manager would be ill-advised to commit the organization to actions based on such an aberration. Statistical tests can keep management from unknowingly taking such chances: they keep one honest.

Managers should not fear statistics, but be thankful they are there.

In this chapter, we will introduce the most important statistical tools likely to be used in an introductory program of low-cost research. The chapter assumes that the research analyst will make extensive use of a computer to generate the statistics and conduct the statistical tests by using one of the myriad statistical packages currently available (such as SPSS, SAS, Crunch, or SYSTAT). All are available in versions for personal computers. The use of computers has two implications. First, it means that the researcher will never have to actually calculate any of the statistics we will discuss. Thus, we can focus here on making sure the researcher understands what the computer will produce.

The easy access of computers has a second implication, a very serious danger for the naive researcher. Computers are dumb processers. They will take any set of values and by hook or crook crank out any statistics requested. Thus, if males are precoded as 1 in a study and females as 2, the computer can certainly tell you that the average sex of your respondents is 1.6239 with a standard deviation (presumably in sex-ness) of .087962. This, of course, is patently ridiculous. But, there are many occasions on which a similar, not-so-obvious error can easily occur if the researcher asks for statistics which are inappropriate. It is the old GIGO problem: Garbage In, Garbage Out! If statistics are to keep a researcher honest, the researcher must know when and where to use them legitimately. Thus, our goal in this chapter is to describe the use of different kinds of statistics so that they can be requested appropriately.

We will purposely simplify many of the treatments in order to provide the reader with a layperson's understanding that, it is hoped, is not intimidating. Many assumptions and variations in calculation methods are not discussed. It is suggested that, before actually using the statistics described here, the researcher either seek advice from a more experienced user or read further in the readings at the end of the chapter.

We will begin with some basic concepts.

INPUT DATA

If a researcher is going to use statistics properly, it is first essential to consider the kind of data about which descriptive statistics are to be calculated or to which will be applied some kind of statistical test. Statistical analysis, even such simple analysis as counting, requires that each characteristic we wish to study be assigned a unique value. Sometimes, especially in qualitative research with small samples, this value can be a word or a symbol. For example, the interviewer could assign the word "yes" or "positive" or the symbol + to indicate that a respondent liked a product, or a flavor, or a company. Analysis could then produce a statistic called a frequency count of these words or symbols to reveal overall perceptions of various stimuli or various groups of respondents. However, even in these cases, when the sample is large and we wish to do a lot of cross tabulations or plan to use a computer, we will want to assign each measurement a number.

For the computer to either prepare summary statistics or conduct a statistical analysis of some kind, each measurement of our sample population must be assigned a number. These numbers can differ significantly in their level of sophistication. And it is this level of sophistication that determines what should and should not be done to them. There are four categories in which numbers are generally grouped. In increasing order of sophistication, they are (1) nominal numbers, (2) ordinal numbers, (3) intervally scaled numbers, and (4) ratio scaled numbers.

We will discuss each briefly, noting that numbers of a particular higher order status can always be treated as if they had a lower order status. For example, one can always treat ordinal data as if they were merely nominal.

Nominal Data

In a surprisingly large number of cases, the number we assign to some object, idea, or behavior is *entirely arbitrary,* although in some cases a tradition may establish the rules of assignment. If measurements are assigned arbitrary numbers, they are called *nominal* numbers and their sole purpose in the analysis is to differentiate an item possessing one characteristic from an item possessing a different characteristic.

Consider, for example, the assignment of numbers to football players. Each player has a number that distinguishes one player from another. They allow coaches and fans to tell them apart and allow referees to assign penalties to the correct person.

The numbers here have no other meaning than differentiation. Despite what a boastful wide receiver may tell the press, players with numbers in the 80s are not necessarily smarter than those with numbers in the 70s, nor do they deserve bigger salaries. They are probably faster than those with numbers in the 70s, but not necessarily faster than those with numbers 16 to 20 or 30 to 50. The fact that someone has a higher number than someone else does not mean that he is more or less of anything.

Ordinal Data

Ordinal numbers are assigned to give order to measurements. In a questionnaire, we may ask two respondents to rank Brands A, B, and C. Typically, we would assign a 1 to their most preferred brand, 2 to their second most preferred and 3 to their third favorite. Note that, if someone prefers A over B over C, we do not know how much A is preferred to B, or how much B is preferred to C. For example, Gordon may prefer A a great deal over B, but Gary may be almost indifferent between the two giving a slight edge to A. But they would both have the same rankings. It is perfectly permissible to assign any numbers to the respondents' first, second, and third choices as long as we retain the same ordering distinction.

Interval and Ratio Data

The next two classes of data represent a substantial jump in sophistication from the first two classes. The two classes of measurements just discussed (nominal and ordinal) are frequently described by researchers and statisticians as *nonmetric* numbers. Interval and ratio measurements are called *metric* (or parametric) numbers. Most of the sophisticated summary statistics and statistical tests with which the reader is probably familiar (e.g., the arithmetric mean and the correlation coefficient) strictly require metric measurements. For this reason, it is desirable, but not essential, that researchers seek to develop interval or ratio data whenever possible. It should be noted that experience has shown that assuming data are metric when they might be only ranked does not usually produce serious distortions in results. For example, if a magazine reader rates *Time* as 5 on an "informative" scale and *Newsweek* as 4, it may seem safer (more conservative) to interpret these results as only saying that the reader rated *Time* higher than *Newsweek* (that the data are really ordinal). However, making the stronger assumption that one has an interval scale will typically not materially affect one's conclusions.

Interval data are similar to ordinal data in that the assigned numbers order the results. In this case, however, the differences between numbers have an additional meaning. In an interval scale, we assume that the distance or interval between the numbers has a meaning. The difference between interval data and ratio-scaled data is that the latter have a known zero point and the former do not. Thus, we may be able to say that, on a "sweetness" scale, Brand A is as far from Brand B as Brand C is from Brand D (the interval assumption). We cannot say that Brand A seems to be four times as sweet as Brand D! The distinction may be made clear by using two common examples.

A Fahrenheit temperature scale is an example of an interval scale. Any four-degree difference in temperature is like any other four-degree difference. But since the zero point on a Fahrenheit scale is arbitrary, we can say that if the temperature rose from 76° to 80° in the morning and later dropped from 44° to 40° just after midnight, the changes were equal. However, we would be foolish to say that the morning was twice as warm as the night. Is 80° twice as warm as 40°? Is 10° five times as warm as 2°? We can speak confidently about temperature intervals and not temperature ratios.

In contrast, age is an example of a scale with a real, known zero. In this case, we can say that someone who is 40 is twice as old as someone who is 20. In many analyses in marketing, the distinction between interval and ratio-scaled data is not very important managerially.

FIGURE 10–1
Numerical Qualities of Some Typical Marketing Measurements

Non-Metric	Metric
Nominal	*Interval*
Sex	Some rating scales
Marital status	(e.g., semantic differen-
Store/brand last patronized	tial, Likert scales)
Ownership of various items	Knowledge/awareness levels
Employment status	*Ratio*
Ordinal	Age
Occupational status	Education
Brand/store preferences	Sales
Some rating scales	Time elapsed
Social class	Income

Some examples of marketing measurements that fall under each of the four levels of numerical sophistication are given in Figure 10–1.

DESCRIPTIVE STATISTICS

The problem with much research is that it produces too much data. Some of it we will wish to simply report just as it comes and some of it we will wish to relate to other data to show differences, relationships, and so on.

For a great many decision problems, we may be satisfied with a description of the population under study. At the very least, merely looking over the data is a good starting point for later, more sophisticated analyses.

Descriptions of data can take many forms. Take the simple case of the taste test ratings for a new cake mix. We can report the scores that respondents give to each version of the mix as frequency distributions. Or we can portray their scores graphically in a bar chart or histogram as in Figure 10–2. The next step will be to summarize these data in more concise form. This will be particularly desirable if we wish to compare a large number of different distributions such as, say, respondents' ratings

FIGURE 10–2
Ratings of a New Cake Mix

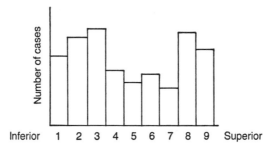

of 10 new mixes on five different taste and preference dimensions each. In summaries, we are usually interested in three features: (1) The frequency counts of various measurements—(how many people assigned a "3" on sweetness to Mix A); (2) Some measure of central tendency—(what was the mean level of sweetness assigned to Mix A); or (3) Some measure of the spread of the measurements—(were the sweetness ratings of Mix A more dispersed than the ratings of Mix B).

Central Tendency

The term *average* is, unfortunately, loosely used by the general population to connote any one of the following:

1. The modal value: the value most frequently reported.
2. The median: the value at the mid-point of a distribution of cases when they are ordered by their values.
3. The arithmetic mean: the result of weighting (multiplying) each value by the number of the cases reporting it and then dividing by the number of cases.

Applying a measure of central tendency is not always straightforward. Suppose 15 respondents rated the sweetness of cake mix A on a seven-point scale as follows (their ratings have been reordered for convenience).

1 2 3 3 3 3 4 4 5 5 6 6 7 7 7

Here, we can see that the mode is 3, the median is 4, and the mean is 4.4, all different! Which is the best measure of central tendency? To some extent it depends on management's interests. If they want to know how the largest segment rated the brand, one would use the mode. If they wanted to know at which point the sample was divided in half with respect to sweetness, one would use the median. If they wanted to weight respondents by the scores they assigned, then the mean should be used.

Not all measures of central tendency can be applied to all kinds of data. The kinds you can use vary depending on the type of data you have, as follows:

Numbers	Permissible Measures
Nominal	Mode
Ordinal	Mode, Median
Interval	Mode, Median, Mean
Ratio	Mode, Median, Mean

It should be noted that, although it is all too frequently done, one should not attempt to compute an arithmetic mean using ordinal data. It is not at all uncommon to hear untrained researchers speak of a brand's average ranking. This is only correct if the researcher is referring to the median or modal ranking.

Here are a few more important suggestions about measures of central tendency:

1. Always compute and look at all the measures of central tendency you can. A median or mode may tell you something the mean does not.

2. In computing a mode, do not neglect the possibility that a distribution is bimodal. The computer will typically report only one mode. But the researcher should scan the frequency counts of all responses or have the computer produce a bar chart (histogram) in order to detect multiple modes where they exist. For example, it would be important to know whether scores of "liking" for your brand or for a major competitor's brand was unmodal or bimodal. If it were bimodal (see Figure 10–2), this would suggest that the brand tends to polarize people into a

FIGURE 10–3
Normal and Skewed Distributions

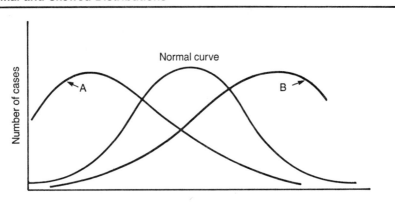

group of likers and a group of dislikers (or "less likers"). This could suggest a possible vulnerability for the brand to an attack on those who like it less.

3. Do not be afraid to compute a median even where the data are grouped (e.g., ages under 10, 10 to 19 etc.). The computer will automatically do this for you.

4. Be sure to compare the median to the mean when you have metric data. Since they are identical in a normal distribution, a comparison will tell you whether your distribution is skewed in any way. Some statistical tests have as an assumption that the underlying data approximate the well-known normal curve. The more the mean and median differ, the more the distribution leans one way or the other.[1] As shown in Figure 10–3, distributions can be skewed positively (Curve A) or negatively (Curve B). Several characteristics of interest to marketers, such as the quantity of a product bought per week or the size of a household's income, will be positively skewed.

---

[1]A second measure sometimes used to test normality is called *kurtosis*, the peakedness of the distribution. It is possible for the data to have equal means and medians, but be so pointy or so square that the assumption of normality of the distribution must be discarded.

Measures of Dispersion

Measures of dispersion indicate the relative spread of the data we are studying. Heights of a line of chorus girls will be much less diverse (spread) than heights of children in a primary school. Measures of dispersion are relatively underutilized by naive marketing researchers. They form an important part of many statistical analysis procedures (e.g., testing whether an experiment's results were due to chance) and they can be useful in their own right.

There is, of course, no such thing as a measure of dispersion for nominal data. It makes no sense to talk about the spread of marital data. Dispersion, however, can be computed for ordinal data. The most common dispersion measures here are: (1) the range from maximum to minimum, and (2) the *interquartile range,* the difference between the 75th and 25th cases. The latter is often used because it produces a measure that eliminates the effects of extreme values at either end of the rankings which would exaggerate the full range.

For metric data (interval or ratio-scaled), the most common measure of dispersion is the *variance* or its square root, the *standard deviation.* Variance is computed by subtracting each value from the mean of all of the values, squaring the results, and then averaging these squared values.[2] The variance has two virtues. First, it tends to weight values far from the mean more than those near the mean. This makes it a relatively stringent measure when incorporated in statistical tests of relationships or of differences. The second virtue is that (assuming we have a normal distribution), it allows us to say something rather precisely about how many cases will fall within a certain distance from the mean (i.e., in standard deviation units).

One can also use the standard deviation or the variance to compare two distributions expressed in the same units. For example, we can compare perceptions of a store in one city with those of a store in another city on both mean and variance. It may be possible that the means are the same in the two cities,

---

[2]Actually, dividing by one less than the number of cases.

but the variance is much higher in one than the other. This would suggest that the store's image is relatively clear in one city and pretty fuzzy in the other. (See Figure 10–4.) In the same way we might compare variances within a city to see whether the store's image is fuzzier for some market segments than for others.

Another role for the standard deviation is to tell us something about the unusualness of a given case. By calculating how many standard deviations a given case is from the mean, we will have a quantitative measure of how typical or atypical it is. We could say, for example, that per capita tuxedo sales in Reno are a lot different from the average for the United States in that only 2 percent of reporting cities have greater tuxedo

FIGURE 10–4
Ratings of Product Quality in Department Store X in Two Cities

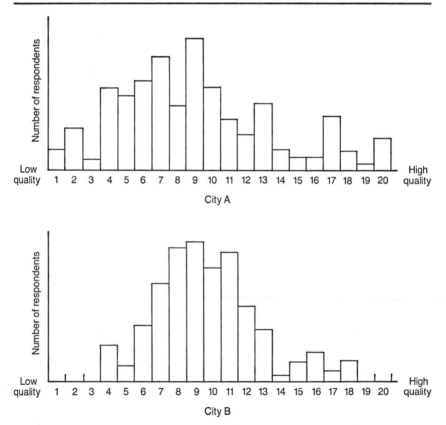

sales. (Indeed, since the Greek symbol for the standard deviation is the letter *sigma,* it is not unusual to hear a member of the research community describe an offbeat colleague as being "at least five sigmas off center!")

A final role of the standard deviation for experienced researchers is in normalizing data. This process is described in Exhibit 10–1.

EXHIBIT 10–1

Normalization

The fact that one can describe a particular case as being so-many standard deviations away from the mean introduces one other important role that this dispersion measure can serve for researchers. As noted earlier, a frequent problem when comparing responses to certain kinds of psychological questions across respondents is that people tend to differ in the proportion of a given rating scale they tend to use. For instance, when rating different stores on an 11-point interval scale, an extroverted respondent may use the full range from, say, 2 to 11 while more restrained respondents may venture ratings only between 4 and 7. If we were to compare only their raw scores, the computer would treat a score of 7 as being essentially the same for both. But, as we have seen, a 7 for the extrovert is just barely above average, but for the introvert it represents outright enthusiasm, the highest score he or she gives.

To accomodate these basic differences across individuals (or, sometimes, across questions), it is customary to transform the original respondent scores into scores measured in terms of numbers of standard deviations. Thus, a computer would be instructed to divide each respondent's original score on a given scale by that respondent's personal standard deviation on all similar scales. This is called normalization of the data. By this procedure, the introvert's score of 7 will get transformed into a higher normalized score than the extrovert's score of 7.

Normalization is also a method for making many different *kinds* of variables comparable, that is, to express them all in standard deviation units. This approach is often used when employing multiple regression equations.

A final measure of dispersion that is of great interest to statisticians is the *standard error*. This measure has much the same meaning and use as the standard deviation, but it describes the spread of some summary measure like a mean or a proportion. Because we know the proportion of cases that fall within specific distances from the mid-point of a normal curve as expressed in standard errors, we can say something about the likelihood that the true mean we are trying to estimate in a specific study is within a certain distance (in standard error units) from the mean we actually did find. Assume that we studied owners of a particular model of automobile and calculated that the mean number of miles driven per year was 10,000 miles and the standard error was 100 miles. We can say that we are 95 percent sure that the true number of miles driven per year for this model is between approximately 10,196 and 9,804 miles (i.e., the sample mean plus or minus 1.96 standard errors).[3] This is because we know that 95 percent of all cases under a normal curve fall between the mid-point and points approximately 1.96 standard errors above and 1.96 standard errors below that mid-point. The band expected to envelop the true mean is often called the 95 percent *confidence interval*.

STATISTICAL ANALYSIS

Statistical analysis helps researchers and managers answer one of two questions: (1) Does a specific result differ significantly from another result or from an expected result, or (2) Is a specific result associated with or predicted by some other result or results or is this just due to chance?

Such analyses will typically be performed on one of three kinds of data: frequencies, means, or proportions. Do more people buy from a jumbled or a neat display? Is the proportion of customers noticing a newspaper ad different for men and women? Can mean miles of automobile driving be predicted from occupation, income, and family size?

---

[3]The confidence level for two standard errors is 95.44 percent.

In the sections to follow, we will introduce the major statistical analysis techniques that a beginning researcher may wish to use. We will organize the techniques on the basis of the kinds of data for which they are most appropriate—nominal, ordinal, or metric. However, we need first to make a brief comment about significance.

Levels of Significance

An important question in statistical analysis is what do we mean when we say there is a very low probability of a particular result being significant. If a probability is very low, we may decide that our actual results are really different from the expected results and take some action on it. But suppose the analysis yielded a .15 chance that the results are really not different? Should we act on this or do we only act if the probability they are not different is .05 or lower? That is, what is the appropriate *level of significance?* In classical statistics, statisticians tend to use either the .05 or the .01 level of significance as the cutoff for concluding that a result is significant. In this writer's opinion, this classical notion is of little relevance to marketing decision makers, especially in this age of computer analysis.

Historically, statisticians have instructed us that good science involves (1) the construction of hypotheses usually in null form (i.e., that there is no difference or association) before the results are in (so we are not tempted to test what we have in fact already found), and (2) the setting, in advance, of a level of statistical significance level beyond which we would reject the null hypothesis. The cut-off is typically stated as the probability of rejecting this hypothesis. Classically, this probability was set either at .05 or .01 depending on how tough one wanted to be before accepting a positive outcome.

But, of course, these levels are arbitrary—why not .045 or .02? Further, they ignore the managerial context. The latter is most important. It must be recognized that the real issue is not whether the data are sufficiently strong to permit us to make statements about the truth, but rather whether the results are strong enough to permit the manager to take action.

Implicit in this action orientation is the view that (1) it is the manager's *perception* of the significance of the result that is relevant—not the researcher's use of some classical cut-off; (2) significance is really in terms of whether the result will lead to action, and (3) significance is ultimately a matter not just of statistical probability, but also of the manager's prior information, his or her prior conviction about which way to act, and the stakes involved. In this conceptualization, it becomes obvious that the researcher's responsibility is simply to report the absolute probability that a result is significant and then let the manager decide whether this is significant in terms of the decision at hand. Significance in some cases (e.g., where the stakes are low and management is already leaning toward a particular course of action) may be acceptable with a .15 probability or better. In other cases where the stakes are larger and management is quite unsure what is best, only a .03 or better probability will decide the matter. In modern managerial decision making, the classical role of the .05 and the .01 levels of significance should be irrelevant.

Nominal Data: The Chi-Square Test

Where we have nominal data, we are forced to analyze frequency counts since there are no means and variances. Two kinds of questions are typically asked of these frequency counts. When looking at only one variable we usually ask whether the results in the study differ from some expected distribution (often referred to as *the model*). For example, we might wish to know whether the distribution of occupations in a target population is different from that found in the market as a whole or in an earlier study. The second kind of analysis we may wish to conduct is to ask whether the distribution of one variable is associated with another, for example, whether occupation depends on the geographical area of the respondent. The appropriate statistical test to use for either type of analysis is called the Chi-square $[\chi^2]$ test. Because it is especially appropriate for nominal data and because it can also be used for higher order numbers, Chi-square may well be the single most frequently used statistical test in marketing research! For this reason, we will describe its use in some detail.

The beauty of the Chi-square test is that it is exceedingly simple to understand and almost as easy to compute. I have calculated χ^2s on backs of envelopes on airplanes, on my electronic calculator during a client meeting and, of course, innumerable times in the classroom. All that is needed is the raw frequency count (F_i) for each value of the variable you are analyzing and a corresponding expected frequency (E_i). The Chi-square technique then calculates the difference between these two, squares the result, and divides by the expected frequency. It then sums these calucations across all the values (cells) for the variable to get the total Chi-square value. (Division by the expected frequencies is a way of making sure a small absolute difference for a case with a lot of respondents expected in it is not given as much weight in the final result as the same absolute difference for a smaller cell.)

Comparison to a Given Distribution

Suppose we have the distribution of foreign and domestic automobiles currently owned by a sample of buyers visiting a New York City used car lot on a random sample of days and nights. We want to know whether this differs from what would be expected if we had obtained a random sample of all New York (or U.S.) car owners. Of our sample of 130 shoppers, 80 said they owned domestic cars, 30 owned Japanese cars and 20 were listed as "other." Suppose further that we have access to a published trade magazine study that says that, in New York, 54 percent of all registrations are domestic, 27 percent are Japanese, and the rest are from other countries. The question is, do the cars of *our* shoppers differ from the expected pattern? The Chi-square for this example is calculated in Table 10–1.

If the analysis is done by hand, the analyst then refers to a Chi-square table that indicates the likelihood of obtaining the calculated total Chi-square value (or greater) if the actual frequencies and the expected frequencies were really the same. (If one is using a computer, this probability will be printed on the output.) If the probability is very low, it means that results are clearly not what was expected. Conversely, subtracting the probability from 1 gives us the probability that the results are really different. For example, a Chi-square probability of .06 means

TABLE 10–1
Actual and Expected Automobile Ownership

Automobile Owned	Actual (F_i)	Expected (E_i)
Domestic	80	70
Japanese	30	35
Other	20	25
Total	130	130

$$\chi^2 = \Sigma\frac{(E_i - F_i)}{E_i} = \frac{(70 - 80)^2}{70}$$
$$+ \frac{(35 - 30)^2}{35} + \frac{(25 - 20)^2}{25} = 3.143$$

that there is a 6 percent chance the two distributions are really the same and a 94 percent chance they are not.

It is important to use the appropriate degrees of freedom when determining the probability. (The computer does this automatically.) In the example above, we estimated the expected number of cases for three cells. Since we started with the total of 130 cases, once we had calculated the expected frequencies in any *two* cells, the remaining cell has no freedom to assume any value at all; it is perfectly determined. Thus, two of the cells (i.e., their values) were free to take on any amount and one cell was not. Therefore, degrees of freedom in this case is two: the number of cells minus one. In a cross-tabulation, degrees of freedom is $(R-1)(C-1)$ where R is the number of cells in a row and C is the number of cells in a column.

Cross-Tabulations

A second research issue involving nominal values is whether two or more nominal categories are independent of each other or are associated. In the earlier example, we might ask whether the distribution of auto types differs between men and women. The Chi-square analysis procedure used in this case is very similar to that in the previous case and the formula is unchanged. That is, we are again simply asking the Chi-square analysis technique to tell us whether the actual results do or do not fit a model.

Suppose we had surveyed 80 men and 50 women in the study and their car ownership profiles were those reported on the left side of Table 10–2. Are these distributions affected by the sex of the shopper or are they independent? To answer this question, we must first construct a set of expectations for each of the cells in Table 10–2 and then go through the cells and, one by one, compute Chi-square values comparing expected to actual outcomes. As in all cross-tabulations, we are testing whether there is *no* relationship between the variables, i.e., they are independent. The first step is to figure out what the expected frequencies would be if the two variables were really independent. This is easy in that, if they were independent, the distribution within the sexes would be identical. Thus, in the present example, we would hypothesize that the proportion of domestic, Japanese, and other cars is the same for the two sexes.

In Table 10–2, we can see that only slightly over half the men (actually 54 percent) have domestic cars, but three quarters of the women do (74 percent). Therefore, we must ask: does the proportion owning domestic cars depend on one's sex or is any seeming association really just due to chance? The expected frequencies based on a no-difference model are given on the right hand side of Table 10–2. (Note that the marginal totals all around have to be the same for the actual and expected frequencies.)

TABLE 10–2
Automobile Ownership by Sex

Automobile Owned	Actual			Expected			
	Male	Female	Total	Male	Female	Total	Percent
Domestic	43	37	80	49.2	30.8	80	61.5
Japanese	22	8	30	18.5	11.5	30	23.1
Other	15	5	20	12.3	7.7	20	15.4
Total	80	50	130	80	50	130	100.00

$$\chi^2 = \frac{(43 - 49.2)^2}{49.2} + \frac{(37 - 30.8)^2}{30.8} + \frac{(22 - 18.5)^2}{18.5} + \frac{(8 - 11.5)^2}{11.5}$$
$$+ \frac{(15 - 12.3)^2}{12.3} + \frac{(5 - 7.7)^2}{7.7} = 5.27$$

The calculated χ^2 is 5.27. Is this significant? If we don't have a computer, we first need to know the degrees of freedom before looking up the table. As noted earlier, the degrees of freedom are just the number of cells in the rows minus one, multiplied by the number of columns minus one. In this case it is $(r-1)$ $(c-1) = 2$. (The correctness of this can be seen by arbitrarily filling two cells of the expected frequency section of Table 10–2. Note that the other four cells can only take on one value given the marginal totals.) In the present case, with two degrees of freedom, we would conclude that there is between a .9 and a .95 probability that the null hypothesis is not true, i.e., that there is a relationship between sex and automobile ownership. It is now up to the manager to decide whether this is enough certainty on which to act (i.e., to assume that female buyers are much better candidates for "great deals on your basic American automobile").

Some Caveats

There are two things to guard against in carrying out a Chi-square analysis since the computation of Chi-square is sensitive to (1) very small expected cell frequencies, and (2) large absolute sample sizes. To guard against the danger of small expected cell sizes, a good rule of thumb is that one should not calculate (or trust) a χ^2 when the expected frequency for any cell is five or less. Cells may be added together (collapsed) to meet the minimum requirement or, if this is not possible, Fisher's exact test may be used.

With respect to total sample size, it turns out that Chi-square is directly proportional to the number of cases used in its calculation. Thus, if one multiplied the cell values in Table 10–2 by 10, the calculated Chi-square value would be 10 times larger and, of course, very significant rather than barely significant as it is now. There are statistical corrections for large sample sizes that more experienced researchers use in such cases. The naive researcher should simply be aware that large sample sizes can result in bloated Chi-squares. And for this reason, he or she should be especially careful when comparing Chi-squares across studies where differences in significance levels may be due to nothing more than differences in sample sizes.

Metric Data: T-Tests

The next most frequently used statistical test in marketing is the T-test. Because it is only applicable to interval or ratio data, it is called a *parametric* test. It is used to compare two population estimations such as means or proportions and assess the probability that they are drawn from the same population. It is computed in slightly different ways depending on whether one is analyzing independent or nonindependent measures.

T-Test for Independent Measures
The T-test can be used to compare means or proportions from two independent samples. For example, the T-test can be used to indicate whether a sample of video rental customers in New York spent more per transaction than a sample in San Antonio. The procedure to conduct this test is first to use a procedure to estimate the (combined) standard errors of these means. (Remember that the standard error is a measure of the spread of a hypothetical series of means produced from the same sampling procedure carried out over and over again, e.g., in New York and San Antonio.) One then divides the difference between the means by the combined standard error (actually a combined standard error of difference in means).[4] This, in effect, indicates how many standard errors the two means are apart. The resulting figure is called a T-statistic if the sample size is small (i.e., under 30) and a Z-statistic if it is large. This statistic then allows us to say something about the probability that two means are really equal (i.e., drawn from a more general population of all customers). A low probability indicates they are different. The same analysis could be conducted comparing two proportions instead of two means.

Independent T-tests can also be used for two other purposes that are often important in research. First, they can test whether

---

[4]To combine the standard errors and conduct this test, the original data in the samples must be normally distributed and have equal variances. If one suspects these assumptions are not met (e.g., the computer printout or a simple graph says so), a more sophisticated analysis should be conducted.

a mean or proportion for a single sample is different from an expected value. Thus, for example, a researcher could determine whether the average household size in a sample differs from the Bureau of the Census figure for the area. Using this same logic, the T-test can also assess whether the coefficients in a multiple regression equation are really *zero* as indicated in Exhibit 10–2.

T-Test for Dependent Measures

Sometimes we wish to see whether the means or proportions for the answers to one question in a study are different from similar means or proportions elsewhere in the same study or in a later study of the same sample. For example, we may wish to know

---

Exhibit 10–2

Testing Regression Coefficients

Multiple regression equations are typically developed to produce a linear combination of significant predictors of some phenomenon. For example, one might develop an equation estimating the ability of age, family size, and/or education in combination to predict the average transaction size of customers at a particular video rental outlet.

The resulting equation will have coefficients for each factor (e.g., age or family size) that are used to produce the predicted transaction size for each respondent. For example, age might have an estimated coefficient of 7.3 cents, saying that for every year a person ages, they will spend 7.3 cents more on an average transaction, with the other factors in the equation held constant. In the process of estimating this coefficient, the typical computer program will also produce a T-statistic and probability which will help us conclude whether the coefficient of 7.3 is really zero. If the computer printout says that the probability is high that it is zero, then the researcher should be inclined to conclude that age is not a valuable predictor and ought to be dropped from the prediction equation (which then should be re-estimated).

---

whether respondents' estimates of the likely selling price of one new product concept is higher or lower than that of another concept. (Note that the means or proportions must be in the same units.) Since this procedure would compare respondents to themselves, the two measures are not independent. In this case, the computer takes each pair of respondent answers and computes a difference. It then produces a T-statistic and an associated probability that indicates the likelihood that the mean of all of the differences between pairs of answers is really zero. If the probability is low, we would conclude that the respondents did perceive the likely prices of the concepts as different.

Metric Data: Analysis of Variance (ANOVA)

One-Way ANOVA
Suppose we want to compare three or more means? That is, suppose we want to ask whether the mean transaction sizes for video rental customers are different across five cities. The parametric test we would use here is called one-way analysis of variance which is, in a sense, an extension of the T-test described above. It will be remembered that, for the T-test, we compared the difference between two means to an estimate of the random variance of those means (expressed as the standard error of the difference). The more general *analysis of variance* (ANOVA) technique proceeds in essentially the same way. It calculates a measure of variance across all the means (e.g., the five cities) and then compares this to a measure of random variance, in this case the combined variances within the five cities. Specifically, ANOVA divides the variance across the cities by the variance within cities to produce a test statistic and a probability of significance. The test statistic here is called an *F-ratio* (of which the T-ratio or T-statistic is a special case). Again, a low probability and a high F-statistic is interpreted to mean that the variance across the cities is greater than chance.

Note that we did not conclude that any one city is different from any other specific city; only that there was significant variance among them all. We may have a hypothesis that a specific pair of cities are different. In this case, of course, we would simply have the computer run a T-test on the difference between the two means.

N-Way ANOVA

Analysis of variance is probably most often used as the primary statistical tool for analyzing the results of experiments. It is highly flexible and can be used for quite complicated designs.

Consider by way of illustration, a simple study of the effects on weekly total sales in a women's clothing store of (1) offering or not offering free coffee, and (2) using each of four different types of background music. Suppose the researcher conducted a fully factorial experiment (i.e., every possible combination) in which each of the four kinds of music was tried out for a specified period of time at sample stores with and without a free beverage service. Hypothetical results for each of the eight combinations offered in five stores for each cell are shown in Table 10–3.

N-way analysis of variance proceeds to analyze these results in the same way as we did in one-way ANOVA. We first compute an estimate of random variance, in this case the combination of the variances within each of the eight cells. We (actually a computer) then calculate *three* tests for significant effects. Recalling the discussion in Chapter 7, the computer program asks:

1. Is there a main effect due to having the beverages present or not, i.e., is the variance across the two beverage conditions significantly greater than the random variance when the music treatments are controlled?
2. Is there a main effect due to the different music types (ignoring beverage treatment)?
3. Is there an interaction effect due to the combination of music and beverage service; that is, are the results in each of the eight treatment cells higher or lower than would be predicted from simply adding the two main effects together?

In each case, the computer reports an F-statistic and a probability of *no* effects. A glance at the means for the various cells in Table 10–3 shows that (1) beverages yield more sales than no beverages, (2) semi-classical music yields the most sales and

TABLE 10–3
Sales Results of Hypothetical Experiment (Sales in $1,000)

Music Type	Beverages	No Beverages	Music Mean
Classical	122	98	
	136	106	
	153	111	
	109	103	
	120	94	
	$\bar{X}_{11} = 128.0$	$\bar{X}_{12} = 102.4$	$\bar{X}_{1.} = 115.2$
Semi-classical	136	111	
	127	119	
	104	104	
	131	121	
	136	110	
	$\bar{X}_{21} = 126.8$	$\bar{X}_{22} = 113.0$	$\bar{X}_{2.} = 119.9$
Middle of the road	97	110	
	110	120	
	95	113	
	107	131	
	122	106	
	$\bar{X}_{31} = 106.2$	$\bar{X}_{32} = 116.0$	$\bar{X}_{3.} = 111.1$
Contemporary pop	86	99	
	85	101	
	93	110	
	78	90	
	93	95	
	$\bar{X}_{41} = 87.0$	$\bar{X}_{42} = 99.0$	$\bar{X}_{4.} = 93.0$
Beverage mean	$\bar{X}_{.1} = 112.0$	$\bar{X}_{.2} = 107.6$	$\bar{X}_{..} = 109.8$

contemporary pop the least, and (3) beverages added to classical or semi-classical music increase sales, but when added to contemporary or pop music *decrease* sales. Are these results statistically significant? The ANOVA results for the data in Table 10–3 are as follows:

	Sum of Squares	Df	Mean Square	F-ratio	Probability
Music main effect	4151.0	3	1383.67	12.764	.000
Beverage main effect	193.6	1	193.60	1.786	.191
Interaction effect	2521.0	3	840.33	7.752	.000
Error	3468.8	32	108.40		

Here, we see that the type of music does have a significant effect: the differences in means with the beverage treatment controlled seem to be real. However, despite appearances, the presence or absence of beverages has no effect. Finally, there is an interaction effect which does indicate that the combination of beverages and classical or semi-classical music is the manager's best bet. It may be that the two create a much more desirable ambience. At least our statistics kept us from concluding that beverages by themselves would be a good addition.

Association: Non-Metric and Metric Data

In many cases, the researcher will wish to know whether variables are associated with each other, either singly or in sets. If variables are associated, we may be able to use one variable or set of variables to predict another. Further, if we have some plausible prior theory, we may also say that one variable or set of variables explains or causes the other (although one must always remember that association is not causation). We have already discussed nominal measures of association using Chi-square. Other measures of association can be computed for both ranked data and metric data.

Ordinal Data: Spearman Rank Order Correlation

Spearman's rank order correlation procedure can compare the rankings of two variables, for example, a department store's rankings on sales personnel knowledge and product quality. Spearman's Rho coefficient indicates whether a higher ranking on one variable is associated with a higher (or lower) ranking on some other variable. If the two rankings move in the same direction, the sign of Rho will be positive. If the rankings move in opposite directions, Rho will have a negative sign. In either case, Rho can range between zero and one; the closer to one, the more we can conclude that the rankings really are associated.

Metric Data: Pearson Product Moment Correlation

This approach seeks the same result as the Spearman analysis, but is used for interval or ratio-scaled variables. The Pearson

FIGURE 10–5
Two Hypothetical Regression Lines

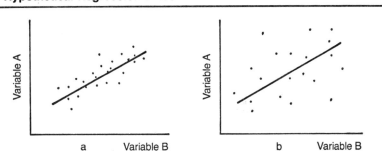

correlation coefficient, called *r*, can be positive or negative and range from 0 to 1. Most computer programs will produce both the Pearson *r* and a probability that the actual value of *r* is zero.

Metric Data: Simple Correlations
Another use of the Pearsonian correlation coefficient is as a measure of the extent to which a straight line plotted through the points representing pairs of measurements fits the data poorly (and has a low *r*) or rather well (and therefore has a high *r*). Figure 10–5 shows a line with a good fit and a line with a poor fit.

Metric Data: Multiple Regression
If one variable is good at predicting or explaining another variable, the researcher may wish to look further to see whether an additional second or third variable will help improve this explanatory power. Multiple linear regression is the technique most often used for this. In a manner similar to simple two-variable correlation described above, multiple regression seeks to construct a linear combination of two or more independent variables (that may be metric or dichotomous[5]) that predict the value of a dependent metric variable. An example would be using age,

---

[5]A dichotomous variable is a special case of a nominal variable where the values zero and one are used to indicate the presence or absence of some charateristic, e.g., being a woman or being married.

income, education, size of household, and sex to predict the amount a person would spend on a visit to a women's clothing store.

If one has a great many variables that *might* be used in such a multiple regression, but the researcher is not sure which to use, there are two basic approaches to finding the best set (using a computer).

Theory driven. The researcher can specify the set of variables in advance—usually on the basis of some theory about which variables ought to predict well. Since the computer will print out a T-statistic measure indicating the probability that the coefficient for any given variable is really zero, the researcher can then look at the initial output and eliminate predictors with high probabilities of being nonsignificant and rerun the analysis. This may have to be done two or three times before the final best set of predictor variables is determined.

Data-driven (stepwise regression). Alternatively, the researcher can ask the computer to look for the best set of predictors among what is usually a very large set of candidate variables using a procedure called *stepwise regression analysis*. Under this procedure, the computer takes the original variance in the dependent variable and proceeds to enter into the equation the predictor with the highest explanatory power (e.g., the highest simple r). It then subtracts out the variance explained by this variable, computes new correlations of each remaining potential predictor variable and the adjusted dependent variable, and then picks the variable with the highest correlation at this step. In this manner, variables from the candidate set are added to the prediction equation until they are all exhausted or some predetermined stopping point is reached (such as when the variance about to be explained at the next step is less than 1 percent).

Stepwise regression is a good technique when one is at the exploratory stage of a study. However, care should be taken with stepwise regression since it has properties that make it possible that a truly significant predictor will be missed because it happens to be highly correlated with a variable entered at an early step in the analysis. Further, if the sample is large enough, researchers should test the model eventually discovered on a different subsample from the one on which it was developed.

Once the multiple regression analysis is done, the researcher will wish to look at three measures produced by the computer program:

Multiple R.   This statistic measures how well the equation fits the data. The probability that this statistic is really zero is important as an indicator that the equation really does predict.

Multiple R^2.   This measure is analogous to the Pearsonian r^2. It indicates the proportion of variance in the dependent variable accounted for by the linear combination of the predictor variables. It is as important as the probability of the multiple R being zero. If one has a large data set, it is often possible to have a highly significant multiple R for an equation that explains very little of the variance in the dependent variable!

Standardized Variable Coefficients.   The researcher will also wish to know the relative contribution of each of the independent variables to the overall prediction equation. One could look at the relative size of the coefficients for each predictor variable to try to learn this, but this would be misleading because the variables are usually in different units (e.g., the coefficient for income may be very small because income is expressed in 1,000s or 10,000s of dollars while sex may have a large coefficient because it can be only 0 or 1). The solution to this dilemma is to convert all of the variables into standard deviation units. The resulting *Beta coefficients* (as they are called) are simply the original coefficients (often called *B coefficients*) divided by the respective standard deviations (see Exhibit 10–1). Those variables with larger beta coefficients can be considered to make more contribution to the overall prediction than those with smaller coefficients.

OTHER MULTIVARIATE TECHNIQUES

Many researchers may already be familiar with the techniques just described and would like to move on to more sophisticated analyses. It is not appropriate to treat more advanced techniques in depth in this volume. However, to acquaint the reader with some of the possibilities, several of the major alternatives will be described briefly. At the end of the chapter, the reader is referred to other sources for further detailed information on the various approaches. A general, useful, nontechnical book to which the ambitious reader may wish to turn for a good overview is *Multivariate Data Analysis: An Introduction,* by Barbara Bund Jackson.

Factor Analysis

Many measurements in a study will be related. In studies with very large databases, it will often be very valuable to ask whether the measures obtained can be reduced to a smaller set of underlying factors to which each of a set of measurements is related. Factor analysis investigates the correlations among measurements and provides the researcher with one or more factors that apparently underlie the data. Factor analysis looks at all the variables in a set simultaneously. None is specified as a dependent or independent measure.

An example of the use of factor analysis is that recently carried out by the United Way of America to help its 297 local chapters evaluate their performance against other comparable local chapters. In the past, chapters had been compared to others like themselves only in total market size. But United Way realized that comparing a city in an economically troubled part of Pennsylvania to a city of the same size in booming Arizona or Florida made little sense. They sought to develop measures that would better describe differences in markets. To do this, the Research Division in the Alexandria, Virginia office of United Way of America assembled 92 indicators on each of its 297 solicitation areas, in part using several of the secondary sources mentioned in Chapter 5. The Research Division then used a factor analysis computer program to reduce this unwieldy set of

92 indicators to a manageable set of five basic factors that seemed to capture much of the complexity of the local social and economic profiles. The five factors were:

1. An income/affluence factor.
2. A type-of-employment/labor-force-structure factor.
3. A factor indicating the relative preponderance of impoverished and/or minority communities.
4. A growth rate factor.
5. A factor indicating the relative age of adults and presence of children in area households.

Note that the labels for the factors were added by the researcher and were not automatically produced by the computer program.

Cluster Analysis

Very often marketers would like to know whether members of a large set of objects being studied (e.g., respondents, stores, countries, and so on) clump together in groups exhibiting relatively homogeneous characteristics. Cluster analysis is designed for this type of problem. It takes whatever information the researcher has on each object and proceeds to develop groupings that maximize the homogeneity within the groups and heterogeneity across the groups. Again, no variable is dependent or independent. In top-down clustering, the analysis begins with all objects in one large group and proceeds to split the group step by step until some homogeneity/heterogeneity level is reached. In bottom-up clustering, the program begins with each object in its own group and proceeds to combine them into groups until the specified stopping point is reached.

The United Way used cluster analysis to partition its 297 local solicitation areas into 12 relatively homogeneous groups based on their scores on the five factors mentioned above. The clusters range in size from 7 to 51 communities. Organizations within clusters now can share performance data and experiences with greater confidence that they are dealing with others facing very much the same kind of market challenges they are.

Discriminant Analysis

Simple and multiple correlation analyses typically have metric measurements on their dependent variables. But sometimes marketers may have a nominal measure that is of interest. Discriminant analysis is a technique similar to regression in that it develops a set of variables that best helps marketers predict whether a given case (i.e., respondent) falls into a particular nominal category.

For example, suppose the United Way wished to understand what variables differentiate three groups; (1) nondonors, (2) new donors, and (3) repeat donors. Discriminant analysis can be used to determine the best combination of predictors of group membership. As with multiple regression, the analysis can also indicate the relative importance of each of the predictor variables in the final solution.

The equation that predicts group membership is called a discriminant function. One complication of discriminant analysis is that there can be more than one discriminant function if the researcher is trying to discriminate among more than two groups. A second important difference from regression is that discriminate analysis does not produce a statistic like R^2 which indicates how well the discriminant function(s) predicts. Typically, researchers take as a measure of success how often the final function(s) correctly predicts a subject's true group membership.

Multidimensional Scaling

Marketers are often interested in understanding how objects in a group are perceived in relationship to each other by target consumers. A brand manufacturer will be interested in understanding which other brands are most and least similar to it in consumers' minds and what these consumers are using as the key dimensions in evaluating the entire set of brands. Multidimensional scaling is a technique used to position objects in some physical or perceptual space. It does so by analyzing one of three kinds of measures: (1) objective measures of an object's characteristics such as an automobile's MPG, acceleration time from 0 to 60 MPH, base price and so on; (2) subjective measures of an object's characteristics such as perceptions of the automobile's quality, road handling, and styling; or (3) subjective measures of similarity or dissimilarity among the objects, letting respondents use whatever dimensions they wish to use to determine those relationships. In all three cases, the computer analysis routine produces a map of the objects relating them in geometric space along one or more underlying dimensions (in a sense like factor analysis). It is then up to the researcher to label these underlying dimensions. When the raw data analyzed include subjective perceptions, the result is sometimes referred to as a *perceptual map.*

Multidimensional scaling studies that use subjective input in the form of either object ratings or similarities judgments can also ask respondents about their ideal object (e.g., their ideal automobile). An automobile industry researcher can then look at which respondents have ideal automobiles near to the researcher's own make (i.e., their natural constituency) or see whether there are sets of respondents with no automobiles near their ideal points. The latter would comprise a potential target for an entirely new product offering.

Conjoint Analysis

A great many consumer choices involve trade-offs between features possessed by different alternatives. For example, when considering which supermarket to use as a major source of groceries, a consumer might have a real set of choices available like the following:

Supermarket A: high prices, good produce, average meat quality, poor parking, short driving time.

Supermarket B: medium prices, poor meat quality, average produce, ample parking, short driving time.

Supermarket C: very low prices, poor produce, good meat quality, ample parking, long driving time.

The consumer's preference ranking of these three alternatives will depend on the extent to which he or she is willing to trade off, for example, poorer produce and a longer drive for lower prices.

Conjoint analysis is a technique for exploring these trade-offs. In a conjoint study, objects such as products, services, or outlets are described in terms of attributes to be traded off. Consumers rank sets of these objects and then the conjoint analysis routine proceeds to indicate the relative value respondents attach to each of the different dimensions. It will also indicate (1) which combination of the specified attributes will be most attractive to the entire population (including combinations not offered in the study), and (2) which consumers will find an existing or proposed combination of attributes most appealing.

Multivariate Analysis of Variance

Often a researcher in an experimental study may wish to see whether there are differences across groups in some set of metric characteristics rather than a single characteristic as in an ANOVA design. In the analysis of variance (ANOVA) example presented earlier, the effects of beverage availability and music type were studied with respect to one outcome: total sales in a women's clothing store. But suppose the researcher wishes to look at the effect of the two types of treatment on:

1. Average length of time spent in a store.
2. Total sales of high-priced clothing.
3. Total sales of accessories.
4. The ratio of items sold at full price to items sold at a marked-down price.

The manager will be interested in this combination of outcomes. Multivariate Analysis of Variance (MANOVA) proceeds in much the same way as ANOVA with similar outputs to answer this question.

REFERENCES

1. Zeisel, Hans. *Say It With Figures.* 5th ed. New York: Harper & Row, 1968.

2. Loether, Herman J., and Donald G. McTavish. *Descriptive Statistics for Sociologists: An Introduction.* Boston: Allyn & Bacon, 1976.
3. Siegel, Sidney. *Nonparametric Statistics for the Behavioral Sciences.* New York: McGraw-Hill, 1950.
4. Jackson, Barbara Bund. *Multivariate Data Analysis: An Introduction.* Homewood, Ill.: Richard D. Irwin, 1983.
5. Sethi, S.P. "Comparative Cluster Analysis for World Markets." *Journal of Marketing Research,* August 1971, pp. 348–354.

SECTION 4

ORGANIZING LOW-COST RESEARCH

CHAPTER 11

ORGANIZATION AND IMPLEMENTATION ON A SHOESTRING

In the preceeding chapters, we outlined both a procedure for planning and implementing a program of low-cost research and a wide ranging set of techniques for actually carrying it out. It was intended that the reader come away from these materials highly motivated to begin or to expand a program of low-cost research. At this point, the major tools that ought to be in the beginner's research arsenal have been presented and some of the psychological and informational barriers to moving forward, one hopes, have been dissipated.

It is now time to tackle the very serious problem of just how to get it all done, particularly within a very limited budget. The glib answer is, of course, to beg or borrow as much as possible and keep the costs of the research as low as possible with the constraint that one always has an obligation to management to provide good as well as cheap research. However, in reality, the task of system-building is more complex. To see some of the ways in which it may be possible to keep costs down, we need to list the basic requirements for carrying out a beginner's research program. These requirements can be roughly divided into three categories: *ideas, people,* and *things.* A partial list of some of the requirements in each of these categories is outlined in Exhibit 11–1.

We will consider some of the tactics available to the low-cost researcher in each of these categories.

EXHIBIT 11–1

Resources Needed for an Extended Program of Marketing Research

1. Money to supplement the manager's limited budget.
2. Know-how to do the following:
   a. Learn from management what decisions they need to make and what information will help them make those decisions.
   b. Estimate the costs and benefits of research.
   c. Develop protocols for observation.
   d. Design experiments.
   e. Design sampling plans.
   f. Write questionnaires.
   g. Train a field force and their supervisors.
   h. Write coding manuals/schemes.
   i. Design and carry out statistical analyses (including any computer programming necessary).
   j. Run focus groups.
   k. Write reports (including preparation of graphics—possibly a separate skill).
   l. Present the results and see that they are implemented.
3. Personnel to do the following:
   a. Conduct and/or supervise interviews.
   b. Mail and follow up questionnaires.
   c. Carry out experiments.
   d. Conduct observations.
   e. Code results.
   f. Enter results.
   g. Run computer programs.
   h. Produce final reports and presentation materials.
   i. Collect and analyze archives.
4. Equipment and facilities:
   a. Rooms for experiments or focus groups.
   b. Telephone equipment (including monitoring facilities) for interviewing.
   c. Computers for:
      (1) Cover letters for mail studies.
      (2) Questionnaires.
      (3) Statistical analyses.
      (4) Report writing and graph preparation.
   d. Software for word-processing, analyses, report publication and graph preparation.
   e. Mailing lists or other materials for sampling.
   f. Libraries for secondary source material.

FINANCIAL ASSISTANCE

Assuming the research manager has been assigned a modest budget for a program of research, how can it be augmented? Several sources of additional funding can be explored.

Immediate Superiors

Chapter 2 outlined an approach in which the knowledgeable and persuasive research manager could demonstrate to management the benefits from additional expenditures on research that will more than justify those expenditures. The research manager needs to follow those steps to get the manager who approved the intitial basic research budget to supplement it because of the value this will bring. The first step is to begin a long-term campaign to educate the manager in the benefit/cost approach to research funding that we have developed here. The manager must learn to appreciate the extent to which the provision of some information in many situations will help make for better decisions even if the stakes are low. The manager must learn that inexpensive information can be very helpful when he or she is most unsure as to what to do.

One problem is that one's superiors may be inhibited by the myths outlined in Chapter 1. The research manager should undertake a subtle, but purposeful, campaign to destroy them. In addition, management should become aware of many of the low-cost research possibilities outlined in this book. At the same time, following suggestions in Chapter 2, the researcher should constantly look for opportunities to point out over and over again how a particular problem that management has just confronted can be helped by research. In a sense, the research manager should force serendipity.

One technique that may be helpful in this regard is the *Unauthorized Cheap But Good Research Demonstration Project.* An occasion may appear when the research manager senses an opportunity to demonstrate (not just describe) how research can help improve a particular management decision. If at all feasible, the researcher should surreptitiously carry through a pilot study of modest proportions using existing funds focused on this decision. While such a strategy is risky, it is hoped that the results of the ad hoc study will be so compelling that management will grant ex-post authorization of the budget to the daring researcher. Peters and Waterman indicate that one of the hallmarks of a well-run organization is its tolerance of organizational mavericks.[1] The researcher might wish to casually lay a copy of *In Search of Excellence* in the manager's in-box.

Other Organization Divisions

If the low-budget researcher is employed by a multidivision enterprise, other low-budget researchers may well be hidden elsewhere in the organization. Jointly undertaken projects typically can achieve much greater payoff than would be possible from each budget separately. On the other hand, it may be that other company divisions may not appreciate the possibilities of research at all. If this is the case, the researcher could from time to time add a few questions to planned studies to suggest the value of research to other divisions. Subsequently, financial contributions for projects could be solicited initially on a marginal cost basis. Once one joint venture is successful, other divisions could be enticed to join the enterprise.

Competitors

There may be certain kinds of projects where participation by competitors (who would obviously share in the findings) would be better than no research at all. For example, a joint study on the effectiveness of industry advertising or distribution channels might appeal to multiple participants. If such projects are to be mounted, any of the firms involved could manage it, for example, the one with the most experience in the type of research contemplated. Alternatively, a joint task force could be established. While this can lead to conflict and, in my experience, will inevitably delay the project, it will at least ensure that each contributor has a say in what the final research design looks like,

---

[1]Thomas J. Peters and Robert H. Waterman, Jr. *In Search of Excellence: Lessons from America's Best-Run Companies* (New York: Harper & Row, 1982).

thus increasing the likelihood they will participate. Of course, the disadvantage of this type of low-budget financing is that there is no confidentiality.

Suppliers or Distributors

Other organizations in the firm's manufacturing/distribution system may be persuaded to participate in a research project that would benefit mutual interests. Despite this mutuality, there is still the possibility that competitors would learn about the project. However, if projects can be designed that are of clear benefit to other intermediaries, they may well be willing to maintain confidentiality.

Trade Associations

Going to competitors or others in the distribution channel may raise antitrust questions in addition to confidentiality problems. Further, joint projects may be aborted or compromised due to wrangling over who is in charge, what gets done, who does it, and how the results are to be used. If these are likely to be problems, it may be useful to induce the industry trade association to take on the projects. If an association does not exist, an accounting firm or university may be persuaded to perform the same function. The obvious advantages are several, not the least of which is that there may be certain cost economies inherent in the tax-free status of the nonprofit association. Further, to the extent intra-industry data will be involved, having the project under the aegis of an association or university may increase respondent participation and candor. Further, the association may be anxious to help if it sees a research study, especially a continuing study, to be a benefit it can offer to those firms who will affiliate in future. For this reason, it is possible that the association may wish to contribute some of its *own* funds to a study from which it will benefit.

Unrelated Organizations

The final, least likely, possibility is that the researcher may encounter other organizations or individuals who are interested in possibly conducting research. For example, a paper products distributor, a food machinery manufacturer, and a meat packer may all be interested in surveying restaurateurs. In such cases, a joint, relatively significant research venture would be feasible. It obviously will require considerable enterprise to discover such a critical mass of participants.

ACQUIRING KNOWLEDGE

All of the activities of a year-long program of research activity can be carried out by the researcher and a separately dedicated staff. Alternatively, virtually all can be carried out by outside agencies. There exist full-service market research agencies that can do virtually any activity a researcher wishes to carry out, as well as organizations and individuals who specialize in certain specific marketing research functions such as conducting focus groups (or focus group recruiting), telephone interviewing, laboratory experimentation, computer programming and statistical analysis, preparation of graphics and so on. Many of these outside suppliers have close competitors, a few have their own proprietary approaches (e.g., unique methods of new product testing

A survey of major U.S. marketing organizations carrying out various kinds of research indicates that consumer products companies were more likely to farm out research than were industrial or financial marketers. The following percentages of budgets were spent for outside research:[2]

Industry	Percent
Consumer products	53
Industrial products	18
Financial services	22
Advertising agencies	36

[2]Dik Warren Twedt, ed., *1983 Survey of Marketing Research,* (Chicago: American Marketing Association, 1983), p. 32.

It will be recalled from Table 2–1 that consumer researchers spend almost five or six times as much as industrial or financial organizations. Advertising research is the task most often farmed out to outside agencies followed by consumer panel research. Unfortunately, there are no data indicating which functions are most often delegated to outsiders by major firms. In my experience, most business organizations do not do their own field interviewing. Field work requires specially trained people who would only be put to work from time to time as needed. Managing such a significant part-time labor force does not appeal to most firms. Outside field research agencies can achieve significant scale economies in such activities that individual firms cannot. Again, because of the specialized skills involved, focus group interviewing is also frequently contracted out, although here it is as often to individuals as to firms.

It is most likely, however, that a beginning researcher with a limited budget will have little financial capacity for hiring a great deal of outside know-how. However, there are a number of other lower cost (sometimes free) sources of assistance that can be utilized. Several of these are covered below in an ascending order of difficulty of acquisition:

Your Own Organization

If your organization has other divisions that in some way work with or prepare analyses or reports, you may be able to secure their assistance. Other divisions or departments that can be accessed are:

Long-Range Planning. There may be economists or others in a long-range planning group with advanced social science training who can be helpful with some kinds of statistical analysis. Economists in particular are likely to be familiar with regression, correlation, and such arcane topics as confidence intervals.

Production Planning/Quality Control. Those who have been trained in these two areas may be familiar with concepts of experimental design and tests of significance (i.e., whether 12 defects per hour constitute a serious quality control problem).

Advertising or Marketing.   Recently hired MBAs with marketing majors may have been exposed to marketing research (possibly) or statistics (probably) courses in their graduate programs.

Electronic Data Processing/Accounting.   These departments will frequently have computer programming experts and/or individuals familiar with handling large data sets.

Public Relations.   These specialists are often skilled in producing newsletters and reports. They may be able to help with graphics, report design, and the like. They may also be familiar with—or can help the researcher evaluate—so-called desktop publishing computer software (to be mentioned below).

Secretarial/Word Processing.   Here is a good place to get advice on word processing software. It may also be a place where one can acquire a secretary who is adept at producing specialized research reports, complex tables, figures, and the like.

Local Colleges and Universities
Institutions with programs in undergraduate or graduate business and economics can be very helpful in several ways.

Professors.   Professors have been known to do consulting and may be hired at less-than-market rates (sometimes *free* consulting help) if the professor believes there will be something publishable or something valuable for the classroom in the work. While business researchers are rightfully concerned about confidentiality of their own studies, most proprietary data can be well disguised for publication or classroom use (the professor will almost always agree to this *in writing,* if you wish). Further, the assistance may well be worth some small potential that information will be leaked to competitors.

The researcher should not be limited for possible sources of help to business schools or economics departments. Psychology or education departments may have people with experimental design, computer, or statistical skills. They may also provide focus group leaders with good group dynamics skills and/or psychological insight. Anthropologists may be helpful in observation studies.

The beginning researcher, however, should be cautious about some hidden costs of hiring professors. If they are not paid or paid at rates under the market, they may not feel under pressure to meet deadlines the researcher sets.

Graduate Students. At institutions with advanced degree programs, master's or doctoral candidates are typically impecunious. Even when they have tuition assistance or support from the school, they almost always need supplemental income. Graduate students can be particularly helpful in implementation (rather than design) roles, especially if they are used in areas where they may have technical training, such as computer programming or statistical analysis. However, one should be cautious abut engaging callow youths, even if they have MBAs or are working on Ph.D.s, to provide advice on problem formulation and research design where seasoned experience is a job requirement.

Assistance to Nonprofits

Researchers in nonprofit organizations can avail themselves of help unavailable to others except at considerable cost. An enterprising nonprofit researcher could tap the following sources.

Pro-bono Professionals. A selected number of professional fields have an ethic that encourages their members to donate their time to voluntary service in worthy causes. For example, the nonprofit research director could seek help from the major accounting firms since they have considerable experience at massive data handling. They typically have computer programmers and statisticians on staff and possibly specialists in report writing whom they may be willing to lend free of charge to the nonprofit organization. An area in which accountants can be of special help is in archival analysis. Their auditors take great pride in being able to delve into records to learn the hidden secrets of an organization. They can have excellent suggestions on where to look for unsuspected marketing insights.

Volunteer Board Members.   Key executives in the private sector have traditionally volunteered to serve on the boards of directors of nonprofit organizations. While some of these board memberships are intended more to add to the executive's resumé or to facilitate business contacts with other board members, in the main, board members can be very hard workers and very helpful. In my experience, nonprofit managers are much more likely to think of stocking their boards with politicians, lawyers, accountants, and heavyweight fundraisers rather than marketing experts. They rarely think of adding research experts. It may not be easy for the research director to convince nonprofit managers of the desirability of having the head of a local multiservice marketing research agency on the board, especially if he or she is seen as potentially taking the place of someone more valuable. However, such individuals can be immensely helpful to the research operation. They can provide direct advice themselves. They can encourage (or assign) their own junior staffers to provide technical advice. They can provide volunteer staff for certain tasks, access to computer equipment and/or software, and opportunities for piggybacking research.

One of the most valuable roles they can serve for the research manager is in *changing the attitudes of top management.* The research manager may have limited influence over the way the organization plans and sets policy. However, an independent, experienced outside director trained in marketing research can keep pointing out to top management how research can help this segmentation decision, that new service decision, that forecasting problem and so on. This intervention will eventually do much to promote business for the research manager. At the very least, the researcher on the board will gradually change the climate so that the research director's future proposals will be better understood and appreciated and, eventually, more often acted on.

Retired Executives.   Many retired executives are anxious to keep active and to use their skills in work they feel is socially productive. In the United States, the Service Corps of Retired Executives has had a long tradition of providing government-sponsored help to small and nonprofit enterprises. While such executives may not be versed in the latest computer and statistical niceties, they can be wise and experienced counselors for the researcher thinking about different ways of formulating and researching management problems.

ACQUIRING PERSONNEL

Research takes people, often a considerable number. As noted earlier, it may be preferable for management to hire outside skills for certain research tasks because these tasks require unusual, precise skills and/or because these skills can be obtained at much less cost (including learning time) than would be involved if the researcher tried to do the task inside the organization. Several additional options are available for low cost/free help.

Volunteers

Most nonprofits and some for-profits (such as hospitals) have volunteers available to them who work anywhere from a few to many hours a week. These volunteers can be used for many of the low-skill research tasks described elsewhere in this volume.

- Address and stuff envelopes for mail questionnaires, keep track of mail returns, and initiate follow-up-mailings.
- Hand out or drop off self-report questionnaires.
- Carry out simple observations such as counting customers stopping at a particular display, counting cars in a competitor's parking lot, or writing down (and later looking up the residence associated with) license plates in a mall parking lot.
- Transcribe archival records, such as addresses in a visitor's guest book or information from expense account vouchers.
- Clip competitive information, such as articles or advertisements from local newspapers or magazines.
- Assist in experiments.
- Do simple analyses if a computer is unavailable.

With training, of course, volunteers can be given more specialized and responsible tasks, such as conducting telephone or personal interviews, coding questionnnaires, carrying out experiments or processing data. Of course, the training component is crucial. At first appearance, volunteers would seem like the ideal low-cost resource. They are often overeducated for the tasks to which you wish to assign them. Some of them will be very dedicated. Volunteers are not, however, without their costs. Those who volunteer often are very difficult to manage. One executive I know has said that he has a "rule of thirds" for volunteers. One third will work very hard without much supervision and encouragement; one third will work if given the right incentives and directions; and one third will hardly work at all.

Part of the difficulty can be laid to the education, social status, and motivation of many volunteers. Many believe that the organization should be very grateful for their help and so are very patronizing in their attitudes. This often leads them to disdain certain kinds of work ("Stuff envelopes—are you kidding; I have a graduate degree in art!"). Others, because they feel they earn more elsewhere or are better educated than the research manager, may argue about the way things are done or go off on their own and try to do things in a better way.

For many activities, relatively poor performance by volunteers may not matter greatly (i.e., stuffing envelopes). However, it is more often the case in research that perseverance and attention to detail are critical if one wishes to draw a representative sample, ask unbiased questions, prove causation, or perform a precise analysis. For this reason, the research manager should be careful about using volunteers unless (1) they are to be trained carefully; (2) it is made perfectly clear to them what standards of performance are expected; and (3) they are told that anyone not performing to the extent and at the quality level the research requires will be "fired." Volunteers usually respond very favorably to being treated as responsible professionals who have an obligation to their organization to do excellent work.

Students

We have already noted that advanced students can be hired by researchers who need specific knowledge skills. Students can also serve as temporary help in carrying out many (or all) of the day-to-day tasks on research studies. There are four academic vehicles for this.

Case Studies

Many professors in management or marketing classes require their students to undertake a real-world case study as a term project. These may be specialized in areas like consumer behavior or marketing research. Typically, these projects are required in advanced courses taken by senior undergraduates or second year MBAs. While many students will already know what organization or problem they wish to study, many are at a loss or are at least open to suggestions by a researcher who contacts them.

Work-Study Programs

Some institutions like Northeastern University in Boston have a work-study program in which students attend class part of the time and work part of the time. While the low-budget researcher would have to pay work study participants to help out on a research project, such workers may command relatively low wages while having a sophistication and an intellectual interest not found in typical part-time employees.

Independent Studies

Many schools permit students alone or in teams to put together independent study projects equal to one or two courses. These could easily be defined to incorporate a specific research project.

Masters and Doctoral Theses

Not all schools have Masters' thesis requirements anymore, although they are more commonly found in Europe. Masters' theses are typically less scientific and less often need to be intellectually earthshaking than Ph.D. theses. A proper match with the low-budget researchers' needs may be possible. Such a match is usually much less likely for a doctoral dissertation. The objective of a doctoral dissertation is to advance some scientific theory or to perfect some methodology. In some rare cases, the doctoral student may be interested in obtaining a real-world site at which to develop data or test a model or some methodology.

If these opportunities appeal to the low-cost researcher, the first step in securing student help would be to write a general letter to the deans of local schools of business indicating an interest in matching organizational research needs and the academic needs of the school and its faculty. A brief description of the organization should be included as well as a general overview of the kinds of projects in which the firm would be interested. An offer should be made to visit the school and discuss the possibilities further with interested faculty. If the school is interested (the dean will likely pass your letter on to relevant staff), the researcher may be asked either to come by or to write a second, more precise description of the company and its current concerns to be circulated to potentially interested students.

As in the case of volunteers, students do not come without costs. Even though they are likely to be at advanced stages of a business program, one should not expect great wisdom and experience or even a great deal of technical competence (except for doctoral students or individuals with special skills such as programming). Further, there are some disadvantages to using students.

1. Students will be interested in the project because of its potential for learning. Thus, the researcher should be prepared to waste some time with them to educate them about the organization and how research is carried out in the real world.

2. They are not employees. Even with volunteers, the organization can exert a great deal of control over what is done. With students, there has to be mutual agreement as to objectives. Managers should be careful not to treat students as if they were employees and, especially, not leave them to do only routine jobs. Students will stuff envelopes if they see it as a reasonable cost of their real-world education or if they see that the organization is picking up its share of the "scut work"

3. Students have other obligations. As a consequence, they may not work as fast as the organization wants and may miss meetings and deadlines that are important.

4. Projects will have to fit into a semester or quarter timetable (except for theses and independent study projects). Students should not be expected to undertake major long-term projects.

5. Students can sometimes be arrogant (especially those from some of the more elite institutions). They will have been exposed to what their professors have been telling them is the very latest management and marketing concepts and technology. If the researcher or organization is not using this technology or is not enthusiastic about it (or, worse still, doesn't *know* about it), students may become patronizing or attempt, none-too-subtly, to offer enlightenment. (This, of course, is sometimes also a problem working with the professors themselves!) For the new research manager this may be a special problem if he or she is still a bit insecure in using new research techniques. On the other hand, a researcher may occasionally find the students to be adept teachers.

Government Services and Public Librarians

To the extent the organization is seeking secondary source data, public libraries and government organizations, such as the Departments of Agriculture and Commerce and the Bureau of Labor, may be willing to do some of the background legwork. Librarians with access to on-line database information retrieval systems may be able to provide the expertise usually needed to cope with these systems and may actually carry out low-cost computerized information searches for the novice researcher.

Database Research Services

If a librarian cannot help, there are now available a number of services that the researcher can pay to do secondary source analyses or to carry out archival research, for example, providing citations to articles by and about competitors or a new technology. Some services may also provide on-line reproduction of the articles themselves.

Salespeople

It is very tempting for a researcher with a low budget who wishes to get data from the marketplace or from customers whom salespeople contact routinely to use the latter as field survey workers.

Rothman's Pall Mall of Canada uses this approach. Sales staff use a portable Telxon computer and a videotex software package, VIEWBASE, to record marketing and sales information when they visit retailers. Among the data that can be collected are: competitive products in stock, point-of-purchase displays in use, amount of inventory, price discounts on display, and retailers' responses to questions. Each evening sales personnel connect their portable computers by telephone to a central computer. Data received from the salespeople then feed into daily reports prepared and available to top management who can, in turn, send instructions via the central computer back out to the field force to follow up on what is learned.[3]

There are obvious cost savings from such a move and one would expect salespeople to have rather high response rates if they were asked to conduct formal interviews with selected customers. However, in this role, salespeople have a number of serious disadvantages:

1. They are likely to resent the assignment (or request). This means they may hurry the work and make major errors of commission *and* omission.

2. If given latitude to select respondents (e.g., as in a quota sample), they may be expected to make choices that are easy to survey or who will either enhance or not detract from the salesperson's own reputation. This will make it more likely they will pick their favorite customers or those with whom they are the most successful. This will give an upward bias to many responses including estimates of planned sales, attitudes toward the firm and, especially, attitudes toward the salesforce.

3. The salesperson may well be tempted to turn the interview into a selling opportunity. This will not only bias the immediate results, but also potentially lose the customer as a possible future research subject.

4. Even if the salesperson doesn't try to make a sale, the customer may be suspicious and hold back or distort answers.

---

[3]"Sales Staff Also Does Some Research," *Marketing News*, September 13, 1985, p. 1, 37.

This does not mean that salespeople cannot be trained to be effective field researchers. They may well see a research project as an opportunity to become involved in broader planning issues and thus enhance their skills and knowledge. However, on balance, because of their basic orientations, salespeople should only be used as interviewers as a last resort. They may, however, be used to carry out observations of interest to the researcher (e.g., noticing which trade magazines are on a customer's desk).

Personnel Department

This department can assist in hiring and training part-time personnel and in conducting evaluations of those in the research project.

Purchasing

This department can help when the researcher wishes to hire outside suppliers for research services. Purchasing professionals can seek out alternative suppliers, establish bidding procedures, and evaluate bidding submissions at least in terms of costs and fulfillment of bidding requirements. They can also (along with company lawyers) prepare a contract with the supplier that ensures that the researcher's needs are met as required, on time, and at the lowest possible cost.

Securing Low-Cost Samples from Outside Research Services

There are several organizations which maintain pools of respondents who have agreed in advance to participate in research studies, thus cutting nonresponse problems and achieving overhead efficiencies.

National Family Opinion (NFO)

This organization has a sample pool of 220,000 families who have agreed to return self-administered questionnaires without compensation. Many separate panels of 1,000 each are maintained, each generally representative of the U.S. population as a whole. They can be hired by the low-budget researcher. Since characteristics of the households are already known, NFO can also construct highly controlled panels of specific kinds of households for particular marketing research purposes (e.g., older women for a new anti-aging cosmetic or families with young children for certain toys).

Market Facts Consumer Mail Panel
This pool of 70,000 will respond to mail questionnaires and test products. Respondents will also keep records over time. Again, Market Facts' system permits careful selection of a very specific sample or several matched groups that can each be exposed to different experimental treatments (e.g., different ads, products, even questionnaire designs).

Piggybacking
Many independent survey organizations, both locally and nationally, permit researchers to add (piggyback) a few questions onto a survey designed for other purposes. Sometimes this can also be done within the researcher's own organization where marketing questions can be added to researh done by other departments such as public relations or personnel. These other studies, of course, should be selected carefully to make sure their topics don't influence marketing results.

Omnibus Surveys
Other research suppliers carry out studies in which a number of organizations pool their questions in a single instrument (or series of instruments). This, of course, permits them to share overhead costs. However, it also means that the researcher's questions will be mixed in with an unknown set of others. These could cause major or minor biases depending on the particular study. The Roper Organization, a Starch INRA Hooper Company, administers Limobus™. Limobus interviews 2,000 adult Americans in their homes face-to-face every month. In a recent ad, they claim that: "Sample size, and composition are tailored to your needs. A simple question asked of 2,000 respondents costs 90¢ per interview, asked of 1,000 respondents, it's $1.10."

Outside Computerized Databases

Several organizations make available databases comprising various kinds of market data, usually disaggregated at the city, census tract, or zipcode level. These are often based on U.S. Census or other data. Specific secondary analyses can be carried out by suppliers of these data or the raw data tapes or discs can be purchased for analysis on the researcher's own computer. For example, Sammanesh Data Systems, Inc., 1413 177th Avenue N.E., Bellevue, Washington makes available updated county level economic and demographic data files that can be run on IBM PC/XT/ATs at a cost of $75 to $90. Sammanesh also makes available similar data produced by R.L. Polk on a zipcode basis. These are available for $2.00 per zipcode.

Cooperating Businesses

One final source of personnel for research available only to non-profit organizations is the private business firm. United Way has been fortunate in this regard. The accounting firm of Arthur Andersen and Co. made 10 of its offices available for a detailed worksite study United Way wished to carry out.

ACQUIRING EQUIPMENT

Low-cost research usually does not require a great deal of physical hardware. Most equipment needs are for computers, telephones, software and temporary facilities. The following possibilities may help keep these costs low.

Focus Group Rooms

One's own home or the company conference room or cafeteria can be used for focus group interviews. These locales obviously can bias respondents and the spaces will not be equipped with the two-way mirrors or videotaping capabilities available in professional sites. Still, the ambience can be made very pleasant and audio tape recording is usually still possible.

Telephones

Volunteers or staff may be willing to allow their home telephones to be used for limited interviewing provided their costs are reimbursed.

Computer Software

In my opinion, no one who wishes to undertake a continuing program of research should be without the following kinds of software. They are listed in decreasing order of importance.

Word Processing
Word processing software such as a Microsoft Word, Wordperfect, or Wordstar is essential for drafting proposals, writing questionnaires, developing observation protocols, or coding manuals and preparing final reports. Word processing programs with mail/merge capabilities can prove especially valuable for mail studies where they can be used to prepare labels and write cover letters customized to each respondent. Software capabilities to prepare tables or simple columns of figures will be desirable features of chosen word processing software.

Statistical Software
Some spreadsheet programs have fairly robust capabilities for data manipulation and table preparation. However, investment by the researcher (both financial and intellectual) in a statistical package will be well worthwhile over the long run. The most extensive statistical software packages commonly found in the major research agencies are SPSS, SAS and, less commonly, BMD. All are available in mainframe and PC versions. The PC versions are called: PC SAS, SPSS PC+, and BMDP/PC. However, these systems are relatively complex, relatively expensive, and require considerable time to learn. The beginning researcher may want to consider these packages as software to move up to. Less expensive statistical packages such as ABSTAT, Crunch, and SYSTAT are available at much less cost, yet they contain all of the major statistical procedures discussed in this volume. The reader will have to investigate these programs extensively to

see which is most compatible with their own organization's computer and the researcher's own orientation to computers (e.g., whether text-driven or menu-driven software is preferred). Some of the less expensive programs have limits on the number of cases or the number of variables per case they can handle so the researcher should give some thought as to what the system's maximum capacity should be.

Graphics Software

Otherwise very dull reports can be significantly improved in attractiveness and clarity through the use of effective graphics. There are now a wide range of graphics software packages available for this purpose. Most do the standard bar and pie charts and several will produce three-dimensional presentations. The researcher should review the alternatives, in particular paying attention to labeling capabilities and the complexity that can be obtained for related sets of data. Attention should also be paid to whether the graphics package is compatible with the word processing and/or statistical software the researcher has chosen.

Desktop Publishing

Recent developments in desktop publishing offer the researcher a wide range of capabilities for composing final documents and questionnaires with very elaborate and attractive headlines, borders, drawings, and flow charts as well as the standard graphs, tables, and text. This software represents a significant advancement over early combinations of word processing and graphics programs. Desktop publishing can add considerable drama to each research report.

Other kinds of software also being developed that may eventually save low-budget researchers time and money are programs to help prepare questionnaires, develop and monitor samples, and guide and monitor telephone interviewers (as described in Chapter 8).[4]

---

[4]Ellen Burg, "Computers Measure Interviewers' Job Performance," *Marketing News*, March 14, 1986, p. 36.

The researcher interested in this software may find some or all of it available elsewhere in the organization or among friends. Because each software package has its own idiosyncrasies, the researcher is urged to take two steps. First, considerable investigation should be carried out among friends or through published independent evaluations (such as those in *PC World*) before making an investment. Once the researcher has made the effort to learn the software, it is often mentally difficult to change even though the original choice was less than optimal. Second, attention should be paid to compatibility among software systems both in style of use and interchangeability of materials (e.g., data files, tables, text, graphs). It is frustrating to prepare a nice table or graph in a statistical package and then find that it must be retyped to fit into a word processing program. The popularity of integrated systems like SYMPHONY and FRAMEWORK represents one response to this annoying problem. Unfortunately, these integrated programs do not as yet contain very sophisticated statistical capabilities.

An incomplete list of software and prices available in early 1987 is reproduced in Appendix C.

APPENDIX A

MAJOR SECONDARY SOURCES

A. General Sources of Information
   1. *Encyclopedia of American Associations.* (Gale Research Company, Detroit, Mich.). Directory of individual associations, each of which can be a valuable source of information on its industry.
   2. *American Statistics Index.* (Congressional Information Office, Washington, D.C.). Lists all data available from federal government sources. Updated monthly.
   3. *Federal Statistics Directory.* (U.S. Department of Commerce, Washington, D.C.). Provides names, addresses, and telephone numbers of people involved in preparing U.S. government statistics. Individuals can explain data and indicate whether special analyses can be obtained and at what cost.
   4. *Encyclopedia of Business Information Sources.* (Gale Research Company, Detroit, Mich.). Details a wide array of information sources including those in the general literature.
   5. *Statistical Reference Index.* (Congressional Information Office, Washington, D.C.). Guide to selected state and private statistical publications.
   6. *Directory of Mailing List Houses.* (B. Klein Publications, P.O. Box 8503, Coral Gables, Fla.). Lists sources of mailing lists for surveys (and other marketing purposes).
   7. *Bureau of Census Catalog.* (Superintendent of Documents, U.S. Government Printing Office, Washington, D.C.). Regular listing of Bureau of Census reports such as those listed below.
B. Federal Government Statistics
   1. U.S. Bureau of the Census
      a. *Census of Population.* The mammoth decennial measurement of the characteristics of the general (consumer) population. Collected at the neighborhood block level in years

ending in zero. Reports aggregate these data by census tract, county, city, Standard Metropolitan Statistical Area, state, and the total United States. Computer tapes of subsamples of the total census are available at modest cost. Census Bureau will also prepare an analysis run to your specifications for a negotiated fee.

 (1) *Current Population Reports.* Updates of various census measurements based on yearly, smaller surveys. Includes reports on: general population characteristics (age, marital status, etc.), status of minorities, and poverty status of the entire population.

 b. Census of Housing. Collected at the same time as the Census of Population. Provides data on type and size of structure, condition, occupancy, rents, and value of real estate. Reports proportion of households with various kinds of equipment including stoves, dishwashers, telephones, air conditioners, etc.

 (1) *Current Housing Reports.* Annual series updating the Census of Housing. Based on smaller sample.

 c. Census of Various Industries. Collected every five years in years ending in "two" or "seven." Provides data on number of firms, employees, and sales by type of firm disaggregated to the city level. Separate censuses are available as follows:

 (1) *Census of Retail Trade.*
 (2) *Census of Wholesale Trade.*
 (3) *Census of Service Industries.*
 (4) *Census of Manufacturers.*
 (5) *Census of Mineral Industries.*
 (6) *Census of Transportation.*
 (7) *Census of Agriculture.*
 (8) *Census of Government.*

 d. Industry Updates. Each of the series listed above is updated monthly or annually in the following documents:

 (1) *Monthly Retail Trade.*
 (2) *Monthly Wholesale Trade.*
 (3) *Monthly Selected Service Receipts.*
 (4) *Annual Survey of Manufacturers.*
 (5) *Current Industrial Reports.*
 (6) *Minerals Yearbook.*
 (7) *Agricultural Statistics and Commodities Yearbook.*

e. *Statistical Summaries.* The above annual data along with other information are summarized in other ways by the Census Bureau. These publications include:
   (1) *Statistical Abstract of the United States.* The most general compendium of statistical information. A good place to begin searches for secondary data. Available in paperback.
   (2) *County Business Patterns.*
   (3) *State and Metropolitan Area Databook.*

2. Other sources
   a. *Federal Reserve Bulletin.* Statistics of interest to the banking and finance industries. Published monthly. Data on transactions, interest rates, savings, department store sales, prices, and international trade and finance.
   b. *Monthly Labor Review.* Data on employment, wages, hours worked, and wholesale and retail price indices.
   c. *Commerce Business Daily.* Provides synopses of planned procurements, sales, and contracts to be awarded by U.S. government. Valuable for those considering doing business with the government.
   d. *Overseas Business Reports.* Provides information on an annual basis on economic conditions in various markets and selected facets of doing business in those countries.
   e. *Department of Agriculture Reports.* The Department conducts a wide variety of experiments and other studies designed to help improve the sale of agricultural products. Studies include those on alternative pricing and packaging strategies and store display techniques.
   f. *Statistics of Income.* Compiled by the Internal Revenue Service from income tax returns of individuals and organizations. Published annually.
   g. *U.S. Industrial Outlook.* Historical data from the Bureau of Industrial Analysis on 200 industries with projections for 10 years into the future.
   h. *Business Cycles: Handbook of Indicators.* Monthly report of 70 critical economic indicators.
   i. *Survey of Current Business.* Monthly report by the Bureau of Economic Analysis on 2,600 statistical series of interest to business. Includes data on the state of the economy, personal consumption, foreign transactions, income, and employment.

     j. Selling to the Military. General information, description of items purchased, and location of purchasing offices.

     k. Economic Indicators of the Farm Sector. Five volume set of detailed information on farmers and those who supply and support them.

     l. Business Conditions Digest. Monthly report from the Bureau of Economic Analysis on business indices.

     m. Economic Indicators. Monthly report from the Council of Economic Advisors.

     n. Consumer Expenditure Survey. Study made every 10 years by the Bureau of Labor Statistics outlining broad expenditure patterns for major socio-economic groupings.

C. State and Local Data

Sources of data for states, counties and individual localities will vary by area. Some likely sources of such data in many communities are the following:

    1. *Local media.* Local newspapers and radio and television stations are likely to maintain information on local population and industry characteristics in order to attract national and local advertisers. They also provide data on their own audiences.

    2. *State or local Chambers of Commerce or development agencies.* These organizations also maintain area data on population characteristics, labor force size and type, industry structure, and other environmental characteristics. Their objective is to attract new industries to the state or community and their data should be interpreted in light of this objective.

    3. *Commercial Banks.* Major institutions prepare local data for their own financial officers as well as selected clients.

    4. *State Departments of Labor or Industry.* These departments report employment and industrial output data for their areas.

    5. *State Departments of Alcoholic Beverages, Motor Vehicles, and Agriculture.* These departments typically collect data on sales, employment, and tax revenues in their sectors.

D. Private Data

    1. *Almanac of Business and Industrial Financial Ratios.* (Prentice-Hall). Reports size, sales, and operating ratios on many industries. Each industry is stratified into 12 categories by size. Based on Internal Revenue Service tax data.

    2. *Consumer Market and Magazine Report.* (Daniel Starch and Staff, Inc.). Demographic and consumption data on households. Includes rates of purchase and ownership of automo-

biles, major appliances, personal products, and services. Also reports magazine audience data. Based on national probability sample.

3. *A Guide to Consumer Markets.* (National Industrial Conference Board). Consumer market data compiled from secondary sources.

4. *Million Dollar Directory.* (Dun and Bradstreet, two volumes). Describes product lines, locations of offices, sales, and employment of companies with assets over $500,000. Based on company data.

5. *Moody's Manuals.* (Moody's). Volumes containing corporate financial data (sales, profit and loss, balance sheet status) for the following:
    a. Banks and finance.
    b. Industrial organizations.
    c. Municipalities and governments.
    d. Public utilities.
    e. Transportation.
    Based on company reports. Updated regularly.

6. *Predicasts.* (Predicasts). Abstracts other organizations' forecasts on 500 indicators and develops a consensus.

7. *Rand McNally Commercial Atlas and Marketing Guide.* (Rand McNally Company). Maps and marketing data for over 100,000 cities and towns. Based on other secondary sources.

8. *Sales Management Survey of Buying Power.* (Sales Management Magazine). Population, household income and retail and product category sales for states, cities, and Standard Metropolitan Statistical Areas. Develops specialized indexes of "buying power" available in each market.

9. *Thomas Register of American Manufacturers.* (Thomas Publishing Company). Annually lists addresses of headquarters, branch offices, and corporate subsidiaries of manufacturers.

10. *United Nations Statistical Yearbook.* (United Nations, New York). Includes population, industrial output, international trade, and other commercial statistics for member nations.

11. *Directory of Conventions.* (Successful Meetings Magazine). Lists all conventions held in the United States annually.

12. *Selected stock brokerage reports.* Stock brokerages frequently prepare analyses on specific industries and/or competitors.

13. *Business Index.* Available in reference rooms of most libraries. This source catalogs under appropriate indexes articles from over 800 periodicals of interest to businesspeople.

14. *FINDEX: The Directory of Market Research Reports.* Reference guide to published, commercially available market and business research. Available in most libraries.
15. *Directory of Industry Data Sources.* (Ballinger Publishing Company). Provides secondary sources of information on industries. Also describes indexing and bibliographic database services. Gives detailed descriptions of primary data sources including addresses for ordering information.
16. *State Profiles.* (Woods and Poole Economics, Inc.). County by county economic and demographic data and forecasts for selected years 1970 to 2005.
17. *Slater Hall Information Products.* Sells specially designed CD-ROM discs containing government data such as the 1982 Census of Agriculture, GNP and other economic time series and updated and projected 1980 Census data. CD-ROM discs can be read by special inexpensive devices that can be attached to many personal computers.
18. *The 1985 Sourcebook of Demographics and Buying Power for Every Zip Code in the U.S.A.* (CACI). Demographic characteristics, buying power indexes for major consumer products and services, top-5 SIC business statistics, 1970 and 1980 census data on selected characteristics, and national and state rankings on key variables. Also available on magnetic tape.
19. *Professional's Guide to Public Relations Services.* (Public Relations Publishing Company). Describes a wide range of electronic and printed databases or sources of databases of interest to public relations specialists.
20. *European Markets. A Guide to Company and Industry Information Sources.* (Washington Research Publishing). Provides marketing and financial information on companies marketing in 17 Western European countries.

E. Syndicated Private Field Studies
The following are some of the major suppliers of specialized field data. In most cases, the services are purchased on an annual basis and may be for some or all of the source's database. Many services provide specialized reports or analyses on request.

1. *Dun's Market Identifiers.* (Dun and Bradstreet). Provides three by five inch cards updated monthly on over 4,300,000 establishments. Each record includes names and addresses, SIC codes, name of chief executive, and number of employees. Can be used for sales leads, mailing lists, or building market profiles or sales quotas.

2. *Nielsen Retail Indexes*. (A.C. Nielsen Company). Audit data collected six times a year on 1,600 supermarkets, 750 drug stores, and 450 mass merchandisers. Data include beginning and ending inventories and intervening purchases by brand in selected categories. These data are then used to estimate brand sales at retail. Nielsen also reports out-of-stock conditions, store promotions, and prices charged. Also includes extent of retail advertising in major media from other sources. Data collected only for cooperating outlets.

3. *Audits and Survey's National Total Market Index*. (Audits and Surveys, Inc.). Similar to Nielsen in focusing on retail sales, but reports data for all outlets in particular product categories (e.g., including convenience and neighborhood stores). Includes estimates for automotive, electrical, and photographic products.

4. *Selling Areas-Marketing Inc*. (SAMI). Reports warehouse shipments provided by cooperating retailers on computer tape. Only covers selected markets, not all of United States.

5. *National Purchase Diary Panel*. (National Purchase Diary Panel Inc.). Obtains diary records from 13,000 families who keep monthly records on about 50 product categories. For each purchase includes data on where bought, what bought, price paid, and intended use.

6. *Nielsen Television Index*. (A.C. Nielsen Company). Uses electronic device to estimate number of televisions in United States tuned to particular programs and characteristics of their audiences. Reports national data every two weeks and overnight data in selected major metropolitan areas.

7. *Starch Advertisement Readership Survey*. (Daniel Starch and Staff Inc.). Tests magazine ad readership in consumer, business, and farm publications, and newspapers. Based on recognition technique where sample consumers are presented with copies of magazines and asked about selected ads as to whether they remember the ad, whether they associated the ad with the brand or company name and, finally, whether they read most of the copy. Based on quota samples.

8. *Simmons Media/Market Service*. (Simmons Market Research Bureau, Inc.). Surveys a national probability sample of over 15,000 households. Uses two personal interviews for each household to secure magazine readership data, a self-report of purchase and use of products in 500 categories, and a diary of television viewing behavior.

9. *CACI/Source Products.* Provides diskettes containing demographic data, housing data and employment data for 1980, current year and five-year projections. Can be obtained for counties,
census tracts, or zipcodes. Customers may purchase diskettes
as needed for analysis on a personal computer.

10. *Donnelley Marketing Information Services.* Donnelley's *Con-
quest* system is an interactive database, access to which is obtained by payment of an annual fee. Users then can acquire
data similar to CACI's on customer demographics by zipcode
and census tract. However, Donnelley also can develop profiles
based on nonstandard area definitions such as circles or poly-
gons. They also make available: sales potentials for 21 categories of retail outlet, maps of target areas, and lifestyle profiles
of 47 different consumer groups. The interactive feature permits the researcher to combine Donnelley's various databases
with data from other secondary sources or from the organization's own studies. Donnelley also has capability of developing
detailed mailing lists for specific market target areas.

11. *BehaviorScan.* (Information Resources, Inc.). This latest development in retail sales measurement technology provides data
on product and brand sales collected through optical scanners
now used in many retail outlets.

12. *IMS International.* Provides data on pharmaceutical product
sales at the retail level in over 50 countries worldwide.

13. *STARTER.* (Burke Marketing Services, Inc.). Provides contin-
uous tracking of consumer awareness, claimed trial and repeat
purchases for nationally introduced new packaged goods.

14. *PRIZM.* (Claritas). Provides 40 psychographic profiles describing every zipcode area in the United States. Links profiles to
product and service consumption. Permits user to locate zipcode
with types of customers ideal for a specific product or service
offering.

15. *National Scantrack.* (A.C. Nielsen and Company). Tracking of
supermarket sales data through Universal Product Code scanning data.

APPENDIX B

ON-LINE DATABASES FOR MARKETING[1]

ABI/INFORM. (Data Courier, Inc., Louisville, Ky.). Bibliographic citations and abstracts; 680 international business and management journals.

ACCOUNTANTS. (American Institute of Certified Public Accountants, New York, N.Y.). Bibliography for accountants; 250 periodicals and selected books, pamphlets.

ADTRACK. (The Kingman Consulting Group, Inc., St. Paul, Minn.). Every ad of a quarter page or larger covering 98 percent of the ad revenues in 150 major consumer and business publications through 1984.

AMERICAN MEN AND WOMEN OF SCIENCE. (R. R. Bowker Company, New York, N.Y.). Biographies of 130,000 active scientists.

AMERICAN PROFILE. (Donnelly Marketing Services, Stamford, Conn.). 1970 and 1980 census data, current year updates and five-year projections. 400,000 records searchable by 160 characteristics. Searcher can define own geographic boundaries.

AP NEWS. (Associated Press, New York, N.Y.). 90,000 news stories as recent as 48 hours old.

ARBITRON INFORMATION ON DEMAND. (Arbitron Ratings Company, New York, N.Y.). Audience demographics and psychographics for 200 television and 250 radio markets.

ARTHUR D. LITTLE/ON LINE. (Arthur D. Little, Inc., Cambridge, Mass.). A. D. Little's own reports of industries, technologies, markets, economic trends, and companies. Over 1,150 reports since 1977.

---

[1]Basic source for this listing is: *ONLINE ACCESS GUIDE*, Vol. 2, No. 2, March-April, 1987.

BIZDATE. (Source Telecomputing Corporation, McLean, Va.). Business news magazine with information culled from other sources (e.g., UPI, U.S. Dept. of Agriculture) updated 55 times per day.

CANADIAN PRESS INFORMATION NETWORK. (Canadian Press, Toronto, Canada). News from major Canadian and American Wire Services, updated continuously.

CENDATA. (U.S. Census Bureau, Washington, D.C.). Detailed demographic data on the United States and selected data on 200 foreign countries. Economic data from manufacturing to foreign trade. Press releases. Updated daily.

CIS (CIS INDEX). (Congressional Information Service, Inc., Bethesda, Md.). 200,000 records of all print publications of congressional hearings, reports, documents, committee prints and publications. Public law records to 1983.

COMMUNICATIONS DAILY. (Television Digest, Washington, D.C.). Daily newsletter and other information on communications and information industries.

DAILY REPORT FOR EXECUTIVES. (The Bureau of National Affairs, Inc., Washington, D.C.). Tax developments in Congress, the Treasury, IRS, the White House and the Courts.

DATA INFORMER. (Information USA, Chevy Chase, Md.). Newsletter and inexpensive access to data from 200–300 business, government, and nontraditional databases.

D&B–DUN'S FINANCIAL RECORDS. (Dun's Marketing Services, Parsipanny, N.J.). Up to three years of financial statements, 14 operating ratios, comparisons to industry. Covers 700,000 companies, 98 percent of them privately held.

D&B–DUN'S MARKET IDENTIFIERS. (Dun's Marketing Services, Parsipanny, N.J.). Profiles of more than 2 million companies, 90 percent private, with 10 or more employees or $1 million or more in sales. Includes executive names and files on all branches.

D&B–INTERNATIONAL DUN'S MARKET IDENTIFIERS. (Dun's Marketing Services, Parsipanny, N.J.). Profiles of 530,000 companies in 133 countries.

DISCLOSURE ONLINE. (Disclosure, Inc., Bethesda, Md.). Information on 10K and 10Q reports and other materials reported by 10,000 companies to Securities and Exchange Commission.

DONNELLEY DEMOGRAPHICS. (Donnelley Marketing Information Services, Stamford, Conn.). Demographic data on individual markets from 1980 census with current year estimates and five-year projections.

DORIS (DEMOGRAPHIC ONLINE RETRIEVAL INFORMATION SYSTEM). (CACI, Inc., Fairfax, Va.). Demographic data from 1970 and 1980 censuses plus current year updates and five-year forecasts. Sales potential estimates for 145 products.

DOW JONES QUOTES. (Dow Jones News/Retrieval, Princeton, N.J.). Current and historical quotes on major U.S. stock markets.

DRI FINANCIAL AND CREDIT STATISTICS DATA BANK. (Data Resources, Inc., Lexington, Mass.). 14,000 time series on banking and finance both United States and foreign.

ELECTRONIC LEGISLATIVE SEARCH SYSTEM. (Commerce Clearing House, Inc., Chicago, Ill.). Tracks legislative bills in U.S. Congress and all 50 states.

ELECTRONIC YELLOW PAGES. (Market Data Retrieval, Westport, Conn.). Ten million listings in 4,800 telephone directories.

FIND/SVP REPORTS AND STUDIES INDEX. (Find/SVP Information Products Department, New York, N.Y.). Data on over 11,000 studies done by over 500 research firms. Quarterly updates.

INTERNATIONAL BUSINESS CLEARINGHOUSE. (Baxter Worldwide Inc., Culver City, Calif.). Lists of goods and services, real estate, and business enterprises for sale worldwide.

INVESTEXT. (Business Research Corporation, Boston, Mass.). 60,000 full-text research reports on 1,500 large, 1,000 smaller emerging, and 1,500 foreign companies.

JAPAN WEEKLY MONITOR. (Kyodo News International, Inc., New York, N.Y.). Weekly financial and industry news on Japan.

LEXIS. (Mead Data General, Dayton, Ohio). Over 3 million cases and other documents on American, English, and French case law. Includes statutes, codes, and regulations. Citation searches.

MANAGEMENT AND MARKETING ABSTRACTS. (Pergamon InfoLine Inc.). Bibliography of articles from 100 international management journals.

MANAGEMENT CONTENTS. (Information Access Company, Belmont, Calif.). Bibliography of 200,000 entries from 700 business journals, newsletters, books, etc.

MOODY'S CORPORATE NEWS–INTERNATIONAL. (Moody's Investors Service, Inc., New York, N.Y.). News and financial information on 3,900 public and private corporations in 100 countries.

MOODY'S CORPORATE NEWS–U.S. (Moody's Investors Service, Inc., New York, N.Y.). News and financial information on over 13,000 publicly held American companies.

MOODY'S CORPORATE PROFILES. (Moody's Investors Service, Inc., New York, N.Y.). Descriptive and financial profiles of 3,600 companies traded on the New York or American Stock Exchanges or over the counter.

MRI 10 MEDIAMARKETS. (Mediamark Research Inc., New York, N.Y.). Audience estimates for major media in the 10 major U.S. markets. Includes survey data including audiences' product usage.

MRI BUSINESS-TO-BUSINESS. (Mediamark Research Inc., New York, N.Y.). Data on purchases of business products and magazines by 4,000 professionals and managers surveyed annually.

MRI NATIONAL STUDY. (Mediamark Research, Inc., New York, N.Y.). Data from semi-annual survey of 20,000 U.S. adults on media and product consumption.

NATIONAL NEWSPAPER INDEX. (Information Access Company, Belmont, Calif.). Full indexes on *New York Times, The Wall Street Journal,* and *Christian Science Monitor* since 1979 and partial indexes on *Los Angeles Times* and *Washington Post* since October 1982.

NEXIS. (Mead Data General, Dayton, Ohio). Full texts of over 8 million articles from *New York Times* (since 1980), *London Financial Times,* plus over 125 U.S. and foreign magazines, newspapers, newswires, and newsletters.

PATSEARCH. (Pergamon InfoLine Inc., McLean, Va.). Information and graphic displays on over 1 million U.S. patents since January 1975.

PREDICASTS. (Predicasts, Cleveland, Ohio). Over 11,000 forecasts updated monthly, time series over 25 years updated annually.

PR NEWSWIRE ASSOCIATION. (PR Newswire Association, Inc., New York, N.Y.). 300 daily news releases from 10,000 news sources.

PTS MARS. (Predicasts, Cleveland, Ohio). Over 30,000 citations on marketing and advertising.

PTS PROMPT. (Predicasts, Cleveland, Ohio). Citations in 1,200 international publications on markets and technology.

REUTER MONITOR. (Reuters, Ltd., New York, N.Y.). Data on commodities, securities, currencies, U.S. and international economics, the energy industry, and general international news.

SIMMONS' STUDY OF MEDIA AND MARKETS. (Simmons Market Research Bureau, Inc., New York, N.Y.). Media audiences and product usage for 3,900 brands in 800 categories for 19,000 U.S. adults. Includes demographic and psychographic information.

STANDARD AND POOR'S CORPORATE DESCRIPTIONS. (Standard and Poor's Corporation, New York, N.Y.). Audited data submitted by 8,000 publicly held companies plus various published articles and reports.

SUPERSITE. (CACI Inc.–Federal, Arlington, Va.). 1960, 1970, and 1980 census data with current update and five-year forecasts for any defined geographic area. Provides demographic data, sales potentials, and psychographic (ACORN) profiles.

TRADEMARKSCAN. (Thomson & Thomson, North Quincy, Mass.). Active and registered trademarks on file with U.S. Patent and Trademark Office.

WHO OWNS WHOM. (Dun & Bradstreet, Ltd., London, England). Listing of parent and subsidiary companies throughout the world.

WORLD PATENTS INDEX. (SDC Information Services, Santa Monica, Calif.). 3 million patent references from 24 major industrialized countries and two international patent organizations.

APPENDIX C

COMPUTER SOFTWARE USEFUL FOR RESEARCH

The readers should be warned that (1) this is a highly selective list; (2) the programs listed in many cases will be revised, updated, or abandoned by the time the list is read, and (3) many more complex, faster, and probably cheaper programs will appear monthly. The reader is urged both to explore these programs and, in the course of exploration, inquire as to what the latest is in any area. To aid this exploration, journals like the *Journal of Marketing Research* now review software from time to time. Further, the *Marketing News* published by the American Marketing Association, Chicago provides a directory of software once a year, with periodic updates. The 1986 version included the offerings of 178 organizations. (This list is the principal source of the examples to follow.)

Note: This listing is restricted to software in selected categories and excludes wordprocessing and desktop publishing. To simplify, software is only included if (1) it can be run on a PC-XT and its compatibles/clones and (2) price was available and was under $2,000. Most such programs will also run on a PC-AT and, presumably, faster computers that are expected in the near future. The researcher with Apple or HP equipment is urged to look at the *Marketing News* guide for software appropriate to their systems.

	Source	Cost (1986)
Statistical Analysis and/or Reporting System		
ABtab	BB and A, Inc., Canon City, Calif.	$895.00
USTATS	Wm. C. Brown Publishers, Dubuque, Ia.	$ 99.95
TABULYZER	Business Research & Surveys, West Orange, N.J.	$435.00
EXEC*U*STAT	EXEC*U*STAT Inc. Princeton, N.J.	$495.00
STATPLAN II	The Futures Group, Glastonbury, Conn.	$ 99.00
SNAP	IMS MICROS, New York, N.Y.	$1,900.00
Statistician's MACE 2.0	Mace, Inc., Madison, Wisc.	$195.00
Master Tab	Marketing Data Research, Tacoma, Wash.	$250.00
VERBATIM ANALYZER	Marketing Metrics, Paramus, N.J.	$179.50
MathStat	Mathematica Policy Research, Princeton, N.J.	$750.00
MICROSCALE w/Systat	Mediax Interactive Technologies Inc., Black Rock, Conn.	$1,450.00
MICROTAB	Microtab, Inc., Newton, N.J.	$475.00
Number Cruncher Statistical Systems	NCSS, Kaysville, Utah	$ 79.00
ANSWER-TABS 5	Orchard Associates Inc., Wilmette, Ill.	$995.00 up
Statpro 2.0	Penton Software Inc., New York, N.Y.	$795.00
SURVEY	Persimmon Software, Mobile, Ala.	$ 99.00
SuperStat	Process Applications Inc., Charlotte, N.C.	$300.00
P-Stat/mr	P-Stat, Inc., Princeton, N.J.	$695.00
SAS-PC	SAS Institute, Inc. Cary, N.C.	N/A
SIGSTAT	Significant Statistics, Provo, Utah	$595.00
PC-BMD	Scott M. Smith, Provo, Utah	$200.00
Spring-Stat	Spring Systems, Chicago, Ill.	$300.00
SPSS/PC+	SPSS, Inc., Chicago, Ill.	$795.00
The T.A.B. Program	Suburban Software, Ridgewood, N.J.	$495.00 up
Surveytab Ver 4.01	Surveytab, Glen Burnie, Md.	$499.00
SYSTAT	Systat, Inc., Evanston, Ill.	$495.00
STRATPRO	Wadsworth Professional Software Inc., Boston, Mass.	$795.00
EzStat	Wolf/Altschul/Callahan Inc., New York, N.Y.	$ 50.00
UNCLE	World Research Systems Ltd., Palatine, Ill.	$1,000.00 up
Data Base Management		
Paradox	Ansa Software, Belmont, Calif.	$695.00
REFLEX: THE ANALYST	Borland International Inc., Scotts Valley, Calif.	$ 99.95
PRODAS	Effort, New York, N.Y.	$1,505.00
DataBanker	S.I. Inc., Waltham, Mass.	$500.00

	Source	Cost (1986)
Survey Design and/or Analysis		
Profile abc	Bardsley & Haslacker, Inc. Mountain View, Calif.	$349.00
SRS	Congressional Systems, Inc., Dallas, Texas	$149.95
The Survey System	Creative Research Systems, Petaluma, Calif.	$500 to $900.00
Telofacts 1	diLithium Software, Beaverton, Oregon	$44.95
CAPPA	Scientific Press, Palo Alto, Calif.	$2,000.00
Maps and Graphics		
STATMAP	Ganesa Group, Rand McNally, Chicago, Ill.	$250.00
PictureIt	General Parametrics Corp., Berkeley, Calif.	$700.00
Speech*Maker	GRAPHIC M*I*S, Springfield, Ill.	$ 70.00
PC-SLIDE	Interactive Market Systems, New York, N.Y.	$995.00
MAXpc	National Planning Data Corp., Ithaca, N.Y.	$495.00
PIG	Pennwell Software, Tulsa, Okla.	$ 49.95
RANDMAP	Rand McNally & Co., Chicago, Ill.	$995.00
Desktop Information Display System (DIDS)	Sammamish Data Systems Inc., Bellevue, Wash.	$750.00
Quick Map	Sammamish Data Systems, Inc., Bellevue, Wash.	$295.00
STATGRAPHICS	Statistical Graphics Corp. Princeton, N.J.	$695.00
Atlas	Strategic Locations Planning, San Jose, Calif.	$349.00
Decision Support		
Expert Choice	Decision Support Software, Inc., McLean, Va.	$495.00
Sherlock	Marketing Technologies Inc., Denver, Col.	$345.00
GRUNTWORKS	Marketools Inc., Barrington, Ill.	$395.00
MaxThink	MaxThink Inc., Piedmont, Calif.	$ 60.00
Other		
+FORECAST	Computer Software Consultants, Inc., Binghamton, N.Y.	$149.00

	Source	Cost (1986)
TELEVIEW II (CATI System)	The Research Group, San Mateo, Calif.	$ 99.00
Ci2 System (CATI System)	Sawtooth Software, Inc., Ketchum, Idaho	$495.00 up
SmartForecasts I	Smart Software Inc., Belmont, Mass.	$495.00
PC-MDS (Scaling, Conjoint, Cluster)	Scott M. Smith, Provo, Utah	$400.00
MICROBJ (Box Jenkins)	Stratix, Inc., Burlingame, Calif.	$295.00
NUAMETRICS	Stratix, Inc., Burlingame, Calif.	$195.00
XTRAPOLATOR	Stratix, Inc., Burlingame, Calif.	$195.00
EASY CASTER	TMS Systems Inc., Blacksburg, Va.	$295.00

INDEX